D1240055

Religious Naturalism Today

Religious Naturalism Today

The Rebirth of a Forgotten Alternative

Jerome A. Stone

STATE UNIVERSITY OF NEW YORK PRESS

Published by
State University of New York Press, Albany

© 2008 State University of New York

For information, contact State University of New York Press, Albany, NY
www.sunypress.edu

Production by Kelli W. LeRoux
Marketing by Fran Keneston

Library of Congress Cataloging-in-Publication Data

Stone, Jerome Arthur, 1935–
   Religious naturalism today : the rebirth of a forgotten alternative /
Jerome A. Stone.
       p. cm.
   Includes bibliographical references and index.
   ISBN 978-0-7914-7537-9 (hardcover : alk. paper)
   ISBN 978-0-7914-7538-6 (pbk. : alk. paper)
   1. Natural theology.   2. Naturalism—Religious aspects.   3. Philosophical
theology.   I. Title.

BL183.S76 2008
210—dc22   2007048682

10 9 8 7 6 5 4 3 2 1

I have great faith in a seed. Convince me that you have a seed there, and I am prepared to expect wonders.

—Henry David Thoreau, *Faith in a Seed*, iii

Our responsibility to our forefathers is only to consult them, not to obey them. Our responsibility to our descendants is only to impart our most cherished experiences to them, but not to command them.

—Mordecai Kaplan, *The Meaning of God in Modern Jewish Religion*, p. 98

A humanistic religion, if it excludes our relation to nature, is pale and thin, as it is presumptuous, when it takes humanity as an object of worship.

—John Dewey, *A Common Faith*, p. 54

To my friends in
Collegium, the Highlands Institute,
IRAS, Meadville-Lombard Theological School,
Unity Temple UU Congegation, the Unitarian Church of Evanston,
and everyone fighting for the Chicago Wilderness

Contents

Foreword

In *Religious Naturalism Today*, Jerome Stone has accomplished several things at one and the same time. His subtitle points straightforwardly to the most obvious—the author has provided an enormously useful and detailed map of what he considers to be a "forgotten" religious alternative. In his sketches—some lengthy, some very brief—he brings several dozen thinkers to our attention, interprets their contributions, and assures the future of this work as an indispensable vademecum for religious naturalism. In this respect, this book serves as a kind of Baedeker, a guide for visitors to a region of mind and spirit that while it is strange to most readers, is beloved for others.

There is more to Stone's achievement in this volume: nature and naturalism are for us today urgent subjects for religious reflection. If we recount the ways in which the last two centuries of scientific knowledge have impacted our lives, what will top the list? The recognition that nature is constitutive of who and what we are as human beings. Whether or not we believe that there is something more, nature is so significant that all our beliefs must be reformulated so as to take nature into account. Whether it is our view of the world, our image of ourselves, or our beliefs about God—everything must be rethought in response to our knowledge of how deeply we are rooted in natural processes. Science has reimaged nature for us in ways so profound that we still have yet to take its measure. We know that nature is no longer "out there" or "over against us." It is deeply within us; nature is who we are.

This being so, the question of considering nature *religiously* or *spiritually* obviously assumes a central place on the human agenda. Jerome Stone recognizes this, and the trend of thought that he surveys, religious naturalism, is important for all of us, whether or not we locate ourselves within the stream that this book charts

Stone has presented his work as invitation, offering readers access to a conversation, not as a manifesto or set of dicta that require obeisance. He himself has made decisions among alternative possibilities in ways that enable us to retrace his process and make our own decisions. Is it possible or necessary to hold to a concept of God within this *natural* worldview? If so, what ideas about God are commensurable with the new worldview? How is sacrality defined in this framework? What spaces or values can count as sacred? Can we find both power and goodness in nature? Must we view nature as impervious, unconcerned with human values? Must we accept nature as we find it or should it be transformed? Is there grace within the framework of religious naturalism? What does it mean to be *religious* in a naturalistic mode? These are the kinds of questions that Jerome Stone has raised and the responses to which he maps in this book. Since he shares his own journey of insight and response with us in these pages, he encourages us to wrestle with the same questions and formulate our own responses—whether or not we finally name ourselves with his name of religious naturalism.

Vademecum—go with me, be my companion, journey with me. This book is an ideal companion and guide, the perfect example of a vademecum for traversing a great and urgent spiritual landscape.

Philip Hefner
Professor of Systematic Theology Emeritus
Lutheran School of Theology at Chicago

Preface

Religious naturalism, a once-forgotten option in religious thinking, is making a revival. It seeks to explore and encourage religious ways of responding to the world on a completely naturalistic basis without a supreme being or ground of being.

Who are the religious naturalists? Historical roots go back at least to Spinoza. Former religious naturalists included George Santayana, Samuel Alexander, John Dewey, Roy Wood Sellars, John Herman Randall, Mordecai Kaplan, Ralph Burhoe, founder of *Zygon*, and such Chicago theologians as Henry Nelson Wieman, Bernard Meland, and the later Bernard Loomer. Recent religious naturalists include William Dean, Willem Drees, Ursula Goodenough, Charley Hardwick, Henry Levinson, Karl Peters, myself, and perhaps Gordon Kaufman. Several articles in the 2000 issue of *Zygon: Journal of Religion and Science* are on religious naturalism.

While its origins may be traced back to Spinoza, this study starts in the early twentieth century with George Santayana and Samuel Alexander.

What might be called the classic period of religious naturalism starts with George Santayana's *Interpretations of Poetry and Religion* in 1900 (Santayana, 1989). There followed a florescence of writings in the religious naturalist vein, largely but not exclusively in the United States. These writings were philosophical, theological and literary. This period lasted for almost half a century until Henry Nelson Wieman published *The Source of Human Good* in 1946 and then left the Divinity School of the University of Chicago the following year (Wieman 1946). There followed a hiatus until Bernard Loomer's *The Size of God* was published in 1987. (It had been presented in 1978.) During this hiatus religious naturalism, when mentioned at all, was viewed largely as a quaint relic of the past. Randolph Crump Miller of Yale, who taught a course in Naturalism or Empirical Theology at Yale Divinity School, was like a voice crying in the wilderness (Miller 1974). Since the publication of Loomer's essay, however, there has been a rebirth of religious naturalism. There have been a number of publications by and studies of religious naturalists and, significantly, the movement has found various institutional homes.

The purpose of this book is to trace this story and to analyze some of the issues dividing these religious naturalists, issues which a religious naturalist must face. My hope is threefold: that people casting about for a credible religious outlook might be aware of this approach and to realize that here is a tradition with immense religious and conceptual resources, that religious naturalists might face some of the issues dividing us, and finally that everyone might realize that there is a new major dialogue partner in the chorus of religious and theological voices.

One issue facing religious people with a naturalist outlook is whether the object of our religious orientation is the whole of the universe or a part of it, such as a creative process within it or the sum of creative and challenging factors. A second is whether we can reconceive the idea of God within a naturalistic framework and if so, what attitude should be taken toward it. Third, whether the object of the religious orientation has the quality of power or goodness, is morally ambiguous or determinate. Likewise, should our religious response be awe toward the whole, aspiration to grow toward the lure of goodness, or something more complex. Again, what sources of religious insight does naturalism explore, the world as understood scientifically or by an appreciative perception? What role do religious traditions play? Finally, what is it like to act and feel as a naturalist with religious leanings?

Any religious position today must be judged at least in part by its potential for empowerment and liberation. Generally speaking, religious naturalism has not grown out of a context of struggle for caste, gender, or class justice. However, it does have emancipatory significance in at least two respects. First, it represents the dismantling of the oppressive aspects of traditional theism. Not only that, it articulates an alternative religious stance which is at least as fulfilling and definitely more empowering than much traditional theism. Second, by being more in tune with the approaches and results of the sciences, it challenges the authoritative stance of some of the more religiously oriented conservative political and social movements. These two points are not insignificant. In addition, as readers of this volume will discover, specific religious naturalists have been especially focused on questions of social justice and individual empowerment.

The overall division of this volume falls naturally into two periods, before and after the thirty-plus year hiatus between 1946 and 1987. Part one deals with the birth of religious naturalism, from Santayana to Wieman. Chapter 1 deals with the philosophers who developed this viewpoint: Santayana, Samuel Alexander, John Dewey, George Herbert Mead, Roy Wood Sellars, and John Herman Randall. Chapter 2 presents the views of theologians: the early Chicago school (George Burman Foster, Gerald Birney, Shailer Mathews, and Edward Scribner Ames), the humanists, the Unitarian Frederick May Eliot, and the later Chicago school (Henry Nelson Wieman, Bernard Meland, Bernard Loomer, and Ralph Burhoe), Mordecai Kaplan and Jack Cohen. Chapter 3 analyzes some of the issues debated between these early naturalists and presents a variety of attempts to develop a naturalist view of the mind. Too recently published to study are Richard Carrier's *Sense and Goodness Without God*, André Comte-Sponville's *The Little Book of Atheist Spirituality*, Michael Dowd's *Thank God for Evolution*, and Robert C. Solomon's *Spirituality for the Skeptic.*

With the exception of the Interlude, this book will mainly study philosophers and theologians. This is partly a result of the limitations of the author's training, in part because a number of theologians and philosophers have been religious naturalists. It does mean that there will be a variety of source materials, such as that explored by Catherine Albanese in *Nature Religion in America*, which will not be utilized in this study.

The Interlude between the first and second parts briefly explores religious naturalism in literature. Part Two depicts the rebirth of religious naturalism following Loomer's presentation of "The Size of God." Over twenty current writers are presented. Chapter 4 analyzes three different sources of religious insight among contemporary religious naturalists, including experiences of grace and obligation, nature both as appreciated and as the object of scientific study, and the hermeneutics of religious and literary traditions. Contested issues are discussed in chapter 5, including whether nature's power or goodness is the focus of attention and also on the appropriateness of using the term "God." Chapter 6 sketches the contributions of other recent religious naturalists. Chapter 7 ends the study by exploring what it is like on the inside to live as a religious naturalist.

Since finishing the manuscript for this book I have discovered that George Riggan, former Professor of Systematic Theology at Hartford Seminary Foundation, can be read as a religious naturalist (Riggan 1973, 473–480) and that Owen Flannagan has an excellent discussion of naturalism in recent American philosophy (Flanagan 2006, 430–452).

I have discussed portions of this book with most of the living writers who share this view and am deeply indebted to their criticisms and encouragement. Thanks to William Dean for inspiring me, Charles Milligan for help with Bernhardt, Emanuel Goldsmith for help with Kaplan, Donald Crosby, Cedric Heppler, Nancy Hutton, and Henry Levinson for their kindnesses in research. Creighton Peden has been a constant inspiration and guide. Tim Philbin of William Rainey Harper

College and also the Interlibrary Loan Department of Riverside Public Library have been most helpful in securing books and articles. The academic community owes a deep debt to Nancy Ellegate and Allison Lee of SUNY Press for their work.

Introduction

What Is Religious Naturalism?

Defining Religious Naturalism

Religious naturalism is a type of naturalism (Stone 2000). Hence we start with naturalism. This is a set of beliefs and attitudes that focuses on this world. On the negative side it involves the assertion that there seems to be no ontologically distinct and superior realm (such as God, soul, or heaven) to ground, explain, or give meaning to this world. On the positive side it affirms that attention should be focused on the events and processes of this world to provide what degree of explanation and meaning are possible to this life. While this world is not self-sufficient in the sense of providing by itself all of the meaning that we would like, it is sufficient in the sense of providing enough meaning for us to cope. The term "nature," of course, has many meanings. I take it that here nature includes the worlds of culture and human history.

Religious naturalism is the type of naturalism which affirms a set of beliefs and attitudes that there are religious aspects of this world which can be appreciated within a naturalistic framework. There are some events or processes in our experience that elicit responses that can appropriately be called religious. These experiences and responses are similar enough to those nurtured by the paradigm cases of religion that they may be called religious without stretching the word beyond recognition. (This is adapted from Stone 1993. *Zygon: Journal of Religion and Science* has a number of articles by religious naturalists in the 2000 volume.) As Charles Milligan, lifelong student of American religious naturalism, puts it, by religious naturalism "I take to be any naturalistic world view or philosophy in which religious thought, values and commitments hold an important and not merely incidental part. Or perhaps more simply, where religious discourse plays an integral role" (Milligan 1999).

One of the best definitions of naturalism is that of Arthur C. Danto in *The Encyclopedia of Philosophy*. "Naturalism, in recent usage, is a species of philosophical monism according to which whatever exists or happens is *natural* in the sense of being susceptible to explanation through methods which, although paradigmatically exemplified in the natural sciences, are continuous from domain to domain of objects and events. Hence, naturalism is polemically defined as repudiating the view that there exists or could exist any entities or events which lie, in principle, beyond the scope of scientific explanation" (Danto 1967, 448). Personally, I place great emphasis on the phrase "in principle," since there are many things that science does not now explain. And perhaps we need some natural piety concerning the ontological limit question as to why there is anything at all. But the idea that naturalism is a polemical notion is important.

One of the difficulties in giving a definition of religious naturalism is that it has classically been defined as the opposite of "supernaturalism." However, many theologians today repudiate the notion of the supernatural. Nevertheless, as I try to show below, in contrast to naturalists of a religious orientation, these theologians refer to a dimension of reality which is other than the natural world. Many contemporary religious naturalists accept the term "naturalism" and I have continued to employ the term, despite difficulties in giving a degree of theoretical precision to the term. Furthermore, many religious naturalists find a congenial working relationship with some of these theologians because of a common interest in the processes of this world. It should be noted that the contrast term to "natural" in "naturalism" is not "culture" or "artificial."

Charley Hardwick, whose *Events of Grace* is a recent naturalistic theology, utilizes a similar approach. Drawing on the philosopher Rem Edwards, he finds four basic features in naturalism.

> These are: (1) that only the world of nature is real; (2) that nature is necessary in the sense of requiring no sufficient reason beyond itself to account either for its origin or ontological ground; (3) that nature as a whole may be understood without appeal to any kind of intelligence or purposive agent; and, (4) that all causes are natural causes so that every natural event is itself a product of other natural events. (Hardwick 1996, 5–6; Edwards 1972, 133–141)

Hardwick adds that there are two additional features which most naturalisms have included. "These are: (5) that natural science is the only sound method for establishing knowledge, and (6) that value is based solely in the interests and projects of human beings." Hardwick finds these last two as problematic and unnecessary for the basic definition of naturalism. I am in agreement with him on this. For my part I am strongly committed to the value of science, but find that assertions like number five are often used to denigrate partially verified information or to downplay the value of appreciation or insights couched in pictorial images. In addition, we should expand beyond our anthropocentric approach to values. My growing appreciation of the nonhuman world and of the increasing difficulty of nurturing this appreciation and how this relates to our environmental crises have helped me question assertions like number six. Just because human values are anthropogenic, at least in part, does not mean that they should be exclusively anthropocentric.

Hardwick goes on to indicate the implications of naturalism for religious thinking. He holds that both classical and revisionary theisms generally have three things in common. These are: "(1) that God is personal, (2) that some form of cosmic teleology is metaphysically true, and (3) that there is a cosmically comprehensive conservation of value" (Hardwick 1996, 8). On Hardwick's view a naturalist theology, or roughly what I have called religious naturalism, involves the denial of these three theses and a reconception of religion involving an alternative view.

At this point the question needs to be raised as to whether or not religious naturalism is a social construction, perhaps even a figment of the author's desire to find people who think like him or her. The question is based on a misleading dichotomy. Religious naturalism is neither a clearly delineated natural object (analogous to a solar system) nor a pure fictive object (analogous to a constellation). Rather, like a galaxy, it is a cultural genus whose contours are clear enough once discerned (Delwin Brown 1994, 75–76).

This book does not pretend to achieve verisimilitude. But it does strive for accuracy in its portrayal. To shift the image, this book is like a portrait. Those who know my work will recognize my hand. But it is hoped that the figures themselves will be recognizable; in fact this is a group portrait. Unlike most group portraits, however, the portraitist is clearly stationed within the group being portrayed.

This notion of a portrait as a joint product of the artist and the subjects depicted is the hermeneutical image which follows from the epistemological stance developed in the author's *The Minimalist Vision of Transcendence* in which experience, understanding, and knowledge are seen as transactions between what we call the subject and the object (Stone 1992, 127–135).

Astute readers will note that I have not attempted a definition or theory of religion. I have defined religious naturalism as that type of naturalism that is similar enough to what we take as paradigm cases of a religious orientation that the term "religious" may be used. By this logical maneuver I have avoided the necessity of formulating a theoretical definition of religion. It is important to have an adequate and sensitive conception of religion, but the burden of formulating such a notion is one which religious naturalism can sidestep. Naturalists have frequently come up with a simpleminded understanding of religion. One of the best treatments of religion by a religious naturalist is Loyal Rue's *Religion Is Not About God* (Rue 2005). There is a complexity to the human religious response that overflows many attempts to theorize about it. Keeping an openness about our understanding of religion might free naturalists in their thinking. Note that religious naturalism is not the same as a naturalistic explanation of religion, although a complete religious naturalist position should include such. I offer a tentative definition of religion in the conclusion. Religious naturalism is about reconceiving the object of religion and about the orientation of affections to this world.

There are some alternative notions of religious naturalism associated with Ursula Goodenough and David Oler. For Goodenough naturalism with a religious orientation involves developing our interpretive (or theoretical, I would say), spiritual, and moral responses in the context of our scientific understandings of nature (including humans). It is a generic term for mindful approaches of these three types to our scientific understandings of the natural world. The one rule is that you cannot change the scientific understandings to fit or support your beliefs (Goodenough 2004). Her own version of religious naturalism, stressing a sense of awe and wonder, fits within this broader understanding. For David Oler religion is about moral transformation. As a consequence he is concerned about the potential for idolatry of the natural in Goodenough's viewpoint. Both of these thinkers are treated more fully in what follows, but I suggest that this issue is worth serious consideration for both friends and critics of naturalism that claims to be religious.

Who Are the Religious Naturalists?

The three pivotal figures, in terms of one or more of whom many contemporary religious naturalists orient themselves, are George Santayana, John Dewey, and Henry Nelson Wieman. I agree with Arthur Danto who sees Santayana as the stimulus for much naturalism in America (Danto 1967, 450). Santayana immediately influenced John Herman Randall. Dewey's most direct influence has probably been on Wieman and myself. However, Wieman may have misunderstood Dewey, as we shall see below. And Dewey's influence on myself, evident especially on my pluralism, is modified by the presence of other influences, especially Bernard Meland. There are many similarities between Dewey and Mordecai Kaplan. Citing Eric Goldman, Allan Lazaroff suggests that "Dewey's direct influence on Kaplan is difficult to trace, however, because most early twentieth-century American reformers were Deweyites before they ever read Dewey" (Goldman 1977, 123; Lazaroff 1990, 173). Kaplan did credit Dewey "with teaching him to think pragmatically and functionally about life in general and about education in particular" Lazaroff 1990, 186). The third pivotal religious naturalist was Wieman who influenced Karl Peters, Charley Hardwick, and myself. And while there was probably little influence between Wieman and Kaplan, Emanuel Goldsmith has demonstrated many parallels between these two giants of American religion (Goldsmith 1990, 197–220).

One way of getting a synoptic view of the religious naturalists is to note that the two major roots of religious naturalism in American are Columbia University in New York, where Santayana was read and Woodbridge, Randall and Dewey taught, and the Divinity School and Department of Philosophy of the University of Chicago where Henry Nelson Wieman and certain others of the Chicago School of Theology (George Burman Foster, Edward Scribner Ames, and Eustace Haydon) taught and where Meadville Theological School next door helped provide a matrix for religious humanism. Marvin Shaw has referred to or at least implied that there is a difference between "Columbia naturalism" and "Chicago naturalism," a difference partly manifested in the fact that Santayana and Dewey primarily influenced philosophical circles while Wieman's main influence was theological (Shaw 1995, 15–18). The difference between these two groups is also manifested in their views of whether the object of the religious orientation, that in the world toward which religious or quasi-religious attitudes and behavior is directed, is primarily its power or its goodness. A further difference is that Santayana and his followers distanced themselves from personal commitment to a religious orientation while Wieman, as well as Peters, Hardwick, and myself—who were strongly influenced by Wieman—were passionately committed to their religious outlooks. In other words, the Columbia naturalists tended to appreciate religion critically, while the Chicago naturalists tended to construct a religious outlook to which they could be passionately committed (Shaw 1995, 13–31).

It may come as a surprise to some readers to discover that many religious naturalists use the term "God" to describe the object of their religious orientation (as distinct from those naturalists, such as Santayana, who uses the term "God" or "gods" in describing human religions). To sort through this issue I propose the following typology. On the topic of God I find that religious naturalists tend to fall into three groups: (1) those who conceive of God as the creative process within the universe, (2) those who think of God as the totality of the universe considered religiously, and (3) those who do not speak of God yet still can be called religious. In the first group belong, among others, Shailer Mathews, Henry Nelson Wieman, Ralph Wendell Burhoe, Karl Peters, and perhaps William Dean. In the second belong Spinoza, Samuel Alexander, George Burman Foster, Frederick May Eliot, the later Bernard Loomer, and others. The third includes Usrula Goodenough, Donald Crosby, Willem Drees, myself, and others.

What distinguishes my use of the term "religious naturalism" from that of some others is my inclusion of the first two groups within the term. This is a controversial usage and is one of the ways in which my conception of religious naturalism differs from religious humanism. As used in this book, religious naturalism is the more inclusive term. To conceive of God either as the creative process within the universe or else as the entire universe considered religiously fits within the definition of naturalism as used in this volume. There is no reference to a supreme reality distinct from and ontologically superior to the universe in these two views. Hence the first two groups may be considered as types of religious naturalism. Perhaps the term "naturalistic theism" might be appropriately used for these views. In this case naturalistic theism would be that variety of religious naturalism that continues to use the traditional term "God," although within a rigorously naturalistic sense.

Related Views

There are some related and overlapping views that it is helpful to distinguish from religious naturalism. The first is empiricism. Religious naturalism often has an empirical orientation, although the nature of this empiricism varies widely. Bernard Meland and others have a broad conception of empiricism, what I have called a "generous empiricsm" (Stone 1992, chap. 4). Further, thinkers such as William James and Douglas Clyde Macintosh are empiricists in religious epistemology but develop notions of God that do not fit the generic definition of religious naturalism as developed here. Finally, it should be clear religious naturalism need not be committed to an empiricist foundationalism.

The second view, which overlaps religious naturalism, is materialism or physicalism. Hardwick claims that a consistent and honest empiricism will be a physicalism. This is not, of course, old-fashioned mechanism, but it is still an insistence on the physical basis of all reality. Danto asserts that naturalism is compatible with a consistent idealistic view (Danto 1967, 448). There is a strong leaning toward physicalism in my own thinking. However, this is a philosophically strong position to maintain. Both for reasons of conversation with indigenous and neopagan religious thinkers who have experienced what they term spirits who are not part of this material world and also in order not to preclude my own growth in this area by dogmatically foreclosing the possibility of such experiences, I do not unequivocally affirm physicalism. However, I do suspect that at the end of the day whatever spirits there are will be found to have a material basis. The world is full of patterns that can be replicated across time and space, but I have always found them to have a physical reality when they exist. Perhaps it is best to say that while naturalism does not logically entail materialism or physicalism, most religious naturalists tend toward a generous materialism that allows for much of what we designate by the terms "mind" and "value."

A third orientation related to religious naturalism is religious humanism. In many ways the religious naturalists who do not use God-language are close to religious humanism. I am referring here to the viewpoints of classical humanists such as John Dietrich and Curtis Reese during the time of the Humanist Controversy (the 1920s) or the signers of the *Humanist Manifesto* of 1933. Clearly these humanists are naturalists in that they focus on this world and deny the reality of God, soul, or heaven. I believe that they could also appropriately be called religious naturalists because their devotion to science and human betterment is analogous to the devotion of those whom we normally call religious. (See my critique of the *Humanist Manifesto*, Stone 1992, 196–202.)

There were writers earlier in this century who are often labeled humanists, albeit religious humanists, who can be distinguished from the humanists of the 1920s and 1930s. These include George Burman Foster of *The Place of Religion in Man's Struggle for Existence* and Edward Scribner Ames in his book *Religion*. It seems to me that they are close to Shailer Mathews who carefully distinguished himself from humanism. As Marvin Shaw points out, these are not merely verbal disputes, but involve basic attitudes and orientations, namely openness to resources of grace (Shaw 1995, 17–30). Shaw appropriately calls them naturalistic theists. In *American Philosophies of Religion* Wieman and Meland referred to Ames, Dewey, Mathews, G. B. Smith, and themselves as "empirical theists" (Wieman and Meland 1936).

William Murry has distinguished older humanists of the 1920s and 1930s from many contemporary humanists. Among the characteristics of this newer humanism, as he describes it, is an openness *"to wonder and mystery and transcendence in a naturalistic framework"* (Murry 2000, 84;

see also Murry 2007, 25–59, 107–115). The older humanists might be considered as religious naturalists, if their passion for truth and justice are read as analogues of a religious orientation. However, the attitude of the newer humanists, as described by Murry, are definitely cut from the same cloth as religious naturalism.

Some of us find a significant difference of basic stance between some varieties of religious naturalism and that of many humanists, religious or otherwise. "The issue is that of openness to resources and challenges beyond the humanly manageable." Thus some varieties of religious naturalism have "a greater sense that we are not masters of our fate, that we need to recognize the worth of, to nurture and be nurtured by, this-worldly grace and judgment" (Stone 1993a, 35).

In short, religious humanism can be seen as one variety of religious naturalism, because the commitment of these humanists to the search for truth and the struggle for justice is the naturalistic analogue to commitment to the transcendent in traditional theism. (This represents a shift in my view; formerly I drew a line between religious naturalism and humanism. See Stone 1999.) Further, the religious humanists, represented especially by the humanists of the 1920s and 1930s, are to be distinguished from those newer humanists who have a deeper sense of wonder and mystery. And writers like George Burman Foster and Edward Scribner Ames, who are often called humanists, might better be described as religious naturalists. Indeed, Ames was not asked to sign the *Humanist Manifesto* (Wilson 1995, 91).

Another issue concerns process theology. Process thinkers often consider themselves as naturalists and thus as religious naturalists. However, there are significant differences between them and the group I am delineating. Their panentheism allows them to speak of God as immanent within the world and hence of themselves as naturalists. However, theirs is a different type of religious naturalism. Process theology has become a rather loose term. For those aligned with Hartshorne at least, there is one entity which is different from all others in being surpassable by no other entity except itself in a future state. It has maximal relatedness and compassion and often is conceived to confer objective immortality through its memory. These three characteristics of being: (1) surpassable by none except itself, (2) supremely related and compassionate, and (3) conferring conservation of value make it different from the writers grouped together in this book as religious naturalists. Thus, as I understand it, the God of process theology, while deeply immersed within this world, is so ontologically distinct and superior as to fall outside of naturalism as I understand it. To conceive of an entity which is surpassable by none except itself is not naturalist. Immanentist yes, naturalist no. As Robert

Mesle, an astute expositor of process theology, puts it, the difference between process theism and process naturalism, which I think is a type of religious naturalism, is "not naturalism vs. supernaturalism, but the question of whether the world of finite, natural creatures is unified in such a way as to give rise to a single divine Subject" (Mesle 1993, 127).

As an illustration of this, in his *Religion and Scientific Naturalism*, David Griffin develops a Whiteheadean view that he calls "naturalistic theism." He is using the term "naturalistic" in a different manner than that used in this volume. "Variable constitutive divine influence would be understood as *part* of the normal pattern of causes and effects, *not* an interruption of this pattern. Such a position could be called 'naturalistic theism,' or 'theistic naturalism.' It would be naturalistic, because it would reject the idea of any supernatural interruptions" (Griffin 2000, 40). In developing this theism, Griffin asserts that: "The supreme power of the universe is pure goodness, pure unbounded love. . . . Far from being a remote, inaccessible creator, this God is intimately involved in the origination of each event in the universe. Each experiential event in the world receives from God its 'ideal aim'" (Griffin 2000, 97). Griffin is correct in using the term "naturalism" of this view in so far as it repudiates a supernatural interruption of the natural order. However, this process God is a supreme power, the only entity involved in the origination of every event and giving to each its ideal aim. This surely is a God who is radically different from the rest of the universe. This is another example of the same word, in this case "naturalism," being used is two radically different senses. Given the cogency of Griffin's use of the term within his framework, which is part of a well-recognized philosophical movement that had received its classical form by at least the 1920s, one can concede the validity of his use of the term as it functions within his conceptual schema. At the same time our use of the term is part of a well-recognized philosophical movement that is at least as venerable in age.

It should be noted that there are a number of other versions of what might be called revised theism that would claim to be naturalistic or at least repudiate supernaturalism. Indeed, many theologians today reject the term "supernatural" as having connotations of miracle, divine intervention, or even a two-level reality. For them there is a strong this-worldly orientation and a real immanence to God. However, at the end of the day for them, there is "a dimension," which we humans can call God, that is in some sense not reducible to this world. This dimension does not appear in the group of thinkers that I distinguish as naturalists with a religious bent.

Furthermore, many religious naturalists find a congenial working relationship with some of these theologians because of a common interest in the processes of this world. Joseph Sittler, John Cobb, Philip Hefner, John Haught, and Wentzel van Huyssteen may be taken as well-known examples of such theologians. Paul Tillich's claim that God is the ground of being, not the supreme being, may be taken as typical. Tillich is not a naturalist in the sense that we are using the term. His ground of being is so ontologically distinct from any being that it is not either the entire world or a process or entity within it. "God as the ground of being infinitely transcends that of which he is the ground" (Tillich 1957, 7; see the section "Beyond Naturalism and Supranaturalism," Tillich 1957, 5–10).

What is the difference between religious naturalism and pantheism? The answer is that these are intersecting concepts. Spinoza is often called a pantheist and this study claims him as the first major religious naturalist, while Bernard Loomer, toward the end of his career, spoke of the entire interconnected web of existence as God. Those naturalists who identify God with the entire universe would qualify as pantheists by most definitions. It is important to note that these thinkers usually identify a certain aspect of the universe as God or the universe when considered from a certain regard or perspective. Samuel Alexander, for example, considered God as the universe insofar as it was evolving toward a new and higher level. Edward Scribner Ames referred to God as the world in certain aspects and functions, namely, orderliness, love, and intelligence or order, beauty, and expansion. F. M. Eliot spoke of God as a symbol for the experiences of a moral imperative, of the orderliness and of the purposiveness of the world. On the other hand, those naturalists who identify God with part of the universe, such as Wieman for whom God is the integrative process within the world, that would not be pantheists.

Paul Harrison, the founder and president of the World Pantheist Movement (WPM), undoubtedly the world's largest religious naturalist organization, writes that "pantheism holds that the universe as a whole is divine, and that there is no divinity other than the universe and nature" (Harrison, 1999, 1). Note that he uses the word "divine" rather than "God." Harrison also points out that to say the universe as a whole is divine does not mean that every individual part of it is divine. "It doesn't mean that oil slicks or bits of chewing gum stuck to the pavement are divine," or nuclear weapons, factory smokestacks, or mass murderers (Harrison 1999, 71). He informs me that recently the WPM has dropped the use of the term "divine."

The World Pantheist Movement has developed a Pantheist Credo (with the proviso that it is intended as a guide and statement of consensus, not as binding on members). The first clause reads: "We revere and celebrate the universe as the totality of being . . . It is self-organizing, ever-evolving and inexhaustibly diverse. Its overwhelming power, beauty, and fundamental mystery compel the deepest human reverence and wonder." The third clause starts: "We are an inseparable part of nature, which we should cherish, revere and preserve in all its magnificent beauty and diversity."

Paul Harrison distinguishes scientific pantheism, which is the focus of the World Pantheistic Movement, from idealistic and dualistic pantheism. While idealistic pantheism might be considered logically compatible with naturalism, as Arthur Danto affirms, religious naturalists typically are not idealists (Danto 1967, 448). Dualistic pantheism would seem to be incompatible with the naturalistic basis of religious naturalism.

A frequent view of pantheism is that it envisions absorption into the infinite ocean of being as a spiritual goal or a prospect after death or perhaps even that the identity of the individual human self with the great ocean of being is the true picture of reality. However, Charles Milligan suggests than pantheism in the past century or so has pictured a real independence and autonomy to the human self, a viewpoint which he himself endorses (Milligan 1987).

There is a similarity between those religious naturalists who speak of the entire universe in religious terms and the advocates of the Gaia hypothesis. Generally, however, these religious naturalists would use religious language of the entire universe, at least in certain aspects, rather than just the planet Earth. Furthermore, the Gaia hypothesis is often linked with interesting but debatable scientific hypotheses about the self-corrective nature of global biochemical processes which are not essential to religious naturalism.

Who Uses the Term?

Who uses the term "religious naturalism" to designate their own views? The term "naturalism" was used in the 1920s, '30s, and '40s to designate a general philosophical position differentiated from two other widespread philosophical views, idealism and dualism, as well as from popular theism and the modified theism of liberal theology. (See Krikorian 1944 and Danto 1967). Wieman's widely read *Source of Human Good* distinguishes "the newer naturalism" from the "older naturalisms, which tended toward reductive materialism" (Wieman 1946, 6. See 6–9). Wieman refers to the chapter on "Categories of Naturalism" by William Dennes in Krikorian's book. Two explicit corollaries which Wieman draws from his naturalism are significant. One is that nothing has causal efficacy except material

events and nothing has value except material events and their possibilities, understanding material events to be "not merely pellets of inanimate
matter" but also "biological, social, and historical forms of existence"
(Wieman 1946, 8). Naturalists generally will agree that biological and
historical forms are basically material, highly developed but none the
less material. Many naturalists, starting with Alexander, Sellars, Dewey,
and Smuts in the 1920s, developed a nonreductive form of naturalism,
often taking an "emergentist" viewpoint whereby novel forms, such as
life and human culture emerge from while still remaining rooted in
the material world, thus allowing for the distinctiveness of biological
and human existence and values as idealism had earlier insisted while
yet retaining the universality of the material world, plus its possibilities
(Alexander, 1920; Sellars 1922, 260–286; Dewey 1981; Smuts 1961).
However, some naturalists, such as Arthur Danto, assert that naturalism
is logically independent of materialism, while others, such as Charley
Hardwick, like Wieman, explicitly develop a materialist (or physicalist)
religious viewpoint.

The term "religious naturalism" was in frequent use at the University of Chicago's Divinity School and its *Journal of Religion* in the 1940s
and 1950s, if not earlier. (I owe thanks to Nancy Hutton and Cedric
Heppler for their help here.) In 1929 Wieman titled his review of E.
S. Ames *Religion*, "Naturalism Becomes Religious." In 1958 Wieman
published an entry "Naturalism" in *A Handbook for Christian Theology*
(Wieman 1958). In 1963 his "Reply to Weigel" refers frequently to
"religious naturalism" and to "the religious vision in naturalistic terms"
(Wieman 1963, 363–377).

At the same time George Perrigo Conger, in *The Ideologies of Religion*, refers to religious naturalism as a view with which he has sympathy
(Conger 1940; I have not been able to secure a copy of this book). Also
in the 1940s Edwin R. Walker, H. H. Dubs, and N. P. Jacobsen are using
the term to refer to a then-contemporary type of religious thinking (H.
H. Dubs, 1943; Jacobson 1949; I owe the references in this paragraph
to Nancy Hutton and Cedric Heppler).

Thus the term "religious naturalism" was in frequent use among
certain theological writers in America in the early 1940s. However,
there was a nearly complete hiatus in the use of the term from 1946 to
1987, a gap that will be discussed briefly at the beginning of part two.
This hiatus is the reason why this volume is subtitled *The Rebirth of a
Forgotten Tradition*.

Around 1955 Bernard Meland wrote an unpublished paper on "The
Roots of Religious Naturalism" (Meland 1955; see also Meland 1962,
130). Meland uses the term in a wider sense than used here, includ-

ing, for example Whitehead among the naturalists. Earlier, in *American Philosophies of Religion*, Wieman and Meland placed "Evolutionary Theists" (John E. Boodin, Robert Calhoun, and others), "Cosmic Theists" (including Whitehead and F. S. C. Northrop), Religious Humanists and Empirical Theists (including Ames, Dewey, Mathews, and themselves) within the larger category of those "rooted in the tradition of naturalism" (Wieman and Meland 1936).

Some contemporaries, for example, Cohen, Goodenough, Hardwick, and Crosby have acknowledged that their views are forms of religious naturalism (Hardwick 2003, 112; Crosby 2003, 118). Hardwick refers to his view as "naturalistic theism." Robert Corrington refers to his work as "ecstatic naturalism" and in correspondence has indicated his willingness to be included in this group portrait. While Loyal Rue does not use the term for himself, he was one of the first, along with Michael Cavanaugh, to introduce the term into the discussions in the Institute on Religion in an Age of Science (Michael Cavanaugh 2000). Rue provides a helpful description of religious naturalism as a religious viewpoint and a fascinating glimpse of its possible future growth after the coming ecological holocaust (Rue, 2005, 361–368). Willem Drees is not sure whether or not he is a religious naturalist, but he is one of the most careful students of it as a movement (Drees 1998; Drees 2000; Drees 2006). Some writers use a term analogous to "religious naturalism." Karl Peters, for example, describes his view as "theistic naturalism." Gordon Kaufman writes that "religious naturalism" is not his preferred term and that he does "not much like living in a box, especially if the specifications of the box are defined by others" (Kaufman 2003, 95). He does say, however, that he is willing to be included as a religious naturalist provided that it is made clear that the biological and cultural realms are to be included in the description of the human condition. He prefers to use the term "biohistorical naturalism."

I believe that most of the remaining contemporary writers included in this portrait of religious naturalists have been given a chance to demur at their inclusion and have declined.

There currently is a slightly different use of the term "religious naturalism" that needs to be recognized (Goodenough 1998, xvii; Goodenough 2004, 1–2). The ideas it connotes and the writers it denotes overlap considerably with those of the term as used herein. In this view religious naturalists are those who find in the natural world (usually construed as including culture and history) inspiration and resources for their religious and spiritual life. This could include many theists who find such inspiration, besides the naturalistic theists such as Wieman, Burhoe, Peters, and Hardwick. I find this use of the term to be helpful in building much needed bridges to more conventionally monotheistic people. In the era when religion plays a major role in cultural fragmentation and personal animosity, this is very important. However, while giving a friendly nod to those who use this term in this fashion, I refrain from using it that way in this book. In the first place, a selection criterion is needed to determine who is studied in this book. Second, I try to adopt a heuristic attitude of tentativeness in my writings. I am agnostic about whether or not there is more ontological reality to the transcendent than my minimalistic vision penetrates. This book is a historical group portrait of religious people who live and think *as if* there is no ontologically supreme God, soul, or heaven. This portrait should provide resources of a tradition for those who are exploring this worldview.

Can We Prove Religious Naturalism?

Arthur Danto, Wentzel van Huyssteen and others have pointed out that naturalism is presupposed and has not been proven (Danto 1966, 450; Van Huyssteen 1997, 97–98). That is true, but rather beside the point. Like any worldview it cannot be proven. But it does make more sense to many of us than alternate views. One way of putting it is to say that just as the heliocentric theory could be salvaged at one time by multiplying epicycles, so too belief in traditional or revised theism can be salvaged by various strategies. However, the time comes when a simpler theory seems more convincing. I have tried to make a case for my own minimalist outlook elsewhere (Stone 1992, 27–33; see Drees 2006, 114–115; Crosby 2007).

Other Studies

As a scholar of the Chicago School of Theology, Bernard Meland will always remain one of the major commentators on religious naturalism, even though he was not focused specifically on naturalism. (See relevant sections in many of his writings, especially Meland 1962. See also chapter XV, "Empirical Theists" in Wieman and Meland, 1936; "Introduction: The Empirical Tradition in Theology at Chicago" in Meland 1969a; Meland, 1970; and Meland 1984.) Charles Harvey Arnold and Creighton Peden are other historians of the Chicago School and Peden and Stone's two volume anthology, *The Chicago School of Theology: Pioneers in Religious Inquiry*, contains many of the primary texts (Arnold 1966, Peden 1987, Peden & Stone 1996). For the Columbia naturalists, Santayana, Dewey, and Randall, William Shea's *The Naturalists and the Supernatural* is one of the classic studies (Shea 1984). Marvin Shaw's *Nature's Grace* is a very helpful study of Wieman and his treatment of Foster, Ames, and Mathews is significant. His analysis of Wieman as providing "a theistic stance without the supernatural God" represents one of the most significant statements in the historiography of religious naturalism (Shaw 1995, 136–139). Michael Cavanaugh's "What Is Religious Naturalism? A Preliminary Report of an Ongoing Conversation" is a helpful summary of online discussions by some members of the Institute on Religion in an Age of Science, including Willem Drees, Ursula Goodenough, Loyal Rue, and himself (Cavanaugh 2000, 241–252). One of the best overall summaries of convergences and divergences religious naturalism is Donald Crosby's lucid "Religious Naturalism" (Crosby, 2007). Willem Drees has given a very helpful exploration of the theoretical issues in religious naturalism in a recent article (Drees, 2006).

Probably the first person to use the term as a label to describe a group of religious thinkers was Edgar Sheffield Brightman in his 1940 *A Philosophy of Religion*, where he applied it to Samuel Alexander and Henry Nelson Wieman (Brightman 1940, 148–153, 209–216). His criticisms of this view are still relevant and need addressing. His general critique is that the emergence of mind and religious faith from unconscious matter is "an unexplained brute fact." A personal God, on the other hand, explains both matter and mind. "Matter is an order of the divine experience . . . mind is an order of beings other than God which . . . [reflect] dimly . . . the nature of cosmic mind" (Brightman 1940, 231). Naturalists generally would reply that such resort to supernatural explanations is just as unsatisfactory an explanation, for the existence of such a God is likewise "an unexplained brute fact," which merely adds to the principles needing explanation. As I would put it, the notion of God is an epicycle in an unnecessarily complex scheme. Brightman has a further specific criticism of Wieman, that God as the growth of meaning and value in the universe is a creator or increaser of value, but not a conserver of value (Brightman 1940, 153). Most naturalists, even if they have a theistic naturalism, do not adopt the notion of God as the conserver of value. The religious attitude here must be that of resignation, not faith.

Part One

The Birth of Religious Naturalism

Early Religious Naturalism

Religious naturalism is currently undergoing a renaissance. The purpose of part one is to explore some of the major religious naturalists of the early twentieth century, so that we can learn from the strengths and weaknesses of our forbears.

We should start with indigenous traditions. However, to discuss the parallels between religious naturalism and the ways of indigenous peoples is impossible here. I will note that the study of indigenous religions by native scholars is one of the signs of hope in today's world. Respect for these scholars demands serious engagement. For Native Americans the pathmaker was probably Vine Deloria (Deloria 1973; Deloria 1999). Milton Chee, John DuFour, Viola Cordova, and Anne Waters have formed a beachhead for Native American philosophers within the Western academy. (See Anne Waters, ed., *American Indian Thought* [Waters 2004]). Ines Talamantez, Apache, heads the graduate program in American Indian religions at University of California at Santa Barbara, which leads students to face the hermeneutical and ethical issues of cross-cultural scholarship. A recent and helpful text by native scholars uses "the sacred" as a generic category in ways that has some analogies to its use by religious naturalists, but the analogy should not be pressed too far, lest we fail to respect the differences among these views (Beck, Walters, Francisco 1992, 3, 8–9). (For an insightful account of native approaches to science, see Gregory Cajete's *Native Science* [Cajate 2000]. For a detailed history of mainstream appropriations and misappropriations of Native American spirituality, see Philip Jenkins, *Dreamcatchers: How Mainstream America Discovered Native Spirituality*, Jenkins 2004.)

In the Euro-American tradition we can start with Bruno or Toland. Giordano Bruno, the European monk, was listed by Paul Harrison in his *The Elements of Pantheism*, as the "first truly post-Christian pantheist in Europe" (Harrison 1999, 29). He paid with his life in 1600 for his heresy. Harrison suggests that John Toland "was the first modern pantheist to combine a religious reverence for the universe with respect for science and a belief that everything is made of matter." Toland even projected an organizational basis for pantheism and developed a brief liturgy for its meetings (Harrison 1999, 31; see Toland 1721).

We could give attention to the Enlightenment and the Romantics and Transcendentalists, especially Wordsworth and Emerson, above all to Grandfather Spinoza, but consideration of space urges restraint.

Interpreters of Spinoza disagree, but surely his phrase "God or nature" (*Deus sive natura*) indicates that he is a forerunner of contemporary religious naturalism. There is one strand in religious naturalism (William Bernhardt, Charles Milligan, William Dean, Thomas Berry, Brian Swimme, and Donald Crosby) that echoes Spinoza in his non-anthropocentric approach to religion. Further, his body-mind monism is another common theme among religious naturalists, although they have not cornered the market on this view. Not all religious naturalists today would follow Spinoza in his rejection of human freedom, but those who affirm freedom or at least some notion of responsible choice often overcome dualism by finding an analogy to choice in some parts of the nonhuman realm, particularly animals with nervous systems, a plasticity that human choice and responsibility is rooted in and emergent from. Finally, an important theme in Spinoza bears pondering. His intellectual love of God is a third level of knowledge above sense perception and rational knowledge. I suggest that rather than a superempirical form of cognition, Spinoza was driving at a form of insight or appreciation of the whole system of nature. This is similar to John Dewey's imaginative sense of the whole. Samuel Alexander was able to bring this notion to life. (See "Spinoza and Time" in Alexander 1939, 374–378.)

In many ways Emerson paves the way for religious naturalism. He had a strong sense of the immanence of the divine in the world. However, his idealism, as in his concept of the Oversoul, kept him from being clearly a religious naturalist. Comments like the following show that Emerson's idealism places him outside of religious naturalism: "Nature is the symbol of spirit. . . . Man is conscious of a universal soul within or behind his individual life. . . . There seems to be a necessity in spirit to manifest itself in material forms; and . . . beast and bird, acid and alkali, preëxist in necessary Ideas in the mind of God" (Emerson 1982, 48–49, 54). As Bernard Meland said, "What Emerson saw was not trees, lakes and planets, but the 'Over-Soul' incarnated" (Meland 1933a, 444). Catherine Albanese finds in Emerson a confusion between nature as real and sacramental and nature as a passing show obscuring the Absolute behind it. From this confusion the heritage of Emerson became an ambiguity between seeking harmony with nature and attempting to master it, including both the wilderness preservation movement and the attempt of the mind-cure movement to leave lower for "higher" nature (Albanese 1990, 82, 87). Thus I find Emerson's legacy for religious naturalism to be mixed.

While religious naturalism, as constructed in this book, starts with Spinoza and has roots within the Western tradition, we could also start in India with the Carvaka writers, the skeptical and materialistic Hindu heterodox thinkers (Radhakrishnan and Moore 1957, 227–249). Issues of publishing economy urge restraint.

Again, the Mahayana Buddhist notion that samsara is nirvana might be considered as an affirmation in a different language of the sacredness of this world. If spirituality is not "understood as crossing a metaphysical boundary into the supernatural, but rather as a matter of dissolving our habits of exclusion and relinquishing our customary horizons for what we allow to be relevant—a process of restoring our original intimacy with all things—Buddhism can be seen as a profoundly spiritual tradition. It is a spirituality devoted to erasing the fearful anguish of feeling utterly alone in this world and to resuming full presence as an appreciative and contributing part of it" (Hershock 2005, 6).

If "Heaven and Earth" point to the creativity of all things, then the neo-Confucian affirmation that humans form a triad with heaven and earth may be read as a counterpart to the naturalist's imaginative grasp of the whole. Zhang Zai's *Western Inscription* which he placed on the wall of his academy reads in part: "That which fills the universe I regard as my body. . . . all things are my companions" (Wing-tsit Chan 1963, 497). When this is seen as an imperative as well as a declaration, the ethical and spiritual tasks of religious naturalism may be viewed as a yin-yang alternative between the Confucian "investigation of things" and "cultivation of the heart-mind" and the Daoist going with the flow of the Dao. (For Daoism, see any translation of the *Dao De Ching*; for Confucius see Hall and Ames 1987, 12–17, 195–249; for Neo-Confucianism, Fung Yu-lan 1953, vol. II, 491–496; Siu-chi Huang 1999, 68–76; and the contributions by Mary Evelyn Tucker, Michael C. Kalton, Tu Weiming, Joseph A. Adler, Toshio Kuwako, John Berthrong, Robert Cummings Neville, Robert P. Weller, and Peter K. Bol in Tucker and Berthrong 1998.)

The extent of the congruence between neo-paganism and religious naturalism remains to be explored. There are obvious difficulties, particularly for those, such as the author, who are rooted in monotheistic or Enlightenment sensibilities. I tried to address these difficulties in "On Listening to Indigenous Peoples and Neo-pagans: Obstacles to Appropriating the Older Ways," (Stone 1997). Since writing that essay I have seen the need to explore further the degree to which techniques of magic involve an extension of what I have called a generous empiricism and to which they involve an ignoring of the need for empirical safeguards (Stone 1992, 111–168). One of my Wiccan friends pointed out that, whereas I was interested in openness to uncontrollable and unmanipulable resources of grace, she was interested in manipulating forces for good. This may be partly a matter of emphasis, perhaps even on my part, a well-fed and well-nurtured male with a strong ego who has discovered a need for an occasional stance of receptivity. It may also represent a different fundamental orientation.

Since starting this study more and more religious naturalists have been brought to my attention. For instance, Alton Jenkins has drawn my attention to Lloyd Geering of New Zealand and reminded me of the British scholar Don Cupitt. However, I have had to acknowledge my limitations and draw this project to a conclusion.

Chapter One

Philosophical Religious Naturalism

The details of our story start with philosophers: George Santayana in the United States and Samuel Alexander in England followed by American pragmatists (Dewey, Mead), John Herman Randall, Roy Wood Sellars, and Jan Christiaan Smuts.

George Santayana: Religion in the Life of Reason

George Santayana, who taught philosophy at Harvard from 1889 to 1912, was one of the most creative religious naturalists. He rejected the ontological validity of religious beliefs, but affirmed the importance of their role in human life. He developed a rich naturalistic hermeneutics of religion in Western civilization which remains an inspiration and resource for contemporary religious naturalism.

A good way to grasp Santayana is to note how he distinguished between facts and ideals. At their best both poetry and religion articulate human ideals. They do not describe facts. He writes in the Preface to *Interpretations of Poetry and Religion*, "The excellence of religion is due to an idealisation of experience which, while making religion noble if treated as poetry, makes it necessarily false if treated as science. Its function is rather to draw from reality materials for an image of that ideal to which reality ought to conform" (Santayana 1989, 3; for the distinction between poetry and religion, see the Preface, and chapters I and X of *Interpretations of Poetry and Religion*). In the last sentence of this book he writes: "Poetry raised to its highest power is then identical with religion grasped in its inmost truth; . . . then poetry loses its frivolity and ceases to demoralise, while religion surrenders its illusions and ceases to deceive" (Santayana 1989, 172).

Religion differs from poetry and other products of the imagination in its pragmatic effect. Religion "differs from a mere play of the imagination in one important respect; it reacts directly upon life; it is a factor in conduct. Our religion is the poetry in which we believe" (Santayana 1989, 20). The imagination enforces duties powerfully when it pictures them "in oaths sworn before the gods, in commandments written by the finger of God upon stone tablets, in visions of hell and heaven, in chivalrous love and loyalty, and in the sense of family dignity and honour" (Santayana 1989, 11).

The error which Christianity committed, but paganism did not, was to confuse idealization with description of fact. This fallacy, the root of all superstition, is to think that for poetry to be religious, to be the inspiration of life, it must conceal that it is poetry and deceive us about the facts. What makes superstition is the failure to distinguish between objects of imagination and facts to be described and understood. "Men became superstitious not because they had too much imagination, but because they were not aware that they had any." There is a further distinction which Santayana immediately makes, religion differs from superstition in its moral worth. "For religion differs from superstition not psychologically but morally, not in its origin but in its worth" (Santayana 1989, 68).

Santayana's criticism of liberal trends in religion is that they collapse description and imagination. The liberal school is "merely impoverishing religious symbols and vulgarising religious aims; it subtracts from faith that imagination by which faith becomes an interpretation and idealisation of human life, and retains only a stark and superfluous principle of superstition. For meagre and abstract as such a religion may be, it contains all the venom of absolute pretensions. . . . Mythology cannot become science by being reduced in bulk, but it may cease, as a mythology, to be worth having" (Santayana 1989, 4; see "Modernism and Christianity," in *Winds of Doctrine*, Santayana 1913, 48–53).

Santayana's main treatment of religion is in *Reason in Religion*, Volume III of the five volume *Life of Reason*. Here we find rich insights and hermeneutics mixed with overgeneralizations and rank anti-Semitism (Henry S. Levinson's *Santayana: Pragmatism and the Spiritual Life* and Marvin Shaw's dissertation are helpful. See Levinson 1992 and Shaw 1968).

His starting point is superstition, the most primitive element in religion. (He sees superstition as having never been totally overcome in the history of religion. His term is the "life" of religion, not its evolution.) Finding an aspect of superstition to appreciate rationally will be difficult. It is not difficult to find an aspect of superstition to criticize. Superstition is an attempted science, motivated by the desire to understand, to foresee, or to control the world. However, its claims are arbitrary chimeras, founded on a confusion of efficient causes and ideal results.

The critical aspect of Santayana's naturalistic hermeneutics is clear at the beginning. To appeal to the supernatural is to remain in the obvious, in what is plausible and easy to conceive. Moral and particular forces are easier to imagine than universal natural laws.

For example, the key to appreciating miracles is the obviousness of its supposed connection between the physical event and its "spiritual" or psychological cause. "If the water of Lourdes, bottled and sold by chemists, cured all diseases, there would be no miracle. . . . But if each believer in taking the water thinks the effect morally conditioned, if he interprets the result, should it be favorable, as an answer to his faith and prayers, then the cure becomes miraculous because it becomes intelligible and manifests the obedience of nature to the exigencies of spirit" (23/190 The first page reference is to *Reason in Religion*, Santayana 1905; the second reference is to the one volume abridgement of *The Life of Reason*, Santayana 1953). He next deals with sacrifice and prayer. Sacrifice starts off as propitiation of an envious god, but soon suggests that what was once a bribe easily becomes a friendly distribution, giving to each participant what is due by convention, however little it may be deserved. In religious ritual people find satisfaction in fulfilling in a seemly manner what has been prescribed.

Then new religious sentiments appear. In agricultural contexts, for example, sacrifice becomes a ritual of thanksgiving. So in Christian devotion, which often follows primitive impulses in a more speculative fashion, the cross is not merely the payment of a debt or an amount of suffering to be endured, but rather an act of affection and an affirmation that God wished to assimilate himself to humans, instead of declaring forgiveness from on high.

If sacrifice can become thanksgiving, it can undergo an even nobler change, pointing out the wisdom of renunciation. We are invited to give up the inordinate and foolish part of our will. When religion achieves this stage it stops misrepresenting material conditions, and learns to express spiritual goods. Of course, the pathology of this is that sacrifice may merely achieve an emotional catharsis instead of a moral improvement.

His discussion of prayer continues the distinction between the physical effects of religion and its spiritual value. "Prayer, in fine, though it accomplishes nothing material, constitutes something spiritual. It will not bring rain, but until rain comes it may cultivate hope and resignation and may prepare the heart for any issue. . . . A candle wasting itself before an image will prevent no misfortune, but it may bear witness to some silent hope or relieve some sorrow by expressing it." Both physical dependence and spiritual dominion can be expressed in worship and supplication to God for aid. "Physical impotence is expressed by man's appeal for help; moral dominion by belief in God's omnipotence." This belief could easily be contradicted by events, "if God's omnipotence stood for a material magical control of events." However, faith can survive any outward disappointment, because it does "not become truly religious until it ceases to be a foolish expectation of improbable things and rises on stepping-stones of its material disappointments into a spiritual peace. What would sacrifice be but a risky investment if it did not redeem us from love of those things which it asks us to surrender?" (47–48/201).

Here we begin to glimpse the rational development of religion. "In rational prayer the soul may be said to accomplish three things important to its welfare: it withdraws within itself and defines its good, it accommodates itself to destiny, and it grows like the ideal which it conceives" (43/198). The functional approach to religion manifests itself in the ideal of deity, which is the ideal of humanity freed from those limitations that a wise person accepts, but a spiritual person feels as limitations. Humans are mortal. Therefore the gods must be immortal. The religiously advanced person tries to see everything as they do, under the form of eternity. This is the goal of reason. The gods are just. They are no respecters of persons. It is our ideal to become like this. It would be embarrassing to indulge in selfish prayer. The impartial majesty of the divine mind will be imagined and thus will tend to pass into the human mind.

Santayana now moves to a discussion of mythology. He has already asserted that the first function of religion is propitiation, which comes before the construction of a mythology. Cult comes before fable and worship precedes dogma.

As with his discussion of prayer, Santayana rejects a simple identification of myth with empirical truth. Even when people acknowledge a Providence, they still have natural aversions and fears. Among sane people, prayer has never stopped practical efforts to secure the desired results.

The function of prayer is not simply magic or compensation, but transformation. If a myth was originally accepted it was not for its obvious falsehood; it was accepted because it was understood to express reality metaphorically. Its function was to exhibit some piece of experience in its totality and moral outcome, just as in a map we reduce everything in order to examine it in its relationships. Put another way, the function of myth is to present events in terms relative to spirit.

The two factors in mythology are "a moral consciousness and a corresponding poetic conception of things." Thus the role of reason in religion again becomes clear. Had fable started with an adequate explanation of human values, its pictures, even if the external notions they built upon were wrong, would have shown that a world so conceived would have contained the ideals and prizes of life. "Thus Dante's bad cosmography and worse history do not detract from the spiritual penetration of his thought." *The Divine Comedy*, in other words, "describes the Life of Reason in a fantastic world" (55–56/204). One function of mythology has been to change religion from superstition into wisdom, from a justification for magic into an ideal representation of moral goods. Gods are representations of our ideals. The function of the gods is to interpret the human heart to us and to help us discover our ambitions and, as we emulate the gods, to pursue these ambitions.

Among the common folk the poetic factor usually predominates. Historians and theologians tend to concentrate on the hypostasized forms of mythology, instead of the moral factor. Apollo was not only a sun god. He became the patron of culture and thus had moral functions. Alongside of Apollo there were the poetic figures of Helios and Phaëhton, minor deities who could also express the physical operation of the sun, but did not express the moral factor.

Sometimes a religious mind will outgrow its traditional faith without being able to reformulate the natural grounds and moral values of the precious system in which he or she can no longer believe. In such cases the dead gods leave ghosts behind them, because the moral forces which the gods once expressed remain inarticulate. To regain moral freedom and put knowledge to rational use in the government of life, we must rediscover the origin of the gods. We must reduce them analytically to their natural and moral constituents, and then rearrange this material in forms appropriate to a mature reflection.

In tracing the natural history of the mythologies, Santayana restricts himself to the classical Greek and Roman and the Christian, the only two likely to have any continued effect on the Western mind, since they are the best articulated and the best known to us.

The Vedic hymns constitute a sort of prehistory of Greek mythology for him, much like the Greek in spirit but less articulate. (This is a continuation into the history of myth of the old idea of Sanskrit being closest to the primitive Indo-European language. A knowledge of the Puranas and Epics would have disabused him of this idea.) Likewise one studies the religion of the Hebrews to discover the roots of the Christian tradition.

For Santayana an overview of the history of Christian dogma moves from this prehistory to the story of two transformations: first the

Patristic adaptation of Hebrew religion to the Greco-Roman world and then the adaptation to the Teutonic spirit in Protestantism. In the first metamorphosis the mythology of the Hebrews was refined, changed into a religion of redemption, and equipped "with a semi-pagan mythology, a pseudo-Platonic metaphysics, and a quasi-Roman organisation" (69/210). In the second transformation, Christianity received a new foundation in the faith of the individual; and, as the traditions thus undermined gradually became attenuated, it was transformed by the German mind into a romantic, mystical pantheism. Throughout all these changes Christianity retained an indebtedness to the Jewish religion for the core of its dogma, cult, and ethics.

The religion of the Hebrew prophets was basically superstitious, for it had a material and political ideal and virtue was recommended as a magical way to propitiate the deity and ensure public prosperity. The idea that "virtue is a natural excellence, the ideal expression of human life," was not possible to those "vehement barbarians" [*sic*] or their "descendants and disciples, Jewish, Christian, or Moslem." Yet the rational element could grow from this crude religion because "by assigning a magic value to morality they gave a moral value to religion" (73–74; the abridged edition has a slightly different wording, 212–213). The imaginary aim of restoring the kingdom of Israel by propitiating Jehovah was a myth which covered a genuine dedication to the ideal.

At the same time that the prophets were changing the tradition, it was being crystallized. Scripture was codified, written, and proclaimed to be divinely inspired through Moses. (Santayana conflates Scripture with the Pentateuch here.) Santayana unleashes his invective here. "What was condemnable in the Jews was not that they asserted the divinity of their law. . . . Their crime is to have denied the equal prerogative of other nations' laws and deities." The Jews "rendered themselves odious to mankind by this arrogance, and taught Christians and Moslems the same fanaticism" (76–77/214–215). Many of us share his abhorrence against fanaticism, but one suspects that the sharpness of his pen here is driven by anti-Semitism.

However, the calamities that befell Israel produced a significant spiritualization in its religion. Sorrow endured for the Lord became blessedness and a token of mystical election. While the prophets and psalmists showed the beginning of asceticism or "inverted worldliness," the early Christians (and Essenes) made this reversal explicit. True, the old mythology remained in the background. The kingdom of God would be established soon. Yet gradually the idea of a theocracy, the kingdom of God, receded or else became spiritualized. Its joys were eventually conceived as immaterial, contemplative, and reserved for life after death.

Salvation consisted in surrendering all desire for worldly things. Thus the prophet's idea of prosperity merited by virtue changed to the belief that prosperity was alien to virtue.

Santayana sees the history of Jewish and Christian ethics as a series of pendulum swings between irrational extremes. In between the extremes is a point of equilibrium from which a sketch of rational religion can be drawn. For example, this point was touched when the prophets realized that right and wrong are determined by human interests, not the arbitrary will of Jehovah, and that conduct creates destiny. But the rational elements in this insight were presented in a mythical form mixed with superstition and chauvinism. Likewise Christianity failed to establish an authentic moral education. Thus a worthy conception of prosperity and the good could not be substituted for the crude ideas of the heathen and Hebrews. Neither were the natural goals of human endeavor recognized and formulated, but everything was left to impulse or contingent tradition. Reason in religion did not triumph.

Then a new form of materialism arose to distort what was rational in the ideas of the prophets. Claims to a supernatural knowledge based on revelation arose. Mythology took on a new shape. The religion of Israel was changed into two formidable engines, the Bible and the Church.

Santayana finds the distinguishing characteristic of Christianity to be the worship of Christ. In a move used by many liberal scholars, he differentiates between the teachings of Jesus, which is Hebraic religion reduced to its essential spiritual core, and the worship of Christ, which is something Greek instead. Like Harnack, he finds the key to early Christianity to be "the Hellenization of Christianity" (Harnack 1902, 215–224).

Unlike Harnack, he finds value in this. Christianity would have continued as a Jewish sect were it not that an infusion of Greek thought made it speculative, universal, and ideal, and simultaneously malleable and helpful in devotions by the adoption of pagan habits. The incarnation of God in humanity, and the making of humanity divine in God are pagan conceptions. Without them Christianity would have lost its theology, which would be no great loss, but also "its spiritual aspiration, its artistic affinities, and the secret of its metaphysical charity and joy" (85/219, Santayana's treatment of Christianity may be seen in a brief form in chapter IV of *Interpretations of Poetry and Religion*).

Not only do Santayana's sympathies with the Apollonian strand of Greek culture come into play here, but also his anti-Semitic sympathies, for he says clearly: "Among the Jews there were no liberal interests for the ideal to express" (85/219). He has completely ignored the Wisdom literature, not to mention the place of the Gentiles in Jewish eschatological imagery.

On this view there were two things which made early Christianity able to spread rapidly. One was the morality and mysticism, beautifully expressed in Christ's parables and maxims, and illustrated by his miracles. This democratic charity could powerfully appeal to an age disenchanted with the world, and especially to the lower classes. The other point of contact early Christianity had with public need was its tapestry of history and the unfathomable mysteries that it held before the fancy. The figure of Christ, with its lowliness, simplicity, and humanity, was at first an obstacle to the metaphysical interpretation that was required for acceptance. But even Greek fable told of Apollo tending flocks and Demeter mourning her lost child. The time was ripe for a mythology filled with pathos. The humble life and sufferings of Jesus were felt in all their beauty while the tragic gloom was relieved by his miraculous birth, his resurrection, and his restoration into divinity.

What overcame the world was not moral reform, which was commonplace, not asceticism, which was urged by gymnosophists and philosophers, nor brotherly love within the community, for the Jews did that. What overcame the world was a new poetry, a new ideal, the crucified Christ. This fable carried the imagination into a new realm. This fable "sanctified the poverty and sorrow at which Paganism had shuddered; it awakened tenderer emotions, revealed more humane objects of adoration, and furnished subtler means of grace" (Santayana 1989, 56).

A further important piece of the Christian poetic fable was the notion of a final judgment. Each person was declared to have an immortal soul, that is, "each life has the potentiality of an eternal meaning, and as this potentiality is or is not actualised, as this meaning is or is not expressed in the phenomena of this life, the soul is eternally saved or lost." The symbolic truth of the Christian fictions helped people understand, "as never before or since, the pathos and nobility of his life, the necessity of discipline, the possibility of sanctity, the transcendence and the humanity of the divine. . . . The supernatural was an allegory of the natural, and rendered the values of transitory things under the image of eternal existences" (Santayana 1989, 62–63).

A related moral truth declared in the Christian poetry is the absoluteness of moral distinctions. While good and evil normally are mixed together, the distinction between them is clear. Some things really are better than others.

> The complexities of life, struggling as it does amidst irrational forces, may make the attainment of one good the cause of the unattainableness of another; they cannot destroy the essential desirability of both. . . . Now how utter this moral truth

imaginatively, how clothe it in an image that might render its absoluteness and its force? . . . In place of the confused vistas of the empirical world, in which the threads of benefit and injury might seem to be mingled and lost, the imagination substituted the clear vision of Hell and Heaven. . . . The doctrine of eternal rewards and punishments is, as we have tried to show, an expression of moral truth, a poetic rendering of the fact that rational values are ideal, momentous, and irreversible. (Santayana 1989, 64, 66)

One interesting insight is Santayana's distinction between metaphor and transformation. Like other Orientals, the poetry and religion of the Jews was filled with violent metaphors, which were abhorrent to the classic mind. "Uniting, as it did, clear reason with lively fancy, it could not conceive one thing to *be* another. . . . But the classic mind could well conceive transformation, of which indeed nature is full; and in Greek fables anything might change its form, become something else. . . . While metaphor was thus unintelligible and confusing to the Greek, metamorphosis was perfectly familiar to him. . . . For instance, the metaphors of the Last Supper, so harmless and vaguely satisfying to an Oriental audience, became the doctrine of transubstantiation" (87–88/220). Now all language may indeed have a metaphorical aspect, but Santayana's distinction between Hebraic and Greek cultures here is worth considering.

The eclectic Christian philosophy, composed of this Christ figure and classical philosophy in a language of metamorphosis, is one of the most elaborate and impressive products of the human imagination. Although the narrow time and space into which the Christian imagination squeezed the world may seem childish and poverty-stricken, this reduction of things to a human measure, this half-arrogant assumption that what is important for man must control the whole universe, made Christian philosophy originally appealing and still arouses enthusiastic belief. Humans are still immature. We are afraid of freedom. We are not satisfied by a good created by our own action. We are afraid to be left alone in the universe. The moral life of man must appear in fantastic symbols. The history of these symbols is the history of the human soul.

When he uses reason to evaluate this Christian dream, Santayana is quite clear that this is not a matter of proof or disproof. "Do we marshal arguments against the miraculous birth of Buddha, or the story of Cronos devouring his children? We seek rather to honour the piety and to understand the poetry embodied in these fables." Note that Santayana has already relegated Christ to the realm of fable and we are left to retrieve something. Note also that this is said within the context of a very controversial dismissal of the literal truth of the poetic element. "Matters of religion should never be matters of controversy. We neither argue with a lover about his taste nor condemn him, if we are just, for knowing so human a passion. That he harbours it is no indication of a want of sanity on his part in other matters." This is as much as to say that the lover and, hence, the religious devotee, lacks sanity in this most crucial matter. "But while we acquiesce in his experience ["satisfaction" in the abridged edition], and are glad he has it, we need no arguments to dissuade us from sharing it. Each man may have his own loves, but the object in each case is different. And so it is, or should be, in religion. Before the rise of those strange and fraudulent Hebraic pretensions . . . [it] could never have been a duty to adopt a religion not one's own any more than a language, a coinage, or a costume not current in one's own country. The idea that religion contains a literal, not a symbolic, representation of truth and life is simply an impossible idea." None of this is subject to proof or refutation. "Philosophy may describe unreason, as it may describe force; it cannot hope to refute them" (97–98/ 226–227).

Santayana sees Christianity as intertwined with pagan elements in its early days, elements which remain to this day among popular Christianity, particularly in the Mediterranean area. This paganization is an improvement for him, because it expressed and inspired spiritual sentiment more generously, whereas without it Christianity would have retained the hostility to human genius so characteristic of Hebraism. Christianity was rendered more congenial and adequate by this infusion of pagan sentiment. "Paganism was nearer than Hebraism to the Life of Reason because its myths were more transparent and its temper less fanatical" (107/232).

In describing this element of paganism Santayana refers to the daily practices of Catholic people, not official theology or ritual. These practices are a particularization of religion, a focus of devotion to particular saints, special festivals, supplications to the Virgin under specific titles. This particularization serves a purpose. A universal power has no specific purpose. It cannot be friendly nor take cognizance of your personal needs.

Religion and philosophy were originally pre-rational, crudely experimental, unconscious of the limits of excellence and life. The Christianity of the gospels was post-rational, it had turned its back on the world. If rational ethics is the ideal rational life of compromise and harmony among all human interests and impulses, post-rational morality arises at times of social dissolution when the support for the rational life has gone. It focuses on one natural interest to fulfill. A partial good is offered as consolation for the loss of the rational ideal. Such partial goods may be a flight above the world, momentary pleasure, mortification of the passions, patience in suffering, conformity to events, etc.

Even more clearly, the Christianity of the later centuries, with its pagan elements, was a post-rational religion. It was acquainted with sorrow and calamity. It became a religion that had passed through both civilization and despair, and finally been reduced to translating the values of life into supernatural symbols. The experience of disillusion forced the imagination to flee the earth and to shape a realm of spirit beyond time and nature, in a posthumous, metaphysical realm.

After pagan custom, the next thing to be intermixed with Christianity was barbarian genius. The conversion of the barbarians was superficial. "A non-Christian ethics of valour and honour, a non-Christian fund of superstition, legend, and sentiment, subsisted always among mediaeval peoples." Pagan Christianity was and always remained an alien religion to the medieval people. "It was thus that the Roman Church hatched the duck's egg of Protestantism." Among these barbarians a religious restlessness brought several gifts, beautiful but insidious and incongruous, including Gothic art, the sentiment of chivalry, and scholastic philosophy. The Christianity infused with barbarianism in the medieval north of Europe was quite different from the pagan Christianity of the south and east. People did not value the renunciation of the things of the earth and the metaphysical glory of its transfigured life. Intricacy took the place of dignity and poetry the place of rhetoric; the basilica turned into an abbey and the hermitage became a school. "Something jocund and mischievous peeped out even in the cloister; gargoyles leered from the belfry, while ivy and holly grew about the cross" (109–110, 112/234–235). Christianity was the occasion and even the excuse for art, jollity, curiosity and tenderness.

This barbarianized Christianity eventuated in Protestantism, the natural religion of the Teutonic peoples, a religion of spontaneity and emotional freedom. It confused vitality with spiritual life. It was convinced of the significance of worldly success and prosperity.   Protestantism is austere and energetic. The only evils it recognizes are seen as challenges to action. Thus Protestantism was attached to the Old Testament, in which the fervor of the Hebrews appeared in its pre-rational and worldly form. It is not democratic like post-rational religions which think of the soul as an exile from another real, a pilgrim toward a distant city.

The Renaissance humanists, if they had not been overwhelmed by the fanatical Reformation and Counter-Reformation, would have been able to reform Christianity, retaining it as a poetic expression of human life, in short, as a form of paganism. Had humanism been allowed to fight for reason with the weapons of reason, it would eventually have

led to a widespread enlightenment without dividing Christendom, in-
flaming venomous religious and national passions, or weakening the life
of philosophy.

Eventually, after the final disappearance of the Christian tradition,
Absolute Egotism appeared in German philosophy. This final expression
of Protestantism marked the definite separation of the Teutonic spirit
from Christianity.

Having given an interpretation of the history of religion in the West,
Santayana returns to some general themes of his hermeneutic of religion.
He first focuses on the conflict of mythology and moral truth. His leading
idea is that if mythology were taken as a poetic substitute for science, the
advance of science would be eliminated. But that has not happened. Myth
originally was a symbol for facts. But eventually it became a substitute for
ideal values and in that substitution became idolatrous.

Twice in European history mythologies have dissolved: first with
the Stoics and then with Protestantism. In both cases mythology, Greek
and Christian respectively, ended in pantheism.

It took a thousand years for Greek paganism to disappear. That
is because religions do not disappear immediately on being discredited.
They need to be replaced. During this millennium, paganism lived on,
in part by influx from the east and in part by reinterpretations. Of these
reinterpretations, the first was developed by Plato and further pursued by
neo-Platonists and Christians in the direction of a supernatural spiritual
hierarchy, a deity and lower levels of angels and demons, and so forth.
Eventually the enthusiasm for ideals degenerated into a supernumerary
physics. At about the same time the Stoics attempted a second reinterpretation of mythology. They explained the popular myths as didactic
fables and identified Zeus with the order of nature. This was a form of
pantheism, which did not provide a solution to the religious problem.
Nature is not and cannot be man's ideal. Since life and death, good and
ill fortune, happiness and misery flow equally from the universal order,
they are declared, in spite of reason, to be equally good. The morals of
pantheism, though post-rational, are not ascetic. The wise man will lend
himself to the labors of nature. In place of the natural ideal are put, not
its supernatural exaggeration but a curtailment of this ideal suggested by
despair. This pantheistic strain entered the Church. As soon as the dramatic
omnipotence of the Hebraic deity was systematized and the doctrines of
creation and providence were pushed to the extreme, ecclesiastical pantheism emerged. The consequences of this for moral philosophy were
appalling, for the sins which God punished were really due to God.

Recent idealism continues this process. It is the final stage of a
mythical philosophy which has been criticizing its metaphors, assum-

ing that they were not metaphorical. Thereby it has stripped them of all meaning and importance. The good, which was once understood as spiritual, was transformed into a natural power. This amounted initially to a misrepresentation of natural things. "The gods inhabit Mount Olympus and the Elysian Fields are not far west of Cadiz" (141/246). However, with the advance of geography these alleged facts, the remnants of former myths, disappear.

From this we may learn that in order to maintain the idea of reason we must distinguish between the real and the rational, for reason involves "action addressed to the good and thought envisaging the ideal." Reason is in the world only insofar as the world supports the excellence and value of each creature and its ultimate desires. But that is a limited support. There is in the world a nonrational principle, which may be conceived as "inertia in matter, accidental perversity in the will, or ultimate conflict of interests" (143–144/247).

In Santayana's view Christianity formed a compromise. It was heir to two dualisms, the contrast in the Gospel between this world and the kingdom of heaven and the Platonic contrast between sense and spirit, between time and eternity. Christianity thus blended the notion of the goodness of this world as created and governed by God and its misery as in need of redemption. Thus it could preach renunciation and asceticism on the one hand and action and hope on the other. Thus the classic naturalistic attitude, the positive valuation of intellect, art, and action, never died out in the West.

For those whose religion is spontaneous and inward, God speaks within the heart. For those for whom religion is a matter of imitation, theology is a matter of physics and history, soon discredited by events. They lack the key to the moral symbolism and poetic validity of theology. Augustine was in both camps. He combined the immediate sense of the presence of God with notions of arbitrary grace and predestination. God as the ideal object of thought and love was combined with God as the ultimate source of sin who could eternally damn innocent babies.

As the centuries passed these ambiguities persisted in Luther and Calvin. Lesser minds repeated these platitudes, not so the ones who thought these issues through. Santayana names Lessing, Goethe, and the German idealists and Emerson and Carlyle. They drew directly from nature and history and the survivals of Christianity became illustrations of universal spiritual truths. This idealistic camp sanctified the world, giving a divine warrant to all facts and impulses. They became apologists for the social conventions of their day. The first idealists were relatively blameless, but the immoral potentialities of this subordination of conscience to whatever exists became evident as this pantheism moved from the seminary into the world. Poets justified their passions, practical men justified their chosen activities, however sordid or inane, and politicians invoked destiny to avoid having to discern rational ends. Pantheism turns the natural world into a self-justifying and sacred system. To worship nature as it is, with all its innocent crimes turned into intentional actions in our mythologies and her unsearchable depths changed into a caricature of barbarian passions, is to subvert all values and to falsify science. Such a disruption of reason is the outcome of mythical thinking. A myth speaks of phenomena as expressions of thought and passion, thus teaching people to look for models and goals of action in the external world where reason finds only instruments and materials.

The next major move made by Santayana in *Reason in Religion* is to turn from religious ideas to religious emotions. Religion is an imaginative symbol for the Life of Reason. Thus it contains symbolic sentiments and duties as well as symbolic ideas and rites. Hence he moves from ideas to emotions, from imaginative history and science to imaginative morals. These sentiments are piety, spirituality, and charity.

Piety for Santayana is a reverent attachment to the sources of our existence and a steadying of our life by that reverence. It is the rational meaning of the mythic representation of our natural conditions. Our awareness that our being is derived, that our spiritual life is a heritage entrusted to us, requires gratitude and a feeling of duty. In another of his pithy phrases he writes, "Piety is the spirit's acknowledgment of its incarnation" (184/260).

We depend on parents, family, ancestors, country, humanity in general, and finally the whole cosmos. None of these are worth venerating as such. After all, piety to humans should be mostly pity. When we turn to the widest object of piety we grant that there is a philosophic or cosmic piety whose object is the entire universe. But we should not personify it and give it the name of God. It is filled with beauty and dullness, cruelty, fire, and mud. We may have society with it. It is our own substance. All our possibilities are hidden in its bosom from the beginning. But our communings with it should be without superstition and terror. It is not wicked, for it has no intention. It is not to blame, for it knows not what it does. Just as we should abstain from judging a parent's errors or foibles, so we should not judge the ignorant crimes of the universe.

Besides piety, which is retrospective, there is spirituality, which is prospective. This is the higher side of religion, which imposes a direction and ideal on the forces of human life, in short, an aspiration. We are spiritual when we live in the presence of an ideal. Spirituality is the rational meaning of the mythic expression of ideals.

The spiritual person does not abandon the world. She is quite ready to use its gifts. The spiritual person recognizes what wealth can do and what it cannot. His unworldliness is really a true knowledge of the world. It is not so much a busy acquaintance as a quiet comprehension and estimation which, while it cannot come without engagement with the world, can very well set such engagement aside.

However, spirituality has a pathology. It is subject to corruption. Its foe is sophistication. Means are pursued as if they are ends and ends are pursued as if they were means to a further end, itself unexamined. So pedantry often displaces wisdom, tyranny government, and superstition substitutes for piety and rhetoric for reason. Further difficulties come with attempts to escape these problems by fanaticism or mysticism. Fanaticism aggresively narrows down concern to only one interest. The mystic passively either accepts all passions or rejects them all. Both represent arrested development of common sense. The Life of Reason is to discover a rational advance over the world as it is, rather than to take the blind alleys of fanaticism or mysticism.

We can find oases of rational episodes in life, patches of science, logic, and affection; but curiosity can lead to illusion, argument can foster hatred of the truth, and love can end in bitterness and even crime and death. The spiritual person therefore cannot be content with a harvest of the accidental fruits of the occasional intrinsic successes of life. Hence for the Life of Reason we may turn to the traditional religions for assistance, once we purge them of their fanciful, dogmatic and fanatic matters. For these faiths present us with a variety of images of excellence with clarity and power. The spiritual person may take one of these as his standard. The rational person goes a step further and relates this standard to the scrutiny of reason.

In addition to piety and spirituality, Santayana speaks of charity. The need for charity is based on the fact that we often assume that our interests are the most important thing in the world, that our ideal should be chosen by everyone. Thus, we need to acknowledge the relativity of our chosen values. This is difficult, because it is easier to become a fanatic, insisting on one ideal, no matter what instincts or interests are stifled, or to become a mystic, sensing the rights of everything so much that we give allegiance to nothing.

In principle we should take all interests into consideration. We should look upon each impulse as something which ought to be satisfied if possible, provided that rival interests permit. It is fanaticism to deny the initial right of any impulse. Reason may have to suppress some impulses, but it should never be inconsiderate in so doing. It should suppress them unwillingly and with pity. There is a conflict of interests in our soul and in society, calling for compromise and restriction, but all parties in the negotiation should be heard with sympathy. This is charity, which is identical with justice. This charity will treat all interests with courtesy, all forms of life with admiration and solicitude.

In religious traditions charity is often motivated and justified by fables, such as Christ's suffering for all sinners. He is said to have loved publicans and sinners. "He understood the bright good that each sinner was following when he stumbled into the pit. For this insight he was loved. . . . The Magdalene was forgiven because she had loved much" (223/274). Her longing was comprehended, not insulted, in her absolution. Charity involves the art of helping people give up their errors without giving up their ideals.

Santayana ends his treatment in *Reason in Religion* by differentiating between a future life and ideal immortality. A future life is an hypothesis about an occult existence with little evidence. Ideal immortality concerns the eternal quality of ideas and validities and reason's affinity to this. As for the evidence for a future life, most of the evidence plays to gullibility and is not worth consideration. Any significant evidence from clairvoyance and telepathy is tenuous at best. Any shred of validity to it points to further natural processes and should not be used to buttress religious doctrines.

Ideal immortality involves the eternal quality of ideas and validities. Immortality also involves the fact that it is eternally true that any sensation or experience in time has occurred. Further one of the pleasures of reflection is its sense of the permanence of truths. Just as Archimedes, studying the laws of the hypotenuse, was engaged in a transcendence over events, so also may we in art and science attain a sense of the unchanging. Further still, every attainment of perfection is an avenue to the eternal. Whoever lives in the ideal and expresses it in society or an art has a double immortality. While alive the eternal has absorbed him. After his death his influence brings others to the same absorption. Reflecting on this he may feel and know that he is eternal.

A fitting way to end our treatment of Santayana is with his reflections on Spinoza in "Ultimate Religion." (Space precludes treating his *The Idea of Christ in the Gospels.* See Santayana 1946.) In "Ultimate Religion" he refers to "the crown of Spinoza's philosophy, that intellectual love of God in which the spirit was to be ultimately reconciled with universal power and universal truth. . . . We stand as on a mountaintop, and the spectacle, so out of scale with all our petty troubles, silences and overpowers the heart, expanding it for a moment into boundless sympathy with the universe" (Ryder 1994, 471–472; see Santayana 1936). Santayana urges us to worship, but not merely the universe as it is, but for what it could become. "If we wish to make a religion of love . . . we must take universal good, not universal power, for the object of our religion. . . . [T]he word God, if we still used it, would have to mean for us not the universe, but the good of the universe. . . . [W]hen power takes on the form of life, and begins to circle about and pursue some type of perfection, spirit in us necessarily loves these perfections, since spirit is aspiration become conscious, and they are the goals of life: and insofar as any of these goals can be defined or attained anywhere, even if only in prophetic fancy, they become glory, or become beauty, and spirit in us necessarily worships them" (Ryder 1994, 474, 476).

Samuel Alexander:
God as the Universe Growing Toward the Ideal

Samuel Alexander was a British philosopher who taught at the University of Manchester from 1893 to 1924. To get a sense of Alexander's time, he was the first Jew to be elected a fellow of Oxford or Cambridge (see John Laird's "Memoir," Alexander 1939, 12) and he was made an honorary member of Ashburton Hall, the women's residence at Manchester where he taught, because he marched in the suffragette parade, a matter of some personal courage given the times (Emmet 1966, vii; for Alexander's role in the suffragette struggle and the movement for women's education, see Laird's "Memoir," Alexander 1939, 48–50).

Best known for his Gifford Lectures published as *Space, Time, and Deity*, the main source for his religious naturalism is the second volume of this work. His motive was to develop an overall view of the evolving universe as depicted by science and to find in it the place of mind, values, and God, that is, to avoid dualism by rooting them within the evolving universe without dissolving them in reductionism. The guiding thread in Alexander is that the universe evolves in emergent levels from space-time, to matter, then life, mind and finally the next emergent level. Mind, for example, is physiological, but not merely such. It is also psychological. This may seem obvious to an educated person of the twenty-first century, but Alexander was one of the first major philosophers to take what we now call the epic of evolution as central to his outlook. Further he was one of the first philosophers, along with John Dewey, C. Lloyd Morgan, Roy Wood Sellars, and Jan Christiaan Smuts to take seriously the concept of emergence as an alternative to the dualisms or idealisms which tried to save a place for mind, values and religion in an increasingly materialistic *Zeitgeist*.

For Alexander the relationship of mind and body is taken as paradigmatic for the relationship between all levels.

Without the specific physiological or vital constellation there is no mind. . . . But while mental process is *also* neural, it is not *merely* neural, and therefore not merely vital. For, that mind should emerge, there is required a constellation of neural or other vital conditions not found in vital actions that are not mental. . . . It would follow that mental process may be expressible completely in physiological terms but is not *merely* physiological but *also* mental. . . . Mental process is therefore something new, a fresh creation, which, despite the possibility of resolving it into physiological terms, means the presence of so specific a physiological constitution as to separate it from simpler vital processes. . . . But at the same time, being thus new, mind is through its physiological character continuous with the neural processes which are not mental. It is not something distinct and broken off from them, but it has roots or foundations in all the rest of the nervous system. It is in this sense that mind and mental process are vital but not merely vital. (Alexander 1920, II, 6–8)

This relationship of "also but not merely" applies to all levels of emergence.

The emergence of a new quality from any level of existence means that at that level there comes into being a certain constellation or collocation of the motions belonging to that level, and possessing the quality appropriate to it, and this collocation possesses a new quality distinctive of the higher complex. The quality and the constellation to which it belongs are at once new and expressible without residue in terms of the processes proper to the level from which they emerge. (Alexander 1920, II, 45)

He carried this view through his theory of value. "The highest values satisfy impulses derived from natural instincts: the search for truth from curiosity, beauty and goodness from the constructive and social impulses (instincts). . . . There are parallels to values among animals and even physical things, although the three highest values [truth, beauty, goodness] are exclusively human. Thus Alexander sharpened his vision of continuity with difference in the universal process of emergence" by extending it to values (Stone 1983, 13).

What is surprising is that Alexander makes a distinction between God and deity. Deity is the next higher level beyond the present toward which the universe is evolving, while God is the totality of the present universe insofar as it is evolving toward deity. In his words, God is the world with a nisus toward, big with or pregnant with, deity. God and deity are not two beings, rather there is one actual being, God, or the universe as a whole insofar as it is moving toward a qualitatively new being, namely deity. God is not an already perfect being, but is rather in the making.

On the surface it is not clear whether "nisus" refers to the universe as a whole insofar as it is advancing or whether it refers to a process within the universe, a leaven driving the rest toward deity. Alexander parallels "nisus" with "tendency" and the metaphor is the world as "pregnant with deity." Thus "nisus" seems to refer to the movement of the whole world toward deity. To speak of the "nisus in the world" would be a loose way of referring to the nisus of the whole (Alexander 1920, II, 346, 367, 418; Alexander 1939, 381).

My contention is that, because of his notion of God as the universe in evolution, Samuel Alexander is one of the first explicit religious naturalists of the recent era. Regardless of whether we feel comfortable with his use of the word "deity" as the next level in evolution, he stands within the stream of those religious naturalists who use theistic language to refer to the universe-as-a-whole in a certain respect, in Alexander's case, as moving towards a new level.

> I do not say, as has been thought, that God never is, but is always yet to be. "What I say is that God as actually possessing deity does not exist, but is an ideal, is always becoming; but God as the whole universe tending toward deity does exist. Deity is a quality, and God a being. Actual God is the forecast and, as it were, divining of ideal God." (Alexander 1920, I, xxxix)

Alexander supplements the idea of God derived from his descriptive metaphysical overview of evolution with the idea of God derived from religious feeling. The metaphysical and the religious approaches are complementary. "The religious description wants authentic coherence with the system of things. The metaphysical one wants the touch of feeling which brings it within the circle of human interests" (Alexander 1920, II, 342).

The world as a whole in its forward tendency acts on our bodily organism and the religious sentiment is the feeling for this whole, the feeling of going out of ourselves toward something greater. "Various emotions enter into the full constitution of the religious sentiment—fear, admiration, self-abasement—but its distinctive constituent is the feeling of our going out towards something not ourselves and greater and higher than ourselves, with which we are in communion" (Alexander 1920, II, 373). Again he writes, "The world as a whole in its forward tendency acts upon our bodily organism and . . . the religious sentiment is the feeling for this whole" (Alexander 1920, II, 376). Alexander can also speak of the nisus of the world toward deity as the object of religious sentiment. "Religion is the reaction which we make to God as the whole universe with its nisus towards the new quality of deity" (Alexander 1939, 383).

We shall see that for Alexander the trouble with pantheism is that good and bad are indiscriminately included in the object of worship. However, the world as a whole, which seems to be the object of worship for Alexander, includes both good and evil indiscriminately. Perhaps the solution is that the focus of religious sentiment for Alexander is not on the world as a whole, but only on the world insofar as it is growing toward deity. Goodness "is directly utilisable for the life of deity, while evil appears as that which deity discards, which accordingly needs transformation before it can be utilised" (Alexander 1920, II, 416).

Alexander refers to the universe as the body of God. Any level can be called, by analogy, the "body" of the level above it. Thus matter is the body of life and life is the body of mind. Indeed all things in the world are "organic sensa" of God. Finally we contribute to God. Since deity is the outcome of the forward movement of the universe, the character of God-in-process partly depends on our actions. We do not merely serve God but help him and, in the measure of our smallness, create deity. "There is not merely reliance upon God but co-operation between the two parties to the religious transaction. We do not merely resign ourselves to something greater, but that something is a partner with us" (Alexander 1920, II, 387).

With Alexander's tendency to find analogies of the human at all levels of evolutionary development, he finds something akin to religion at subhuman levels. "Within the 'minds' of these material or living things themselves the nisus is felt as a nisus towards something unattained, and they have the analogue of what religion is for us. The 'mind' of the stone is a dim striving towards life, which for the stone is an unattained level" (Alexander 1939, 381).

Alexander gives extended treatment to pantheism and theism. For theism, in his view, God is an individual being distinct from and transcending the finite beings of the world. For pantheism God is immanent in the universe. In terms of religious feeling theism appeals to "the personal or egoistic side of the religious consciousness, the feeling that in surrender the worshipper still retains his identity and achieves it in surrender." Theism is "the religion of the 'free' man, who consorts with God on terms which still leave the creature independent according to his finite measure" (Alexander 1920, II, 389). The conceptual (Alexander uses the term "speculative") weakness of theism is its "detachment of God from the finites in his world, and more particularly from the world of nature" (Alexander 1920, II, 390). In particular, the relation of God with humanity is not clearly conceived. "The God of undiluted theism becomes merely the greatest thing in a universe of things and tends consequently in the mythologising imagination . . . to be dowered not with a new and divine quality but with finite qualities on a vaster scale" (Alexander 1920, II, 391–392).

A second conceptual weakness of theism is that God is not conceived as creator in a conceptually clear fashion. If creation is not just a forming of a preexistent material, but rather a bringing into existence of both the material and the form of the creatures, it is hard to grasp how God can lead an existence separate from his creatures.

For pantheism God is immanent in the universe of finite things. This may take either a more popular vague form or it may take a more profound form, as in Spinoza, where everything is only relatively real apart from God. The merits and defects of theism and pantheism are inverses. If theism appeals to the egoistic side of people, pantheism does to the self-surrendering side. A conceptual difficulty for pantheism is how to understand the relationship of God to evil and good and to human freedom. If evil belongs to God, God cannot be worshiped. One of the merits of pantheism is that it supplied the unlabored connection of God and nature and man that theism lacks. Pantheism supplies this connection at the price of submerging the individual into "the nebulous whole." The mature religious sentiment requires in its object of worship elements characteristic of both transcendence and immanence.

Alexander claims that his own view is neither theistic nor pantheistic. God, like all finites, is both body and soul, deity being God's soul, the next emergent level. God's body is all inclusive. All finites are fragments of God's body, though their individuality is not lost in it. But in respect of his deity God should be conceived as theistic (that is, I suggest, transcendent in a naturalistic sense).

Referring to the image of God as a potter in Robert Browning's *Rabbi Ben Ezra*, Alexander's seconds the Rabbi's suggestion that our task as vessels is to slake God's thirst. Our human existence, together with all nature, nurtures God's deity (Alexander 1939, 330). "The numinous mystery still attaches to a world making for deity; and love given and returned is, as it seems to me, as conceivable towards a being, greater than ourselves, who draws us forward to himself by the force of our own aspirations, as to one who draws backward to him the creatures which he created to love him" (Alexander 1939, 331). The notion of God as immanent satisfies the need for an intimacy with God, while deity as transcendent satisfies the independence and freedom of the worshiper and the worth of a person's contribution to deity.

Alexander wrote three significant essays on the seventeenth century religious naturalist Spinoza (Alexander 1927; Alexander 1939, chaps. XIII and XIV). While he disagreed with Spinoza at key points he hoped his epitaph to read, "He erred with Spinoza" ("*Erravit cum Spinoza*," Alexander 1939, 95). He valued Spinoza's naturalism, a philosophical scheme that holds science, morals and religion in a unified whole securing the value of morals and religion, without making them supply the knowledge of the world which science gives. The physical world has a place for religion and beauty (Alexander 1939, 333–334, 347–348; Alexander 1927, 15).

Beyond the value of his naturalism, for Alexander Spinoza is the greatest example of pantheism in the Western world (Alexander 1939, 320).

> The step which Spinoza took . . . is that this infinite being or God is not only the origin of nature but is equated to nature, *Deus sive Natura* is his expression. He is not so much the creator of finites as that they . . . are expressions of him, just as if they were the words he speaks which yet would have no meaning apart from the whole sentence or speech in which they are spoken. (Alexander 1939, 338)

> Spinoza is a pantheist, not in the superficial sense that God is a spirit which pervades all things, but in the truer sense that all things are in God and are modifications of him. (Alexander 1939, 354. For Alexander's discussion of other pantheists, Alexander Pope, Wordsworth, Goethe, and Hegel, see Alexander 1939, 321–322, 346, and 378)

In this profounder pantheism,

> The world is conceived rather as consisting in its parts of existences which owe their being to him, are in a manner shadows of him, possess only a relative individuality compared with his, are fragments of his total existence, and owe their being to their roots in him. (Alexander 1939, 321–322)

I take it that this is Alexander's list of pantheistic metaphors.

The identity of God and the universe is not demonstrated by Spinoza, it is presented as a definition.

> Proofs are nothing but machinery which helps others to secure the philosopher's vision. . . . Spinoza looked out upon the universe and declared it to be God. . . . In like manner the physicist looks out on the universe and sees it to be a system of events. (Alexander 1939, 373)

This vision Spinoza calls the intellectual love of God.

> It arises out of or along with the third or highest form of knowledge, intuitive knowledge. Science or reason, the second kind of knowledge, is the knowledge of true universals. . . . But intuitive knowledge is scientific knowledge seen in its connection with God. (Alexander 1939, 373–374)

> Imagine that any object is conceived in its relation to God, and we have on the one side intuitive knowledge, on the other the union of ourselves with God, which is the intellectual love of God. (Alexander 1939, 376)

> As a practical outcome this intellectual love of God gives us control of our passions, for it takes us out of our isolation and gives us communion with other persons and with God, it secures our true contentment of spirit. . . . It pervades the whole of our action and contemplation with the sense of the abiding reference of it to God. (Alexander 1939, 374)

Alexander, still expounding Spinoza, calls the emotional accompaniment of this vision a "port after stormy seas; the labour of reflection, its doubts, its strenuous pain are replaced by the passionate calm of utter conviction and satisfaction of the mind" (Alexander 1939, 375).

According to Alexander this intellectual love of God:

> is the mystic's love, absorbed in the contemplation of the highest, and though Spinoza does not call it religion, it is in fact religion, where the religious impulse has been founded upon the philosophic synthesis, and the philosophy has taken fire from the emotion which itself excites. (Alexander 1939, 346)

Yet the intellectual love of God is not quite the same as the religious sentiment, since it is basically intellectual and describes its object intellectually. Unless the religious passion is already lit, the intellectual love of God would not rise to religious passion. (For Alexander's discussion of whether Spinoza's treatment of the emotions is too intellectual, see Alexander 1939, 325, 336, and especially 376–377; Alexander 1927, 26.)

According to Alexander, Spinoza "does not altogether escape" the defect of pantheism of not leaving enough room for the independence of the healthy individual from God and for God's need of us (Alexander 1939, 378). Also for Alexander a key question is whether God conceived of as the universe can be the object of worship. The pantheistic Supreme Being contains all things indiscriminately, including evil and good alike.

> Worship demands in its object . . . something which if the predicates of good and bad are inappropriate . . . is yet in the lineal succession of goodness. . . . Hence, instead of a God who is identical with the whole of nature, as with Spinoza, we have to say that only God's body is so identical, but that God's deity, that which is characteristic of him, is lodged only in a part of the world. (Alexander 1939, 379, 383)

In sum, Alexander approves of Spinoza's naturalism, adds evolution and the importance of time, and focuses religious sentiment not on the whole but on the whole insofar as it is growing toward the next higher level.

It may be remarked finally that Alexander was a member of the Reform Jewish community in England and worked on behalf of Jewish refugees and the Hebrew University of Jerusalem and the Jerusalem University Library (see John Laird's "Memoir" in Alexander 1939, 80, 93–94, 96).

The Pragmatists:
Dewey and Mead

Rather than attempt a systematic exposition of the philosophy of religion of John Dewey and George Herbert Mead, this section develops seven themes from them and shows how they can be incorporated into contemporary religious naturalistic philosophy.

Dewey and Radical Empiricism

One of the most important things which contemporary religious naturalism can learn from the pragmatists is to focus on the richness of experience as well as to develop a theory of experience which can legitimate and guide this focus. The term "radical empiricism" has a variety of meanings. I am using it here to mean this focus on the rich texture of experience, a focus which includes aesthetic, moral, emotional and religious experiences. (A rich source of the radical empiricist notion of experience is Bernard Meland. See Meland 1953, 82–87; Stone 1992, 121–127.) What is important here is that experience is seen as valuational.

Dewey has a valuational empiricism.

> If experience actually presents esthetic and moral traits, then these traits may also be supposed to reach down into nature, and to testify to something that belongs to nature as truly as does the mechanical structure attributed to it in physical science. (Dewey 1988, 13)

In slightly different terms, nature has what might be characterized as the objective correlate of our moods.

> Nature is kind and hateful, bland and morose, irritating and comforting, long before she is mathematically qualified or even a congeries of "secondary" qualities like colors and their shapes. (Dewey 1958, 16)

The function of intelligence is to analyze and criticize and perhaps reconstruct primary experience and to refer the refinements of intelligence back to experience for the purpose of enriching itself and clarifying experience. In other terms, various experiences can be valued and the role of intelligence is to discover what is genuinely valuable and to discover its conditions and consequences.

For religious naturalism this means that the starting point of philosophy of religion is neither the construction nor deconstruction of arguments for the existence of God nor the analysis of religious concepts, but rather the exploration of experiences. These experiences need not be conventionally religious, but they are experiences that are especially significant.

Dewey and the Transactional Nature of Experience

Dewey's theory of knowledge has been called "transactional" (Dewey 1925, 198–199; Boisvert 1988, 73–76, 81–87; Sleeper 1986, 23, 69–70, 91–92). That is, he sees a continuing interaction or transaction between knower and known, between experience and the stock of ideas used to understand and transform it. Dewey's example is that of a doctor examining a patient.

> Now, in the degree to which the physician comes to the examination of what is there with a large and comprehensive stock of such possibilities or meanings in mind, he will be resourceful in dealing with a particular case. They . . . are . . . the means of knowing the case at hand; they are the agencies of transforming it, through the actions which they call for, into an object of knowledge. (Dewey 1980, 338)

For religious naturalism in the contemporary world this means that a naturalist philosophy of religion may be understood as a set of ideas both deriving from the felt quality of experience and further transforming experience through the philosophical and scientific concepts used in exploring it. Note that this is neither subjective nor objective. It is neither language nor reality. It is a continuing transaction between these poles.

Dewey and the Reconstruction of Experience

Dewey's naturalistic reconstruction of religion can be of great relevance for contemporary religious naturalism. Religious naturalism should, and often does, involve a generalization and a prescription. The generalization is that all life is change and, until death, growth. The prescription is that life should be changed and growth occur as intelligently as possible. This intelligent growth, this intelligent reconstruction of experience, is central to Dewey. The function of ideals in this reconstruction, for Dewey, is to critique and suggest change. For example democracy as "the idea of community life itself . . . is not a fact and never will be. It is an ideal in the only intelligible sense of an ideal: namely the tendency and movement of some thing which exists carried to its final limit, viewed as completed, perfected" (Dewey 1927, 148).

He is critical of ideals when conceived of as static, vague, unattainable, and accompanied by unexamined formulas. The function of ideals is to critique and suggest changes, to stimulate inquiry and guide and motivate reconstruction. I have elsewhere called this the function of *continually challenging ideals* (Stone 1992, 16–17, 37–40).

At one point Dewey's own idea needs reconstruction. There is not only a fallibility but also a potential for self-deception in human intelligence that Dewey did not stress sufficiently. The needed changes in our reconstruction are probably more radical than Dewey envisioned. The sense of the limitations and possible perversions of our intelligence and social values need to be emphasized continually. This is why religious naturalism needs to emphasize that the reconstruction of experience by intelligent cooperative inquiry may be more radical than Dewey anticipated. We may call this the experience of continually challenging ideals or experiences of situationally or functionally transcendent (as opposed to ontologically transcendent) ideals.

A second area where Dewey's outlook needs reconstruction is that Dewey's outlook seems manipulative. Contemporary environmental studies suggest a lighter and more cautious approach to the world. Dewey is not the crude philosopher of American activism as is sometimes portrayed. Yet the very connotation of the term "reconstruction" can encourage, despite Dewey's intentions, a forging full steam ahead insensitive of consequences. Another favorite term of Dewey, "development," also invokes images of earth movers and poorly designed buildings. Even though we cannot hold Dewey responsible for all of the baggage connected with these words, nevertheless there is not enough sense of caution and sensitivity in his outlook. Although Dewey was a great teacher of teachers, he needed to place further stress on teachableness. His emphasis on active reconstruction needs to be balanced with a stance of openness. Dewey needed a larger place in his philosophy for reflection on receptivity.

The significance of this for contemporary religious naturalism is that our religious traditions are to be reconstructed. All too often the attitude of people toward religion is a dichotomy of either accepting or rejecting it. Our religious traditions are neither to be accepted nor rejected, but to be reconstructed.

Dewey and the Religious Quality of Experience

It is clear that Dewey's reconstruction of the concept of religion separates it from the concept of the supernatural. "I shall develop another conception of the nature of the religious phase of experience, one that separates it from the supernatural" (Dewey 1934, 2). The key to Dewey here is his shift from a conception of religion as a distinct sphere of life related to a distinct transcendent being to a conception of religion as a quality of some of our experiences.

> The heart of my point . . . is that there is a difference between religion, *a* religion, and the religious; between anything that may be denoted by a noun substantive and the quality of experience that is designated by an adjective. (Dewey 1934, 3)

The value of this distinction for religious naturalism is that in the reconstruction of the religious life, we can shift our engagement away from a distinct entity, ground, or process somehow ontologically distinct and superior to the rest of reality toward whatever experiences within this world that have a quality that can be designated as religious.

Today's religious naturalist need not accept Dewey in the specifics of his definition of the religious quality of experience. What is of key significance, however, is the shift in orientation from engagement with a distinct entity, ground, or process to engagement with processes within this world that have a quality that may be designated as religious, at least in a revised sense. Today's religious naturalist may also use other adjectives than "religious," such as "sacred" or "divine."

Dewey and the Sense of the Whole

Dewey sometimes spoke of a sense of the whole.

> In a genuine sense every act is already possessed of infinite import. . . . The boundaries of our garden plot join it to the world of our neighbors and our neighbors' neighbors. That small effort which we can put forth is in turn connected with an infinity of events that sustain and support it. . . . It is the office of art and religion to evoke such appreciations and intimations; to enhance and steady them until they are wrought into the texture of our lives. (Dewey 1944, 262–263)

It is crucial that Dewey chose a series of gardens as his image of the sense of the whole. For Dewey a garden represents work, a reconstruction of the world. For him the meaning of the whole is tied up with the significance of work, of the activity of the self.

But what if the farm or garden runs out? To use the image of a farm, what if erosion, poor management, or global economic conditions force foreclosure of the farm? Where is the sense of meaning? If we tie our sense of worth to our gardens or farms we are on shaky ground. Besides, we cannot always work in our gardens. We might rely on a sense of an ultimate or unconditional meaning beyond our finite endeavors. Or we could draw on Dewey but temper his sense of the significance of work. We need a limited sense of the worth of our being, doing, and having. We can see the actual garden next door. And we can have an imaginative perception of gardens beyond that. This may give added meaning, even zest, to our work in our own gardens, or whatever fruitful labor in which we engage. But we must remember that next year it may become a parking lot. Thus we must temper our aggressiveness and defensiveness and lighten the temptation to despair with a touch of irony and humor.

Religious naturalism can definitely learn from Dewey to have an imaginative sense of the whole. However, we can enrich it with a philosophy of openness, a lifestyle of receptivity to functionally transcendent resources and challenges.

Dewey's God as the Imaginative Unity of Ideals

In Dewey's use of the term "God" in *A Common Faith*, the word "denotes the unity of all ideals ends arousing us to desire and actions. . . . the ideal ends that at a given time and place one acknowledges as having authority over his volition and emotion, the values to which one is supremely devoted, as far as these ends, through imagination, take on a unity" (Dewey 1934, 42). Note the implicit plurality of these ends, the unity supplied imaginatively, and the naturalistic contrast with the Supreme Being of traditional theism. Imagination, be it noted, is not illusory, but a capacity of entertaining possibilities in such a way as to have power over us. Also, this is not merely the unity of ideals. It includes the roots of the ideal in natural conditions, although this is sketchy and seems to come in as an afterthought. "The ideal itself has roots in natural conditions; it emerges when the imagination idealizes existence by laying hold of the possibilities offered to thought and action" (Dewey 1934, 48). For Dewey the term "God" is optional and he prefers the term "the divine" (Dewey 1934, 52, 54). The term is selective. "It involves no miscellaneous worship of everything in general. It selects those factors in experience that generate and support our idea of the good as an end to be striven for. It excludes a multitude of forces that at any given time are irrelevant to this function" (Dewey 1934, 53).

In an exchange with Henry Nelson Wieman which appeared in *The Christian Century* at this time, Dewey's ideas are further clarified. (Dewey's contributions to this exchange were published between February 1933 and December 1934. Dewey's *A Common Faith* was based on the Terry Lectures at Yale given in 1934. See Shaw 1994, chap. 4.) Two points are clarified by Dewey in this exchange. The first point stresses the plurality of these "actors in experience that generate and support our idea of the good as an end to be striven for."

> There are in existence conditions and forces which, apart from human desire and intent, bring about enjoyed and enjoyable goods. . . . Does this admitted fact throw any light whatsoever

upon the *unity and singleness* of the forces and factors which make for good? (Dewey 1933a, 196; italics mine)

The word "God" is:

used simply to designate a multitude of factors and forces which are brought together simply with respect to their coincidence in producing one undesigned effect—the furtherance of good in human life. (Dewey 1933a, 196)

Specifically, this is a rejection of Wieman's conception of God, understood by Dewey to be the "hypostatization" of the "experience of things, persons, causes, found to be good and worth cherishing, into a single objective existence, *a* God."

Furthermore, while some people get an added ecstasy from the concentration of emotion that this unification can bring, this emotion gives no added validity to the idea of God as a unified being. Indeed, a life lived without this concept is not only legitimate, but may even be saner for many people.

Those who choose *distribution* of objects of devotion, service and affection rather than hypostatic concentration are . . . within their intellectual and moral rights. . . . For the great majority of persons this is much the saner course to follow. (Dewey 1933a, 196, italics in original)

It appears that Wieman did not pick up on Dewey's explicit statement of pluralism here, for in his third contribution to the exchange Dewey reiterated his point. Dewey points out that in *A Common Faith* he had referred to "many different natural forces and conditions which generate and sustain our ideal ends." The "unification" of these forces and conditions in the concept of God "is the work of human imagination and will" (Dewey 1934b, 1551).

The second point that Dewey's replies to Wieman make clear is that these natural conditions and forces are to be understood in strictly natural terms, in a sense where the natural includes the human.

Either then the concept of God can be dropped out as far as genuinely religious experience is concerned, or it must be framed wholly in terms of natural and human relationship involved in our straightway human experience. (Dewey 1933b, 394, italics in original)

Furthermore, these forces can be aided by human effort and they do not demand love or adoration.

> The important thing is the fact, the reality, namely, that certain objective forces, of a great variety of kinds, actually promote human wellbeing, that the efficacy of these forces is increased by human attention to and care for the working of these forces.
>
> That which *makes* for good, whether it be singular or collective, demands care, attention, watchfulness. . . . But there is nothing . . . to demand love and adoration. (Dewey 1933b, 395, italics in original)

The task that Dewey leaves the contemporary religious naturalist is to clarify what is to go in the place of love and adoration, which seem to require a personal object and a submissive attitude. For example, some current religious naturalists speak of mystery, awe, or gratitude.

Mead and the More Inclusive Reference Group

Although not himself a religious naturalist, we can use George Herbert Mead's concept of a more inclusive reference. Mead starts with the concept of a generalized other derived from his studies of child development. He posits two crucial stages in the development of a human self: the stage of play and the stage of participating in a game. The difference between the two is that in a game the child must be aware of the attitude of the other players, the participants in the game.

> The attitudes of the other players which the participant assumes organize into a sort of unit, and it is that organization which controls the response of the individual. . . . The organized community or social group which gives to the individual his unity of self may be called "the generalized other." (Mead 1934, 175)

The next step is the notion of a higher or more inclusive reference group which transcends, in a functional rather than ontological sense, the generalized other.

The only way in which we can react against the disapproval of the entire community is by setting up a higher sort of community which in a certain sense out-votes the one we find. A person may reach a point of going against the whole world about him . . . But to do that he has to speak with the voice of reason to himself. He has to comprehend the voices of the past and of the future. (Mead 1934, 167–168)

This is important because the idea of a transcendent norm is possible within a naturalistic outlook. It is reminiscent of Kant's regulative ideals of reason, but clearly within the pragmatic strand of the naturalistic tradition. (See Stone 1992, 16–17, 72).

Roy Wood Sellars:
Evolutionary Naturalism and Religious Humanism

Roy Wood Sellars was one of the first American philosophers to develop a worldview based on evolutionary principles. Co-editor of *Philosophy and Phenomenological Research*, he taught at the University of Michigan from 1905–1906 and 1908–1950 and was involved in writing the *Humanist Manifesto*. (William Schulz claims that Sellars wrote the first draft, Edwin Wilson that he was a major contributor to it. See Schulz 2002, 58–59; Wilson 1995, 26–30.) Sellars differed from the pragmatists in articulating a critical realism in his theory of knowledge (Sellars, 1950, 422–424; Schultz 2002, 119–121). For Sellars naturalism is the philosophical perspective that assumes, not proves, that all existing things are part of the observable processes of the spatiotemporal world. "Nature thus becomes identical with existence and reality" (Sellars 1934, 1; for philosophical assumptions or "perspectives," see Sellars 1961, 174).

Schultz puts it nicely: "Sellars was a neomaterialist, for whom everything could be accounted for in terms of the characteristics and transformations of matter" (Schultz 2002, 121). The term "transformations" is key. Sellars has an emergentist view in which there are four levels of the transformation of matter: inorganic, organic, mental, social. This avoids the twin pitfalls of a dualism that posits separate vital and mental substances and a reductionism that either eliminates these levels or does not articulate a way of thinking of them. Emergence is brought about by the unplanned, increasing organization of matter, making Sellars (with Alexander and Smuts) a forerunner of complexity theory (Sellars 1926, 345).

Based on this theory, Sellars developed his view of religion, paralleling Eustace Haydon, as an adaptive mechanism, a strategy of life. As such, it develops as humans develop (Sellars 1928, 51). Religion can be divided into stages: the mythical, in which the universe is explained in terms of personal agencies, and the scientific, in which the universe is explained in terms of causal laws (Sellars 1918). He later found five stages: religion before the gods, the birth of the gods, their noonday, and the twilight of the gods (the beginning of secularization), and religion after the gods or humanism (Sellars 1928, 51–80, 110–134).

Sellars is clearly a humanist. He was opposed to the liberal theologian's reinterpretation of the term "God." A humanist must "repudiate *with piety* any serious attempt to designate important reality by traditional Christian terms" (Sellars 1941, 51; italics in original). Defined positively, Sellars wrote: "We may define religious humanism, accordingly, as religion adjusted to an intelligent naturalism" (Sellars 1933a, 10; see also Sellars 1931; Sellars 1933).

According to Jon Avery, "For Sellars, this new strategy required a new conception of spirituality.... [He] proposed the cultivation of the values of human life for their own sake rather than for the sake of God. He called his method of reorientation in religion a naturalizing of the spiritual or a spiritualizing of the natural" (Avery 1989, 114). Sellars put it this way: "The idea of the spiritual must be broadened and humanized to include all those purposes, experiences, and activities which express man's nature.... The spiritual is man at his best, man loving, daring, creating, fighting loyally and courageously for causes dear to him" (Sellars 1918, 7–8). This meant a concretizing of devotion, a definite improvement of religion. "The religious man will now be he who seeks out causes to be loyal to, social mistakes to correct, wounds to heal, achievements to further" (Sellars 1947, 158). Indeed, he could refer to the "spiritual fellowship of modern democracy" (Sellars 1916, 14). Dewey would approve and so would Ronald Engel.

John Herman Randall:
The Role of Intelligence in Religion

One of the most profound and sensitive yet neglected philosophers treating religion in the mid-twentieth century was Columbia University's John Herman Randall. His knowledge, if not his viewpoint, would certainly have qualified him to teach in any department of theology in the country. For our purposes his most significant works were *The Role of Knowledge in Western Religion* and *The Meaning of Religion for Man* (Randall 1958, Randall 1968). William Shea's treatment of him in *The Naturalists and the Supernatural* is worth consulting, although Shea's critical perspective is rather different than that propounded here (Shea 1984, 171–202).

Randall reflects carefully on the functions of religion: "first, *celebration*, the social observance, in appropriate ritual form, of the values to which a group is devoted; secondly, *consecration*, the cooperative dedication to those values; and thirdly, *clarification*, the reflective criticism and appraisal of their significance and worth" (Randall 1968, 34). For Randall religious symbols disclose imaginatively "powers and possibilities inherent in the nature of things." They function as "instruments of 'insight' and 'vision' " of what the world might become (Randall 1958, 117). Speaking symbolically, the Divine could be thought of as "the 'order of splendor,' found in our experience of the world" (Randall 1958, 120–121). He is clear about the centrality of vision as a function of religion. "Practical commitment and vision are of course in no sense to be divided or divorced from each other. But men are in the end saved, I am convinced, by vision rather than by works" (Randall 1958, 121; see also Randall 1968 72–74, 82–83).

This insight and vision are not "knowledge" or "truth" in any ordinary sense, certainly not like "the explanatory and verifiable truths of common sense and of scientific inquiry" (Randall 1958, 123). Yet it seems that they do have some cognitive value. What could this be? Randall draws on parallels with the cognitive value of the arts. Utilizing Dewey's treatments of the arts, Randall suggests that the fertility of painting, music, poetry, *and religion* is in their reconstruction of experience. "They may not teach us *that* anything is so. . . . They do not 'explain the world' in the sense of accounting for it; rather they 'explain' it in the sense of making plain its features. But they certainly teach us *how to do* something better. The painter shows us how to see the visible world better" (Randall 1958, 127; italics in original). All this that the various artists and religious people teach us is not knowledge in the ordinary sense. It is rather that they teach us how to discern better the qualities and possibilities of the world. It is like "an art, a technique, of how to see and discern and feel more fully, of how to use the materials of experience to create what was not before" (Randall 1958, 129). It is a *knowing how* rather than a *knowing that*. Such a "know-how" cannot appropriately be judged as "true" or "false." Thus we might speak of religious "knowledge," but not of religious "truth."

Thus we may say that "religion gives us a 'know-how': how to unify our experience through a unified vision of the Divine, of the religious dimension of the world, of the order of splendor. The distinctive character of religious knowledge, which removes it from any competition with other forms of knowing, is that it is . . . an art, a technique, a 'know-how' for opening one's heart to seeing the Divine, for knowing God, in the midst of the conditions of human life in the natural world" (Randall 1958, 133). (Randall uses the term "God" rarely and I suspect that here it is more of a way to bridge the gap to his audience than a technical, systematic term.) Hence we should not speak of religious "truth," a term better used for science and everyday life. Rather we can speak of the adequacy or lack thereof of religious language. Perhaps, remembering the old definition of "truth" as "the adaequation of thing and understanding," we can speak, carefully, of the Truth that shall make you free (Randall 1958, 134).

Religion then "is not primarily a way of understanding and explaining, but a way of celebrating, consecrating, and clarifying" (Randall 1958, 135). Finally, with both the Nazi myth of racial superiority and the excesses of the American Way of Life in mind, Randall urges that "The most important function of intelligence and science in the religious life is to examine intelligently the values it is expressing" (Randall 1958, 140). Even more forcefully, "If religion has no place for intelligence, then it will remain caught in fanaticism, or bogged down in moral sentimentality and intellectual confusion" (Randall 1968, 110).

It is interesting that Randall was a signer of the first *Humanist Manifesto*, although with reservations. According to Edwin H. Wilson, he objected to E. A. Burtt's modification of the Third Thesis of the Manifesto (which denied a mind-body dualism) in the direction of an interactionist position and thought that the last two sentences of the Manifesto concerning human ability to achieve the world of human dreams to be "crass optimism" (Schulz 2002, 64; Wilson 1995, 41–43). In 1953, when the *Humanist* journal solicited responses "twenty years after" the first manifesto, Randall commented on the original *Humanist Manifesto* that it did not express a tragic sense of life, humility, or the need for imagination in religion (Schulz 87).

Jan Christiaan Smuts:
Holism and an Evolutionary Universe

Mention should also be made of a South African general, statesman of international reputation, amateur botanist and authority on grasses, and outstanding amateur philosopher, Jan Christiaan Smuts. He is remembered today outside his homeland chiefly as the probable originator of the term "holism" in his *Holism and Evolution* of 1926. In his lifetime he was a leader of the Dutch Afrikaners in South Africa and he consciously applied his principle of holism after the Boer War to work with the British to develop the Union of South Africa, of which he was prime minister from 1919 to 1924 and then from 1939 to 1948. He organized Britain's Royal Air Force, was an architect of the League of Nations, and represented South Africa at the founding meeting of the United Nations.

For Smuts the universe is full of wholes. A "whole" is a technical term for Smuts. A whole is more than the sum of its parts, otherwise it would be a purely mechanical system. A whole is a synthesis or sum of its parts, a unity so close that it affects the activities and interactions of those parts and makes them different from what they would be without the whole. (My favorite example would be to put a frog in a blender. [Thought experiment, please!] If you turned it on you would have all of the parts, but you would not have a frog. There is nothing mysterious or dualistic about this.) The whole is not something additional to its parts. It *is* the parts in a definite structural arrangement and with interactions that constitute the whole. (Here he does not seem to violate the principle of parsimony.) However, along with emergentist thinking generally, the activity of wholes is creative of something new. For example, a chemical compound has qualities that are new in relation to the chemical elements which compose it.

"Holism" is a term for Smuts which means primarily the operative factor in the world which makes wholes and also the theory concerning it. This factor is a real operative factor, a true *vera causa*. Practically universal, it is expressive of the universe in its forward movement in time, creating new wholes and giving an ever more holistic character to the universe (somewhat like Chardin) and pointing the way to the future. It is the inner driving force behind evolutionary progress, operating through and sustaining the forces and activities of the universe. In a third sense, holism could refer to the totality of the wholes. Just as the term "matter" includes all bits and particles of matter, so "Holism" includes the totality of wholes. (At this point I feel closer to Samuel Alexander, whose "*nisus* toward deity" can, I think, be read without violating the principle of parsimony as does Smuts with his holism as an operative factor.)

Three emergentist thinkers of the 1920s (Samuel Alexander, Smuts, and C. Lloyd Morgan) all thought of the emergence of new characteristics in the universe in terms of stages or levels. For Smuts these stages are matter, life, mind and sometimes personality. (Alexander and Morgan have similar lists. For all of them generalization from the sciences is a key part of deriving their worldview and I think that they would be open to modifying their lists if the sciences suggest it. For example, organic molecules, colloids, and prokaryotes might deserve separate mention on these lists. They are more empirically oriented than a priori in their thinking. When faced with the objection that if Holism is all-embracing it is not capable of confirmation or disconfirmation, Smuts replied that science should also be concerned with all-embracing descriptions, with the universal ground-plan.) At times Smuts could distinguish: (1) material structures, (2) living bodies, (3) animals (or some of them) with central control, (4) animals with conscious central control culminating in personality and society, (5) the state and other organizations and finally, (6) ideal wholes or values, such as truth, beauty and goodness, set free from personality, operative as creative factors on their own account, upbuilding the spiritual order in the universe. His remarks about society and values remain undeveloped.

For Smuts freedom is a function of the whole. The creative mastery of the organism over the environment and its transformation increases with evolution. Organisms are creative in a full sense: metabolism, growth, and evolution. The beginnings of freedom are early in the evolution of life, possibly even earlier, since even matter is creative. With the development of locomotion, freedom increases. In humans, it is a function of the whole personality.

The issue of freedom is still with us. One of the things which emergent thinking can do is to help us understand the issue of freedom by pointing out that the ability to make choices evolved. The development of models and vocabularies adequate to both our scientific understandings and to our need to make responsible choices is badly needed. Perhaps "freedom," is not the best term. "Free will" seems impossibly antiquated. This may be the next important frontier in the development of an adequate naturalistic outlook. I am convinced that the solutions will lie along the path first scouted by the emergent thinkers, including a recognition that the roots of choice lie far back in our evolutionary past.

In *Holism and Evolution* Smuts is reticent to speak of God. Here is where I find that he stays within the bounds of naturalism as employed in this book. (A bold move indeed for a politician in a country with Anglo-Dutch roots.) He is not explicitly religious, but his total outlook is so parallel to many writers treated here that I classify him as a religious naturalist. The universe is holistic without itself being a whole. There is no superior mind or personality. Behind the holistic field of nature is the activity of holism itself, creating and working through wholes. But this outlook can ground our faith or hope in the human struggle for greater good, especially if we resolve through following the pattern of Dutch-British reconciliation and international agencies like the League of Nations to continue the work of whole-making.

Sometime during the late 1920s occurred a significant moment in our story. G. B. Smith, who is treated in the next chapter, offered a seminar at the Divinity School of the University of Chicago in which books by Samuel Alexander, C. Lloyd Morgan, and Smuts were on the reading list. Bernard Meland, who also figures in the next chapter, was in that seminar. Meland will often mention these three together as the "emergent evolutionists." I believe that by his own writings as well as by his influence on process thinkers through his students Schubert Ogden and, above all, John Cobb, Meland helped bridge the notion of "emergence" from these three early writers to today and also helped in the spread of the general acceptance of the notion. Meland put these three writers in the historical context of William James, Henri Bergson, and Whitehead and stressed the notion of emergence as an alternative to reductionism (materialism) and dualism (supernaturalism, Cartesianism, neo-Kantianism, and vitalism). At this point these emergentist thinkers of the 1920s form the roots of much contemporary naturalism (including Ursula Good-enough and Terrence Deacon.) They represent the early emergence of emergentist thinking. (I have decided not to treat C. Lloyd Morgan, author of *Emergent Evolution* [1923] and *Life, Mind, and Spirit* [1925], because in my mind his notion of "Divine Activity" involves an element of transcendence that removes him from a naturalistic outlook.)

Chapter Two

Theological and Humanist Religious Naturalists

The Early Chicago School:
Foster, Smith, Mathews, and Ames

At the University of Chicago Divinity School and related schools there was a period of theological experimentation in the early decades of the twentieth century. Although known especially for their sociohistorical and functional studies of biblical and Christian traditions, as these writers matured they often engaged in theological reflections of a naturalistic inclination. The scholars whose careers developed before the arrival of Henry Nelson Wieman are often referred to as the early Chicago school of theology (Arnold 1966, Peden 1987, Peden and Stone 1996, vol. I). Four of these writers deserve our attention. What is of especial significance for our story is that the naturalistic explorations of these thinkers occurred at one of the major American graduate schools for training ministers and scholars of religion.

George Burman Foster

It was George Burman Foster the theologian who brought early notoriety to the Divinity School of the University of Chicago. He was the center of what could be called "heresy" trials by Baptist ministers and was dropped from the Ministers Meeting, although he never lost his ordination. He was moved out of the Divinity School to the Department of Comparative Religion. It was probably a reference to him that inspired Lyman Stuart to finance the publication of *The Fundamentals*, leading to the fundamentalist movement in America. He was significant in influencing some of the early religious humanists in the Midwest, although there is some question as to whether he himself ended up as a humanist. (For an extensive treatment of Foster with references to the secondary literature, see Jerome A. Stone, "The Line between Religious Naturalism and Humanism: G. B. Foster and A. E. Haydon," Stone 1999; Edgar Towne, 1977).

Later his 1909 *The Function of Religion in Man's Struggle for Existence* is the center of our attention. Here Foster had two ways of conceptualizing God. First, God is the world in its ideal-achieving capacity. Second, just as the modern idea is that the mind is the body in one of its aspects or ways of behaving, so God is the cosmos in one of its aspects or ways of behaving. (Portions of this section are adapted from Stone 1999; see this also for Foster's interpreters.)

"The word God is a symbol to designate the universe in its ideal-achieving capacity" (Foster 1909, 109; also in Peden and Stone 1996, I, 52). There is a real capacity in the universe to which this symbol refers. It is not just a subjective set of ideals.

> The content of our God-faith is the conviction that in spite of much that is dark and inharmonious in the world, reality is on the side of the achievement of values such as ours. But in that case, if our goods are ideals, if our heart's desire be the goals of the true, the beautiful, and the good, if our yearning be for the ideal perfection of ourselves and our kind, if all our time and strength be devoted to such an end as this, we may have the comfort and encouragement of the conviction of its attainability. The evidence of experience is that the structure and function of the universe are such that ideals are by us achievable. . . . The word God is a symbol to designate the universe in its ideal-achieving capacity. It is the expression of our appreciation of existence, when our feelings are so excited as to assign worth to existence. . . . To express the whole matter briefly, our vocation is to achieve ideal values; religion is the conviction that such values are by us achievable, in virtue of our constitution and of the constitution of that whole of which we are a part. Religion, in a word, is self-effectuation. (Foster 1909, 108–110; Peden and Stone, I, 52)

Foster here combines a religious outlook with a consistent naturalism. He unites the search for ideals and the capacities in the actual world to assist the pursuit of those ideals, what I have called the ideal and the real aspects of transcendence. Finally, he has a sense of both the human element in the construction of the God-symbol and the objective reality of the ideal-making capacities, what I call the transactional nature of experience. (For the real and ideal aspects of transcendence, see my *The Minimalist Vision of Transcendence*, Stone 1992, 12–18; for the transactional nature of experience, 127–135.)

Now let examine some details critically. First of all these ideals are achievable. This seems either far-fetched or incautious. Some beauty, truth, and goodness are achievable. But to state that ideals are achievable seems rather bold. Perhaps what Foster wanted to emphasize was that these ideals are not unrelated to our capacities. In the second place prophetic protest against even our values is lacking. There is no note that our ideals need criticism or transvaluation.

Further the implicit unity of ideals and ideal-making capacity here needs examination. The pluralistic possibilities of the divine need recognition (Stone 1992, 14, 16).

Note the phrase, religion "is self-effectuation." As a reaction against throwing oneself passively into the hands of God, there is something salutary here. But surely there is room, even within a naturalistic framework, for a polarity of self-actualization and reception of help. If there are conditions for the production of value, then surely a person can be attentive to and receptive to these conditions without losing autonomy or motivation.

There is something overly strenuous about Foster. Surely it is bordering on fanaticism to urge that "*all* our time and strength be devoted" to the achievement of our perfection. This Puritanism needs to be blended with some Daoist enjoyment. On the other hand, I was formerly surrounded by students who are not strenuous enough. It is hard to talk about the pursuit of values, when consumer oriented people are apathetic or cynical about values in the first place. Is this the Achilles heel of religious naturalism?

Finally note that our yearning is "for the ideal perfection of ourselves and *our kind*." Now I do not think that "our kind" refers to males, white people, or Euro-Americans. I say this in view of his articles on African-Americans and women in which he urges the attainment of full autonomous personality (Foster 1913; Foster 1914; Foster 1921). In all three of these articles there is a welcome emphasis on moral personality with a lack of significant social analysis, except to some extent in the one on labor. In his article on African-Americans he is very aware that self-development requires open doors of opportunity, but his racial essentialism and his ambiguity about the intellectual capacity of "the Negro" (he is "sensuous" yet capable of mental and moral training) are open to criticism. I do interpret "our kind" to refer to humans, and only humans. This is an expression of his Kantian emphasis on personality. An environmentally sensitive theology will need to rethink this.

Foster stresses the symbolic nature of our language about God.

> All our highest ideas are but figurative expressions. Even the concept of a personal God has symbolic validity only. And the function of a symbol is not to give an exact report concerning the nature of an object, but to express the appreciations of the subject. (Foster 1909, 109; Peden and Stone, 1996, I, 52)

Yet along with this goes the affirmation that the symbol of God refers to something beyond the subject, namely, the ideal-making capacity of the universe. It is this combination of symbol plus what the symbol designates that leads me to say that Foster anticipates Dewey's notion of the transactional nature of knowledge.

> Of the symbols used in God-language "personality" holds a special place. Since personality is our highest idea, it must ever be on that account the word which most fittingly symbolizes our experiences of the relation of reality to our ideal values. It is in our human personalities, and, so far as we know, in these alone, that this relation immediately comes to light. (Foster 1909, 109–110; Peden and Stone, I, 52)

This, of course, follows from Foster's high evaluation of personality.

We have been discussing Foster's idea of God as the universe in its ideal-achieving capacity. Foster's second idea is that we need to develop an immanent idea of God just as we have done with the idea of the soul. Just as we can speak of the rising of the sun, even though it is really the turning earth, so we speak of the soul, even though we know today that there is really only a single psychophysiological organism without a separate soul. In like fashion we may speak of God, even though there only a single universe without a separate God.

> There is no such thing as a self-dependent soul freely active or interactive with an organism which we call the body, just as similarly there is no self-dependent deity freely active or interactive within that larger body which we call the cosmos. All this is a survival of primitive animism. . . . I mean that soul and body are not two beings confronting each other as independent and interoperative, but that they are one being

giving account of itself in a twofold manner. . . . I am trying to indicate that the immanence of a free or unfree soul-entity in a body is quite as unintelligible to psychology as the immanence of a free or unfree God-entity in the cosmos is unintelligible to philosophical reflection. (Foster 1909, 21–22; Peden and Stone, 1996, I, 45–46)

The functional approach, displayed in his title, *The Function of Religion in Man's Struggle for Existence* is explicit. His biological image stresses both the creative character of the organism and the role of the environment. This biological imagery is extended to language, art, morality, and religion. Like the eye, they were created by organisms to fill a function.

The gods were created for the sake of the most vital practical interests. They were created in the interest of overcoming the evils that beset the human organism and of appropriating the good that would redound to the weal of that organism. (Foster 1909, 59; Peden and Stone, I, 48)

The function of the concept of God is to express human appreciation of the worth of existence, specifically its capacity to achieve ideals. The function of religion itself, if I read him correctly, is to elicit our courage in the struggle to achieve ideals.

Our vocation is to achieve ideal values; religion is the conviction that such values are by us achievable, in virtue of our constitution and of the constitution of that whole of which we are a part. . . . The worth of such conviction in fulfilling the task is evident. (Foster 1909, 110; Peden and Stone, 1996, I, 52)

Notice Foster addressing the question of illusion. He reverts to the old Romantic metaphor of the rainbow as seen by the child and by the scientist.

To a child a rainbow is a real thing—substantial and palpable; to the

educated man it is an illusion, but it does not deceive him . . . Is it not surprising that we do not reproach our illusions—though our senses deceive us, and our natural anticipations deceive us, and our expectations deceive us? Similarly, many students of religion who have held that religion is an illusion have declared that the illusion was useful. I, too, think there is an element of illusion in religion—think of the phenomena of prayer, in some of its aspects, for example—but I doubt if at bottom it be greater than that in other forms of consciousness. . . . Indeed, the man who *really lives in* religion, deriving the strength and recuperation and meaning of his life therefrom, will not be haunted by this dread of illusion. (Foster 1909, 90–91; Peden and Stone 1996, I, 50–51)

Foster suggests that religion is not the only human creation which involves an element of imagination or fantasy.

It cannot be denied that our god-faith had its origin in human fantasy. But this is not the only human thing that had its origin there. Art is a humanization of the world, too. Aye, so is even science. (Foster 1909, 63; Peden and Stone 1996, I, 48)

Thus it follows that "there never was a false god, that there never was a really false religion; unless you call a child a false man" (Foster 1909, 69–70; Peden and Stone 1996, I, 49). Implied, of course, is a lack of sophistication by the child.

If the validity and value of our ideas and ideals are jeopardized by the subjectivity of their origin, nothing human is valid or valuable. Are not our moral standards, are not our scientific formulae, are not our artistic creations, are not our languages, products of the subjective needs and activities of mankind? But do you discredit the reality and function of these because you made them? . . . If, in a word, religion stands the test of workability and of service equally with other subjective creations like art and language and morality, what more have we a right to demand? (Foster 1909, 102–103; Peden and Stone 1996, I, 51)

It is clear that Foster is trying to point to the subjective element in religion without dismissing it as a mere illusion.

Gerald Birney Smith

One of the strongest proponents of the tentativeness of all human thinking and speaking about the divine was G. B. Smith, teacher of theology at Chicago's Divinity School in the first three decades of the twentieth century. (Much of this section is taken from Stone 1992, 54–58.) For the story of religious naturalism, his most important writing is a late article "Is Theism Essential to Religion?" (Smith 1925; see also Smith 1928.)

This article is a sustained attack on theism. However, it is important to see precisely the concept of theism Smith is attacking. He has in mind a concept of God as creator and governor of the world. This is a concept which provides a theological explanation of nature, a theological anchor for political authority, and a theological interpretation of religious and moral experience, in short, a foundation for nature, society and personal life. The first part of this article is a sketch of the dissolution of this theory through the secularization of these three realms.

Smith's complaint against this view is that it is too definite and too complete to face all of the facts. The theistic hypothesis seems too definite and thoroughly rationalized. A common experience today is the sense of "unutterable wonder as [at] the incalculable spaces disclosed by astronomy and the unimaginable stretches of time suggested by the doctrine of evolution and the almost incredible marvels of atomic structure and action." Science shows us many "mysteries which we do not, and perhaps cannot, know" (Smith 1925, 374–375). Among the facts which theism seems not to face are, first, that science shows us that the evolutionary process seems to be a series of experiments without a clearly defined goal and, second, the presence of evil.

The truth lies somewhere between theism and antitheism, although the theist is nearer right. Part II of the article is a treatment of attempts to have religious values without resort to theism, specifically the work of Edward S. Ames and the humanist Max Otto.

Smith's attack on antitheism (and on religious humanism) is based on his notion that humans are not enough, that we must be related to the nonhuman environment. "In religions man brings his highest ideals and his most precious values into the presence of the vast cosmic mystery which has produced him and which holds him in its power. He seeks to obtain from this cosmic power some kind of a blessing on these values and ideals" (Smith 1925, 374). Although Smith's language is deliberately reticent, the idea of a cosmic power still sounds too much like an ontologically supreme being. There is a superlative and unitary sense to such a phrase which perhaps oversteps the bounds of what we may legitimately assert. Perhaps Smith is on the cusp of religious naturalism.

Smith affirms a strong sense of the worshiper's relationship with this cosmic power and mystery, often using personalistic language.

> The belief in God means that there may be found, not merely within the circle of human society, but also in the non-human

environment of which we are dependent, a *quality* of the cosmic process akin to the quality of our own spiritual life. Through communion with this qualitative aspect of the cosmic process human life attains an experience of dignity, and a reinforcement of spiritual power. The quality of this reinforcement can be adequately expressed only by the conception of a Divine Presence in the cosmic order. . . .

Just what conception of God will emerge from this great experiment we cannot yet tell. But it will express the experience of kinship between man and that quality in the environment which supports and enriches humanity in its spiritual quest. God will be very real to the religious man, but his reality will be interpreted in terms of social reciprocity with an as yet inadequately defined cosmic support of human values, rather than in terms of theistic creatorship and control. The experience of God will take the form of comradeship with that aspect of our non-human environment which is found to reinforce and to enrich our life. Anthropomorphic symbols will frankly be used to promote that experience, but they will not be pressed into exact theological descriptions. (Smith 1925, 375–377)

Smith is more open to the use of personalistic symbols for God, in however guarded a fashion, than most persons of a naturalistic outlook. His use of the terms "quality" and "aspect" are more clearly naturalistic and find echoes in Alexander, Ames, and Dewey. The term "environment" is quite ambiguous for a naturalist, being able to be interpreted in an immanent or transcendent sense.

Two Other Chicago Naturalists

Shailer Mathews, who taught at the Divinity School of the University of Chicago from 1895 to 1933, is known primarily as a scholar of Christian theology, especially of the Biblical period. However, his later writings give us a number of formulations of a naturalistic conception of God.

> *For God is our conception, born of social experience, of the personality-evolving and personally responsive elements of our cosmic environment with which we are organically related.* (Mathews 1931, 226).

Note that this definition is both unitary and pluralistic. The conception is singular although the elements in the environment are many.

Second, this is both subjective, in that it is our conception, and objective, in that it is of elements in our environment. Similar definitions are found in his book, *Is God Emeritus?* and in *Religious Life*, edited by E. Sapir (Mathews 1940, 34; cp. Peden & Stone, I, 1996, 152; Mathews 1929, 54; I have a further analysis and critique of this definition in Stone 1992, 52).

In his earlier work Mathews is not as clearly naturalistic. (It is important in reading Mathews to realize that he is using "naturalism" in a way different from that employed here, that is, a materialistic worldview which excludes the possibility of personality. See Mathews 1924, 4–5. But the issue is not that of how he is using the word.) This incomplete naturalism is found in his use of such notions as that of an immanent God working through the environments of personality, life and matter, or of an infinite Person in the universe of activity analogous to the human personality within our bodies, and "participation of God in the sorrows and struggles of humanity," and "of God's gradual self-manifestation to man through personality and society" (Mathews 1924, 401, 416, 419). However, after his 1924 *Contributions of Science to Religion* his language is more clearly naturalistic.

Another Chicago theologian, Edward Scribner Ames, taught in the philosophy department of the University of Chicago from 1901 to 1935 and was Dean of Disciples house from 1928 to 1945 as well as the pastor of the University Church of the Disciples of Christ. He thought that the idea of God should be revised, just as the notions of mind or soul were being reconceived. When this reconception occurs, God will be understood as the reality of the world in certain aspects and functions. Ames specified these functions as orderliness, love, and intelligence and also as order, beauty, and expansion (Ames 1929, 154, 156; cp. Peden & Stone, I, 1996, 97–99). For Ames God is not a mere projection of human ideals but refers to real aspects or functions of the world.

Ames also thinks of God in terms of what he called "the practical absolute." "God is used as the standard of reference for the adequacy of specific ideals. When a line of conduct is considered, the question arises for the religious man as to whether such conduct is consistent with loyalty with God" (Ames 1929, 178). This "practical absolute" is found in "any type of thinking or practical interest. In reasoning men seek a procedure which validates their arguments. They appeal at last to the nature of reason, to the law of contradiction, or to the sufficient law of reason" (Ames 1929, 180). The scientist assumes the orderliness of nature and regards his experiments as having general validity.

Such a point of reference is found also in our moral life. "Kant's dictum, 'So act that the maxim of our deed may become a universal law,' expresses this craving for the substantiation of individual conduct by a law or principle. . . . This is the way the religious man uses God. God is the judge, the umpire, the referee" (Ames 1929, 180–181). This notion of a practical absolute is analogous to Gordon Kaufman's discussion of the relativizing function of God (Kaufman 1993, chap. 21, esp. 309–314, 319).

Thus for Ames God may be considered both as the world in certain aspects (its orderliness, love and intelligence or else in its order, beauty, and expansion) as well as a standard of reference for our ideals. In terms of my own thinking, there is both a real and an ideal aspect to our experiences of immanent transcendence (Stone 1992, 10–17).

A question comes to mind. When Ames specifies aspects of reality (e.g., order, intelligence, love) which make up what we call God, is the list of aspects complete (e.g., should sublimity be included)? Are these aspects compatible?

The Humanists:
Dietrich, the Humanist Manifesto, and Huxley

The religious humanists of the 1920s and 1930s could be considered religious naturalists in so far as their concern for intellectual honesty and their passion for social justice acted as relatively transcendent factors in their lives and thinking.

We cannot trace the precursors of twentieth-century humanism. Besides such names as Robert Ingersoll, there were several women in the nineteenth century who rejected traditional religion and sometimes the idea of God. Among these were Frances Wright, Ernestine L. Rose, and Elizabeth Cady Stanton. Annie Laurie Gaylor has rediscovered these women for us in her *Women Without Superstition* (Ingersoll 1983; Gaylor 1997).

There has been a tradition of humanism in African American writers. Anthony Pinn suggests that the source of this came from the difficulty of reconciling the experience of oppression with belief in a just and powerful God. Pinn includes Frederick Douglass, Zora Neale Hurston, W. E. B. DuBois, A. Philip Randolph and James Foreman among those who rejected traditional religion. Lewis McGee, William R. Jones, Norm Allen, Jr., and Anthony Pinn are among Black Americans whose this-worldly transcendence may be seen in their struggle for justice.

The immediate roots of religious humanism go back to the formation of the Free Religious Association in 1867 in which radical Unitarian clergy joined others in moving beyond the boundaries of Christianity and to the post–Civil War "Issue in the West" when Unitarian churches debated whether moral character alone was sufficient as a basis for religious fellowship. The Western Unitarian Conference was always less traditional, in part a matter of the frontier. Mason Olds traces the Humanist controversy within the Unitarian churches from 1918 to 1954. The key early humanists in the Unitarian churches were John Dietrich, Curtis Reese, and Charles F. Potter. (See Olds 1996, 33–150.) An important chapter in the history of humanism was George Burman Foster's questioning and his influence on Eustace Haydon, the humanist teacher of world religions at the Divinity School, a leader of the Chicago Ethical Humanist Society, and a drafter of the *Humanist Manifesto*. The key point is that Foster was talking about the death of the supernatural God before 1910, before Dietrich, Reese, or Potter. (For the controversy around Foster, see Edgar A. Towne, "Introduction to Foster," in Peden and Stone 1996; Towne 1977, 165, 168–169.)

John Dietrich

We shall focus on John Dietrich. A German Reformed minister in Pittsburgh, he did not contest his 1911 heresy trial in which he was defrocked and his church was closed because his parishoners supported him. The issues concerned biblical infallibility, the Virgin Birth, the deity of Christ, and traditional views of the atonement. By 1916 he was minister of the First Unitarian Society in Minneapolis (Olds, 1996, 53–97; Dietrich 1989).

Dietrich came to believe that Jesus was not supreme among humanity's religious teachers, further that the scientific method was the best method of achieving the truth. This method was not infallible, but it did show a law governed universe without miracles. His view is somewhat naïve by today's standards for he conceived of a single scientific method and had no significant notion of probability in the world. He advocated what a number of people in the 1920s called "emergent evolution," a view adopted by Sellars, Dewey and others which allowed for a naturalistic account of the richness of human values, not a simple materialism. He was critical not only of fundamentalism but of the liberal biblical hermeneutics of Harry Emerson Fosdick, since Fosdick, according to Dietrich, had only individual taste as a criterion as to what to judge to accept in scriptures. However, I wonder what other standard Dietrich had in setting up his own Bible of Man which he admitted did not have a fixed canon.

Dietrich wished to drop God-language as being more honest than what he termed the liberal's equivocation. However, he rejected the label of atheist, which implied both crude materialism and dogmatism to him (Olds, p. 73). For Dietrich the universe was neither friendly nor unfriendly, but indifferent to humans, thus opposing the humanists Joseph Wood Krutch and Bertrand Russell. Worship will focus on qualities, values, especially love and justice, not on a highest being with these values. And when we admire these qualities in worship we will aspire to them. Almost needless to say, there is no immortality other than a person's influence. He had a naturalistic view of spirit as the personality of a human organism.

He was worried about conformity, about the effect of homogenized news. He took the side of those who thought human nature was malleable enough that we should work on the social environment, even though man's animal nature has not yet died away. Note his construction of "animal," as lower and definitely not cooperative. Carrying this further he felt that we should work on the causes of war, disease, and poverty. Morality is true religion and does not require God. Morality evolves and is the summary expression of person's experience.

John Dietrich used the term "humanism" of his own message before 1918. In 1917 at the annual meeting of the Western Unitarian Conference in Des Moines Dietrich talked with Reese about Reese's sermon of the year before titled "A Democratic View of Religion," which contrasted with an autocratic view of religion. Soon Reese started using the term "humanism." The Unitarian Magazine, *Christian Register*, in 1919 published an article by Dietrich which contrasted a religion based on punishment and supernatural help with a religion which did not look for help or consolation from without. In 1919 Reese became secretary of the Western Unitarian Conference. This is extremely significant for the history of religious humanism, for as the chief Unitarian denominational executive in the Midwestern United States, he was able to facilitate the placement of humanist ministers in pulpits, thus providing an institutional home for religious humanism. A similar event occurred in the Universalist church when Clinton Lee Scott, a signer of the *Humanist Manifesto*, was reelected a trustee of the Universalist General Convention and became state superintendent of the Massachusetts Universalist Convention and also the Connecticut Universalist Convention.

In his life and his sermons Dietrich exemplified the earlier humanist striving for intellectual honesty, truth, and social justice in a nontheistic framework. As such I count him among the religious naturalists of the twentieth century.

The Humanist Manifesto

The successive *Humanist Manifestos* are probably the most well known statements of the Humanist position, at least in the United States. In my

The Minimalist Vision of Transcendence I was quite critical of the first two Manifestos for their Pelagian approach to religion (Stone 1992, 196–202). I have not modified my position on this, although I have since become more appreciative of the intellectual honesty and commitment to truth and social justice of the signers. The major deficiency, speaking from my own specific naturalism, is that for the writers of these two manifestos, religion is the pursuit of ideals and not also an openness to situationallly transcendent resources, what I have called "the real aspect" of relative transcendence. As the first manifesto puts it, "Religions have always been means for realizing the highest values in life. Their end has been accomplished through the interpretation of the total environing situation (theology or worldview), the sense of values resulting therefrom (goal or ideal), and the technique (cult) established for realizing the satisfactory life" (*Humanist Manifestos I and II* 1973, 7). The means of realizing the highest values are worldview, ideal and cult. There is no mention of a reality or realities, even within the natural world, to help in realizing these conditions.

My suggestion is that religious naturalists need to pay attention to these realities. They are not supernatural. In this the humanists are right. However, we need to focus on them. They are the sum total of the physical, biological, psychological, and cultural processes which enable us to strive toward these values. They are to be studied empirically as far as possible. But we should also nurture of an openness and sensitive appreciation of them. This will be the naturalistic analogue to cooperating or transactional grace.

Julian Huxley

Biologist Julian Huxley, first Director General of UNESCO, was a significant humanist writer of the 1920s and 1930s. In *Religion Without Revelation* he calls for a radical transformation of Western religion on a naturalistic basis. The reconstruction is based on agnosticism (thus without reference to a supernatural Divine power), evolutionary natural science, and psychology (Huxley 1941, v, 17). This is a strong agnosticism including God, heaven and hell. "It seems to me quite clear that the idea of personality in God . . . has been put there by man . . . and therefore I disbelieve in a personal god in any sense in which that phrase is ordinarily used. . . . Under the term *personal* god I include all ideas of a so-called superpersonal god . . . or indeed any supernatural spiritual existence or force" (Huxley 1941, 7). "Until . . . the idea of God [is] relegated to the past with the idea of ritual magic and other products of primitive and unscientific human thought, we shall never get the new religion we need.

In that new religion, man must make up his mind to take upon himself his full burden, by acknowledging that he is the highest entity of which he has any knowledge, that his values are the only basis for any categorical imperative, and that he must work out both his own salvation and destiny, and the standards on which they are based" (Huxley 1941, vi–vii). His naturalism implies a belief in the unity, uniformity, and continuity in nature and a denial of the supernatural (Huxley 1941 26–27, 56).

The core of religion is reverence or a sense of the sacred. As the basis for this assertion Huxley draws upon the anthropological and phenomenological studies of Lowie, R. R. Marett, and Rudolf Otto (Huxley 1941, 8, 41–47). Above all mature religion should be linked with intelligence and morality and move beyond convention and superstition (Huxley 1941, 16–17, 41–48, 54). Huxley was an influence for Connie Barlow, who thought of him as the first person to find the sweep of evolution as the modern substitute for the supernatural creator (Barlow 1997, 281–283, 293–296).

Frederick May Eliot:
Unitarian Preacher

Contemporary with the earlier humanists was Frederick May Eliot, Unitarian minister in St. Paul, Minnesota. Eliot was known as sympathetic to humanists, appreciative of what they were doing, especially their stress on human responsibility. He was hospitable to humanists, but was not considered a humanist himself. In 1937 Eliot became President of the American Unitarian Association, the national Unitarian body, a position in which he served for twenty-one years until 1958. For our purposes the significance of Eliot was that he developed a revised theism that falls within the boundaries of religious naturalism as we have defined it.

The substance of Eliot's notion of God can be found in five sermons, published in *Fundamentals of Unitarian Faith* and *Toward Belief in God*. It should never be forgotten that Eliot's theology is expressed in sermons. This is not to say that his ideas lack rigor or depth. Indeed, his sermons contain much substance. But we should not expect a degree of precision in Eliot that we would demand in academic writing.

The marrow of Eliot's divinity can be found at the end of the fifth sermon in his *Toward Belief in God*. "When I say that I believe in God," I affirm my belief in "the reality and significance of three great experiences." First, "that the experience of a moral imperative is real and inescapably important." Second, "that behind all the mystery and darkness of life there is a rational order." Third, that "I am not an accidental collocation of atoms but that I am a child of the universe and heir to all its glories" (Eliot 1928, 93–94). These three experiences are explicated in sermons Three through Five in his *Toward Belief in God*, to which I now turn.

Of the three experiences out of which Eliot says belief in God may be built, he starts with the one which seems to him to be most nearly universal, "namely, the discovery of the reality of the moral law." Eliot first sidesteps the question as to whether there is an objective moral law "apart from the conviction of individual human beings." What he has in mind, he states, "is the conviction of an individual that for him there is a distinction between right and wrong, in some concrete situation in which he finds himself, that has *for him* the validity of final and absolute law" (Eliot 1928, 44, italics in original).

> You are sitting quietly on the sidelines of the game, cool and dispassionate; then suddenly you see that something is at stake in the contest which lifts it out of the realm of sport, at least so far as you are concerned. Something of priceless value is in peril, and you cannot remain neutral or indifferent any longer. That momentary glimpse of moral issues involved in the struggle lifts you to your feet—involuntarily, with no thought for the moment of what it might cost you; and you raise your hand in pledge of your commitment to a cause that is so much greater than your personal life that it has the right to command you with absolute and final authority. (Eliot 1928, 49–50)

Eliot's notion of the moral ideal is fairly broad in scope. It includes the ideal of good workmanship, pride in a job well done. It includes also the ideal of personal honor, of a person who will not sell her opinion or her judgment. Eliot also is moved by the story of Captain Scott and his companions starving and freezing to death at the South Pole. They decided rather than to end their lives to continue to the end cheering each other. Eliot says that he is not saying that if they had killed themselves it would have been cowardly or wrong, but he does say that their heroism does call forth a response from us.

> It is when the summons comes directly to us, though it be in a far less dramatic fashion, that the experience of the reality of the moral law is most truly met. It is when we find ourselves in a situation where the voice of moral idealism speaks to our souls, with immediate and compelling power, that we

discover what the authority of that voice actually is. . . . For us, at any rate, there is . . . an absolute distinction between right and wrong. We may have learned to be humble-minded when it comes to proclaiming the universal validity of that distinction. We may be wholly unwilling to claim final and infallible truth for the particular moral insight which we have found. But for us, in the particular situation where we find ourselves, the voice of moral idealism carries an accent of finality. (Eliot 1928, 55)

The second type of experience which Eliot cites as material for the construction of a notion of God is "a conviction that the riddle of the universe has an answer." Eliot brings together two types of experience which have a similarity. One is the conviction that "comes when circumstances have suddenly dealt" one "a cruel or treacherous blow" and that person cries out for "a meaning behind the veil." The other experience is the "desire for light . . . which drives all the seekers after knowledge everywhere." This conviction comes when "we dare to say that we believe there is an answer, to be found by those who search for it with sufficient skill and patience." This conviction lies behind the work of the scientist and is essentially the same conviction which comes "to many a humble seeker for truth in the course of his ordinary human experience" (Eliot 1928, 69–70; I retain Eliot's masculine pronouns for accuracy).

For Eliot "the foundation for all that searching is the conviction, which no logic can substantiate, that man's mind can move from the known to the unknown because the unknown is not unknowable" (Eliot 1928, 71). After a discussion of the discovery of cosmic rays he specifies the message of this discovery:

> The universe, to its outermost limits, is governed by an order that corresponds to the character of our own minds. Thus far, at any rate, we have not found any place where the things that happen are incommensurable with our intelligence; and that thought is deeply reassuring. It fits in with the basic conviction of religious experience that the riddle of the universe has an answer. (Eliot 1928, 75–76)

The third type of experience that Eliot refers to is the "sense of belonging to the universe—of being at home in the world" (Eliot 1928, 93). This is a "conviction that there is a relation of kinship between us human beings and the great forces of the universe in which we dwell and of which we are a part." Eliot stressed that the language used to express this was poetic, indeed, rather like a gesture. At any rate he is saying, in language that he acknowledges as poetic and gestural, that "we are somehow at home" on this earth, that "we are aware of a kinship with the universe that makes it impossible for us to be lonely. . . . We know that we are not the accidental product of blind, meaningless forces" (Eliot 1928, 83–84). This is a belief "that this world is a friendly place, that underneath all the apparent indifference and even hostility of forces by which we are surrounded there is a unity of purpose and a kinship of spirit which are full of promise for the human soul." This belief is a "continual inspiration to the best kind of living." Since it gives us a sense of being cared for and a motive for caring, it is "the surest source of personal integrity and faithfulness." Indeed, with this conviction "you can live with power and joy," and "all the perplexity of mind and all the conflicts of desire and divided loyalties suddenly disappear" (Eliot 1928, 88, 90–92). At this I want to demure somewhat, suggesting that this language, which I find hyperbolic, is a remnant of a form of theistic piety that continued in Eliot's Unitarian heritage.

To recapitulate: for Eliot the three experiences underlying, indeed constituting, his belief in God are the moral imperative, the rational order of the universe, and a sense of purpose in the universe.

This three part analysis of the experiential basis for belief in God, what could be called Eliot's phenomenology of religious experience, was anticipated in a slightly different formulation in the sermon "Unitarian Faith in God," which was published two years earlier in his *Fundamentals of Unitarian Faith*. Here the first two points are basically the same, although in a different order (Eliot 1926, 26, 28).

In this earlier formulation the third point is that our human aspirations give us a "picture of a universe that is akin to our own best selves, a universe in which we are not aliens or strangers, a universe in which at our moments of deepest insight we feel at home." He dismisses counter examples. "Sometimes, to be sure, we are aware of forces that seem hostile and destructive. . . . But those times do not seem to me typical nor do they seem to me to represent the best and deepest of human aspirations" (Eliot 1926, 30).

At this point three subsidiary topics need to be considered: Eliot's definition of religion, his notion of "conviction" or what I call "religious surmise," and his philosophy of religious language.

First, let us note his conception of religion.

Religion is man's effort to interpret and to appropriate for his own use certain experiences which come to him, usually without conscious effort on his own part, in the form

of self-authenticating convictions—sometimes disturbing and
sometimes reassuring—with regard to himself and the world
in which he is living. (Eliot 1928, 61)

In his comments on this passage Eliot notes first that religion is a
human endeavor, not a result of divine revelation. He notes second that
humans try to interpret these experiences and also to keep and share
them, thus creating outward forms and ceremonies. Third, he comments
that these experiences do not usually come as a result of deliberate effort, but rather after preparatory self-discipline, a sort of expectancy or
waiting. His fourth comment is that experiences of religion are usually
a combination of disturbing or reassuring character. If the experience
only disturbs or only reassures, it is likely to be an unsafe guide, either
morbid or arrogant.

Religion furnishes us with two things, first, "a central belief around
which all the convictions and principles of a man's life can be organized"
and second, "a familiar type of symbolism for the expression of that central belief and its subsidiary convictions and principles." As for the first,
in words reminiscent of Royce, we need "a strong and unifying sense of
purpose in life." Thus, "religion has no more vital contribution to offer
to men that this concept of a great purpose outside themselves, in the
service of which they can find a central purpose for their own personal
lives" (Eliot 1928, 101–102, 104). Furthermore, religion can introduce
purpose into the social life of groups, communities, and nations.

As for the second thing which religion offers, a familiar symbol to
express that central purpose, "the word 'God' is the simplest and most
familiar of all the symbolic forms by which belief in the purposefulness
of the universe can be expressed" (Eliot 1928, 107).

The next subsidiary topic to be considered here is Eliot's notion
that these beliefs are matters of "conviction." They are what I call, with
perhaps a touch more of tentativeness, "surmises." In these matters, the
evidence is, in Eliot's words, "one's own inner conviction," not the evidence of law or science but more like the evidence of the poet.

I have been using the word "know" . . . to designate the high
degree of certainty which attends this experience of feeling
oneself a part of the life of the universe, but it is obviously
not knowledge in the strict sense of that word. There is no
objective certainty about it whatever. It is merely an intuitive conviction, resting upon nothing except one's own inner
experience. You may interpret it as indicating the ultimate
nature of reality, or you may interpret it as a figment of the

imagination.... Neither theory can be demonstrated, and neither theory alters the experience itself. What matters is that we should not be afraid to trust the experience. (Eliot 1928, 92)

Another way that Eliot has of speaking of this is to say that these experiences are "self-authenticating" in that they:

carry in themselves the sign of their own genuineness. They are convictions which cannot always be supported by logic, and very often it is quite impossible to marshal behind them any strictly scientific proof. They cannot be demonstrated as a theorem in geometry can be demonstrated. But nevertheless they are as plainly true, for the man who receives them, as though they could be proved with infallible and final logic. If we use the word "know" in a strict sense, there are very few things that can properly be classed as knowledge. But there are some things which we are so deeply convinced are true that we can say that so far as we are concerned they are known to be true. It is almost as though a special dispensation of knowledge had been vouchsafed to us, almost as thought (sc.) we had been the beneficiaries of a divine revelation.

Eliot goes on to say:

The test of our conviction is our willingness to go ahead and act as though we had final knowledge.... Human experience sometimes brings us face to face with an authority that transcends all our personal desires or reasonings, an authority which for us is final and absolute. (Eliot 1928, 65–66, 68)

The third subsidiary topic here is Eliot's philosophy of language. For Eliot religion is found in depths which lie too deep for words, but gestures, including gestures in words, can give expression to them. Life is bigger than our minds. It cannot be enclosed within the walls of an intellectual system. We need more than arguments to meet crises with courage and serenity.

What we all need, I believe, is some way of expressing the deep convictions which come to us in moments of spiritual insight—convictions which we often cannot prove by cold logic to be worthy of our credence, but which we hold with a tenacity that no lack of proof can shake. It is the business of organized religion to give us the help we need in finding some way to express these convictions. That is the supreme function of the religious teacher, who must be a poet and an artist himself, at least in some degree. (Eliot 1928, 82–83)

Specifically, when it comes to the term "God," Eliot is quite deliberate in his reflections. The word "God" is "the simplest and the most familiar of all the symbolic forms by which belief in the purposefulness of the universe can be expressed." Eliot grants that some people are unwilling to use the term "because it has meant such very different things to different people, and they are afraid of being constantly misunderstood." Remember that John Dietrich, the humanist, was preaching across the river in Minneapolis. Eliot recognizes the difficulty, but thinks the advantages of using the term outweigh the difficulties. Granted we must remember that it is a symbol, not the thing for which the symbol stands. Yet each of us has "a right to put into any common symbol the particular content which his own experience leads him to regard as true."

When I use the word "God," writes Eliot, "I am using a symbol for the reality that I believe exists behind the deepest convictions of my own mind and heart," convictions that he has described in terms "the moral law, the rational nature of the universe, the kinship of my life with the universe, and the element of purposefulness." Furthermore, his conviction is that there is a reality behind these experiences and the term "God" can be used to summarize and symbolize the reality of these convictions and "their authority over my life" (Eliot 1928, 107–108).

Eliot grants that it is theoretically possible to find some better word than "God," such as Julian Huxley's phrase "sacred reality." It means the same thing as God and anyone who prefers to use it may. However, there are practical difficulties. It is cumbersome and awkward. It also lacks power.

We need symbols that will reach down deep into our souls and make their power felt in the innermost recesses of our personality. Important as it is to check up our use of symbols by the most critical intelligence we can find, it is still more important to use our brains to choose symbols that will actually work in terms of influencing human conduct. The word "God" is such a symbol. It has come down to us out of the past, saturated with the spiritual experiences and the religious discoveries of many generations. . . . It is the word most rich in meaning and most powerful in its direct appeal of all the words in the language. It is the supremely valuable symbol for the supremely important realities in any man's life. (Eliot 1928, 109–110)

At this point I believe that I can support my claim that Eliot's theology fits within my broad working definition of religious naturalism. Religious naturalism, as defined in this book, asserts that there seems to be no ontologically distinct and superior realm (such as God, soul, or heaven) to ground, explain, or give meaning to this world, but that yet religious significance can be found within this world. Now Eliot's theology is fundamentally about the religious significance of the universe, not about a God above or behind the universe. Thus I claim that it fits within my definition of religious naturalism.

Within this broad conception of religious naturalism, his specific approach involves three distinctive elements: his tripartite phenomenology of religious experience, his notion of religious conviction as the result of an individual wrestling with these issues, and his philosophy of religious language that supports theistic language.

Now there is a passage which might seem to challenge this conclusion that Eliot can be classified as a religious naturalist. It is found in his sermon on "The Unitarian Conception of Prayer" where he sets forth what he calls "the essence of our belief in God."

Theism is the hypothesis that the ultimate ground of the universe is intelligent will, working out a moral purpose, which we can understand at least to the degree necessary to co-operate . . . for its fulfillment. (Eliot 1926, 62)

This notion of an intelligent will "as the ultimate ground of the universe" seems to have crossed over beyond any viable conception of religious naturalism. However, his notion of prayer in this sermon will help confirm that the main thrust of his approach can be thought of as within the scope of religious naturalism. Prayer, according to Eliot, "is an effort on your own part to see more clearly and to consecrate your life more completely" (Eliot 1926, 63).

I wish now to make a brief assessment of Eliot's approach.

1. I believe that he is correct to give us an analysis of the experential basis of religious thinking and behavior.

2. His tripartite phenomenology is open to question. The sense of the moral imperative needs to be mixed with a sense of critical

questioning. The conviction of a rational order in the universe has an old-fashioned ring of an undeviating causal order with none of the more recent sense of probabilistic tendencies. And the notion of the world as purposive is certainly subject to question.

3. His notion that these ideas are convictions that are the result of personal wrestling needs to be interfused with a critical attitude lest convictions be merely prejudice and a door to fanaticism.

4. Eliot's philosophy of the power of religious language suggests that either theistic language, critically understood, can and should be used or else that the issue of the power of nontheistic language be addressed. By this I mean that we should reflect on the need for a language with power, power to disturb, and power to console. We need to decide whether Eliot is correct. Either we need God-language or we don't. Or perhaps, as I suggest, there are contexts in which God-language, used carefully, is appropriate. If and when God-language is appropriate, religious naturalists and fellow-travelers should think carefully about the contexts within which it can be used. If and when God-language is not appropriate we need to address the power of nontheistic language. Can nontheistic devotional language have religious power? Or should we eschew devotional and liturgical language altogether?

The New Universalism:
Skinner and Patton

Universalism, the belief that God's love extends to all humans and that all will be saved and enjoy the blessings of heaven, was the belief of an American denomination with roots predating the Revolution. In the twentieth century their notion of a wider faith resulted in a movement among some of its members toward a naturalistic religious orientation toward the entire universe drawing on the resources of the worlds religions. Two events signified an openness to theological change among at least part of the Universalist community. Clinton Lee Scott did not lose popularity among the Universalists for signing the *Humanist Manifesto*, for he was reelected as a trustee of the General Convention by a sizable margin. In 1943 at the Universalist General Assembly, General Superintendent Robert Cummins asserted that Universalism must make it "unmistakably clear that *all* are welcome: theist and humanist, Unitarian and trinitarian, colored, and color-less" (Cassara 1997, 268). Two major voices impelling this movement were those of Clarence Skinner and Kenneth Patton. There voices eventually became part of the heritage of the Unitarian Universalist Association when Unitarians and Universalists merged in 1961.

Clarence R. Skinner

Clarence Skinner was Professor of Applied Christianity and later Dean of Crane Theological School of Tufts University from 1914 to 1945. In *A Religion for Greatness*, published in 1945, he developed an early anticipation of religious naturalism. Radical religion, as he puts it, seeks and provides *insight* into the *unities* and the *universals.* "Insight" is a broader term than knowledge. Although its validity must be tested by empirical methods, I suggest that it is akin to what I have called "a generous empiricism" (Stone 1992, 111–168). "Unities" refers to the functional relationship of the parts in a whole. "Universals" pertains to the characteristics of the entire cosmos and all that it contains. Thus radical religion will be a universalism, "a philosophy of life or system of values which stress the largest possible *Weltanschauung*, or world outlook" (Skinner 1945, 14; see pp. 11–30). Skinner illustrates this with quotations from *Chuang-tzu*, the *Upanishads*, Jesus, Paul, Whitman, Einstein, Bernard Meland, and especially the *Tao Te Ching.*

Kenneth L. Patton

Kenneth Patton was minister of the Univesalist experimental Charles Street Meeting House in Boston from 1949 to about 1964. His legacy lives on in the humanistic and sometimes naturalistic worship material he bequeathed to the Unitarian Universalists in *Services and Songs for the Celebration of Life.*

In *Man's Hidden Search: An Inquiry into Naturalistic Mysticism*, Patton develops the theme, reminiscent of Meland, of being at home in the universe. In his poetic language (Patton published a number of volumes of poetry) he writes, "The wind comforts him as fondly as his mother's arms. The sunlight is like his best friend's recognizing laughter. A caterpillar crawling on the back of his hand is as rich and welcoming as his brother's arms across his shoulders. The children on the street of another country are as near to him as his own children. . . . The earth is his home and its creatures are his family" (Patton 1954, 54). Even further, "When his earth becomes a part of the universe, man too becomes at home in the wider universe of which his planet is so humble a part. For the mind of man rides out and out into space, passing galaxy on galaxy. . . . The man who has become at home in the universe is not stricken or subdued thus to discover himself and his home. He is exhilarated. . . . We bring the world into ourselves, interiorize it, lodge it in our organs, in our memory, in . . . our brain. Just as the universe and its creatures live warmly and in friendliness within us, do we live with warmth and friendliness among our fellows and in the starry world" (Patton 1954, 63–64) This results in inner peace, a scaling of expectations to our limitations. "You are not crying for a moon of genius, of immortality, of wealth, power and uniqueness" (Patton 1954, 81). Thus his naturalism is the theory that "the world of nature is one and all-continuous" (Patton 1954, 24).

Coupled with this sense of "at home-ness" is the sense of mystery, "The sheer wonder of the 'thereness,' the 'thatness' of any object, the simple, profound mystery of existence itself, of the texture, the presence of anything" (Patton 1954, 71). He suggests that "If there is anything that we may want to call mystery, will it not lie in . . . the pulses of energy out of which all structures and all powers are woven? . . . if we are properly sensitive and attuned to the flow and unity of the world the nettles of mystery will sting us in everything we touch" (Patton 1954, 84).

Patton makes the religious dimension of this naturalism clear, using the category of mysticism, specifically of naturalistic mysticism. "If there is any rating of human experiences one above the other in regard to worthfulness, that which we call mystical refers to a superiority in qualitative intensity and meaningfulness" (Patton 1954, 95). Contrasting the habitual and the mystical, he continues: "if an action has mystical reasons, it matters not how dull the act may seem in itself, it will be an ennobling experience" (Patton 1954, 95–96). "In his religion a man seeks the deepest knowledge and wisdom of which he is capable. He . . . attempts to assess the measure and meaning of his brief existence" (Patton 1954, 97). "Mysticism is the means whereby men outreach themselves, extend themselves beyond previous confines, stretch the tent of their comprehension and observation to cover a larger plot of the universe" (Patton 1954, 98). Patton says that he uses the term mysticism "to describe a quality of experience, not to define that experience as distinct and separate from other experiences" (Patton 1954, 100–101). There are many forms of mystical experience, but each "has the common property of etching experience in a new clarity, a greater significance, a further penetration of meaning than we have known before. . . . There are moments when the sheerest and simplest sensual experience wears a golden significance. . . . We are stabbed by the is-ness and thatness of things. . . . The experience is not always a source of happiness. Often it brings pain, loss, homesickness, grief." Nevertheless, there may come insights or moments of resolution. "We become aware of an answer to pervading anxieties and wonderments. Many things that seemed unrelated and chaotic fall together into patterns of meaning and rightness. Somehow a resolution has come to us. Most often we can find no words for it." The intensity of these experiences cannot endure, "for the intensity exhausts us" (Patton 1954, 105–106).

Patton finds a major cause for our deficiency in mysticism. "Our emotions, our traditions, our language, our habits of thought, have for centuries been accommodated to the two-storied world. . . . Religion was primarily the staircase by which men could get upstairs. . . . Mysticism has suffered, as has religion in general, by being regarded as strictly a business by which man related himself to the supernatural world and united his being with God's" (Patton 1954, 96). This mystical naturalism will involve a striving "for a fuller realization of human togetherness, of man's unity with nature as a child of earth, and for the emotional significance of new knowledge and experience," even an introduction to the yearnings of our fellow creatures (Patton 1954, 98). Patton faces head-on the question of the richness of this view.

> To one who believes in the two realms, an explanation of life and man in terms of one realm may seem meager and stultifying. The only answer is that expanse and splendor have little to do with the number of realms. One room can be larger than two smaller rooms together. In qualitative terms, the material realm may come to appear so abounding in variety, subtlety, beauty, depth, and mystery that it will include within it the qualities of existence and experience that once were thought to belong to a spiritual realm. (Patton 1954, 100)

A Religion for One World lays the principles and gives details for his Charles Street Meeting House, an experimental church deliberately drawing on the resources of the world's religious traditions in art, symbol, and worship. Here he speaks of religion as involving an emotion of participating within, of kinship with nature and our fellow creatures. The emerging religion will celebrate the universe, centering on the specialized development called life. Hence it will be an impassioned affirmation, a celebration of life (Patton 1964, 119, 125, 151).

David Bumbaugh said of Patton, "It was he who taught a monotone rationalism how to sing; it was he who taught a stumble-footed humanism how to dance; it was he who cried, 'Look!' and taught our eyes to see the glory in the ordinary" (Cleary, 2006).

The Later Chicago School:
Wieman, Meland, Loomer, and Burhoe

It is common to divide "the Chicago School of Theology" into the earlier sociohistorical period and the later period starting with the arrival of Henry Nelson Wieman. (See Stone's Preface to Peden and Stone 1996 I, vi–vii or II, v–vi. Some of the material in this section is taken from Stone, 2005.) Certain writers from this second period are key figures in the history of religious naturalism. The following differs from the standard accounts of the Chicago School by including Ralph Burhoe.

Henry Nelson Wieman

Professor of Philosophy of Religion at the Divinity School of the University of Chicago from 1927 to 1947 and later a member of the Department of Philosophy at Southern Illinois University, Wieman was one of the most influential of the religious naturalists. Charley Hardwick, Karl Peters, and I all acknowledge our indebtedness to him. Although considered rather radical during the period of American interest in neo-orthodoxy, Wieman was brought to the Divinity School to counteract the popularity of humanism, especially as developed by Eustace Haydon, who was not technically a member of the Divinity School but who was significant in the life of that school from approximately 1919 through 1945. (One of the best books on Wieman is Marvin Shaw's *Nature's Grace*, Shaw 1995.)

The impact of Wieman in a period of growing humanism may be gathered from two comments. Charles Clayton Morrison, editor of *The Christian Century*, said, "I have no need of Barth. Wieman is my Barth." Morris Eames of Southern Illinois University said that Wieman's writings had allowed him and others to retain religion in the face of the scientific worldview (Broyer and Minor 1982, 208).

Wieman was passionately concerned to find the truth and avoid error in religion. Error in religion results in personal and social havoc. He wanted religion to be anchored in reality. Now in his understanding, common sense empirical inquiry and its sharpening in scientific method are the best way to find truth in any area. Thus, there is but one method of separating truth from fantasy, the empirical method, and religious inquiry is a species of it, differentiated from other inquiry by its object, not its methods or principles. (See Stone 1992, 149–153 for my exposition and critique of Wieman's empirical method in religious inquiry.)

Specifying the object of inquiry is a key phase of any empirical investigation. Thus much of Wieman's work was spent in refining the definition the object of religious inquiry. Briefly the definition of what we are looking for in religious inquiry is:

> What transforms man as he cannot transform himself to save him from evil and lead him to the best that human life can ever attain, provided that he give himself over to it in religious faith and meet other required conditions. (Wieman, 1975, 273; Peden and Stone 1996 II, 109)

In traditional religious language what can save us as we cannot save ourselves, provided we devote ourselves to it, is God. The soteriological emphasis of this is clear. I like to call this a theology of grace. In fact, it is a naturalistic theology of grace, because Wieman had a naturalistic worldview in which the only things that exist or can accomplish anything are events, relations, and qualities (Wieman 1946, 6; Peden and Stone 1996 II, 86). While he owed much specifically to Stephen C. Pepper's contextualism, this is a process-relational view in a very broad sense that could include Dewey's general orientation in *Experience and Nature*, as well as Whitehead, and much process theology (Pepper 1942).

Now within this naturalistic worldview, that which can transform us as we cannot transform ourselves is the process of integration in the world, or what Wieman eventually called, famously, "creative interchange." Creative interchange can function as a naturalistic equivalent of grace. This idea, which has been called a "truncated idealism," is rooted ultimately in Hegel, but its immediate source of inspiration for Wieman was found in Ralph Barton Perry and William Ernest Hocking. (See Wieman 1985 and Minor 1977, chaps 2 and 3.)

In passing I wish to point out that there is a strong and fruitful principle of cultural and personal critique in this outlook. This principle is rooted in the distinction between the creative good (the process of integration) and created goods. All created goods can be become demonic when treated with idolatry (Wieman 1946, 23–26; Peden and Stone 1996 II, 94–96).

Wieman's thought went through several stages of development. After beginning with a heavy dependence on Whitehead, Wieman worked out a viewpoint in *Normative Psychology of Religion* (1935) and *The Growth of Religion* (1938) in which the process of integration extended beyond human interactions and included the history of the cosmos and biological evolution. By the time of *The Source of Human Good* (1946), his focus was almost entirely on creative interaction in human individuals, groups, and history. In his last period, exemplified by *Man's Ultimate Commitment* (1958), reference to God had virtually dropped from his writing and he referred to creative interchange on the human level as that which is worthy of our dedication. One wonders whether this foreshadows the inevitable trajectory of religious naturalism in general. He is perhaps best known for his penultimate period of *The Source of Human Good*. In this period God is the creative process within the world. In his forthcoming study of Wieman, Cedric Heppler will refine the notion that Wieman went through stages. He will assert that Wieman's concept of God as "that which transforms humans as they cannot transform themselves" remained constant. Only the metaphors that Wieman used changed. There is something to be said in the case of Wieman for this notion of the immaculate conception of ideas, wherein the metaphorical dress does not affect the underlying conceptual organism. However, the changes in Wieman are not just in the central metaphor, but where in the world religious inquiry should focus. His scope of inquiry grew progressively narrower, from the metaphysical to the cosmic to the human.

Marvin Shaw sums up Wieman's contribution in a marvelous *bon mot*. Wieman gives us "The theistic stance without the supernatural God" (Shaw 1995, 136). By the theistic stance Shaw is referring to gifts of grace, what I call an openness to situationally transcendent resources. I would add that in pointing out how created goods can become demonic Wieman has also given us a powerful basis for cultural and personal critique, a parallel to Gordon Kaufman's notion of "God the relativizer" (Kaufman 1993, 312–321).

Wieman's students had serious debates with those of the humanist scholar of world religions at the Divinity School, A. Eustace Haydon. It is quite clear that Wieman, although a religious naturalist, clearly utilized the concept of God, at least until he left the Divinity School. (See Wieman 1930, chapter VI; Daniel Day Williams, "Wieman as a Christian Theologian," Sec. II, in Robert W. Bretall 1963, 76–79.) Wieman had refused to sign the *Humanist Manifesto I* in 1933 but did sign *Humanist Manifesto II* in 1973 based on its footnote saying that signers may not agree with parts of it. (John A. Broyer, "A Final Visit with Wieman," in John A. Broyer and Wm. S. Minor, 1982, p. 86, referring in part to an interview with Mrs. Laura Wieman in 1976.)

The brevity of my treatment of Wieman is not a measure of his significance for our story. Wieman has been written about so extensively that I need go no further.

Bernard Meland

Teacher of constructive theology at the University of Chicago from 1945 to 1964, he was a collaborator with and friendly critic of Henry Nelson

Wieman and a fountainhead, along with Charles Hartshorne and Bernard Loomer, of process theology, yet he remained a persistent critic of what he considered the rationalistic excesses of some exponents of process thought. (For a detailed and balanced discussion of Meland's relation to process thought, see Inbody 1995, 109–173. Portions of this section are taken from Stone 1995.)

Meland's first book, *Modern Man's Worship*, parts two and three, now nearly forgotten, contains some of the finest writings in religious naturalism ever produced. He refers to his view as *Mystical Naturalism*: "natural, in the sense that I take the universe, described by the sciences, as the natural home of man, and the environment in which he must fulfill his life; mystical, in the sense that I affirm the possibility of having religious relations with the *Cosmic Phase* of man's world" (Meland 1934, xi). The naturalistic orientation of Meland's outlook becomes clearer in his conception of worship. Worship may be the means of reorienting a person "in the environment that produced him, and of integrating the human species in the natural order of life that sustains and promotes organic growth" (Meland 1934, xiii). Such worship is essential to the health of humans and is even necessary for our survival. For it is the counterrhythm to the activism which, by itself, is overstimulating and debilitating.

For the early Meland the basic religious question has become, can humans be at home in the universe without cultivating illusions? "The extent of man's intimacy with the life of earth has only recently come to be fully realized. Wherever supernaturalism has influenced human thought, man has conceived his life on earth as only a temporary residence in a vale of tears. His real home is in the skies" (Meland 1934, 146–147; Peden and Stone 1996, II, 221). Liberal religion has not really resolved the issue. "Religious liberals seem to be straddling two world views. Influenced by their ethical ideal, they have recognized the importance of present-day living and have turned with zeal to its tasks; but on the other hand, many of their religious concepts are still cast in a pre-scientific framework, and their religious emotions still seem to respond most readily to that other-worldly temper" (Meland 1934, 147; Peden and Stone, II, 1996, 221). Humanism has brought people halfway. The humanist stands on the shore, suffering from the "cosmic chill," afraid to trust the earth.

Until we accept the universe, "not as an indifferent stage upon which to enact our tragic, human scene; but as the very fountain source of our being, our one and only homeland. . . . until we genuinely orient ourselves in our universe, body and spirit, we are destined as damned souls to wander 'twixt our heavens of illusion and a hell of disillusionment. . . . Man has disowned his universe, and the universe, in turn, has damned his soul" (Meland 1934, 169; Peden and Stone 1996 II, 222–223). Meland acknowledges the tragic dangers of the universe. "No one who faces the cosmic scene in its stern, realistic aspects can fail to see that there is much in the universe that defies and destroys the precarious achievements that man has come to call *good*" (Meland 1934, 148; Peden and Stone 1996 II, 222). We must acknowledge that we are creatures, which implies not only possibilities of fulfillment, but also definite limitations. This transformation of our hopes is "a gain masquerading as a loss." To forsake "hopes and ideals that serve only to lure one away from the home of his spirit" may seem devastating at first, but in the long run it places one on firmer ground (Meland 1934, 166).

However, in the long run Meland has a tempered optimism. "Living in the universe is like swimming in the sea. Before one can live serenely amid its scenes, he must be at home, relaxed, confident of the mutual response between his organism and the environing earth. Transformed in attitude, he becomes transformed in mood. Confidence gives rise to buoyancy. Buoyancy breeds serenity" (Meland 1934, 170; Peden and Stone 1996 II, 223). What we need is to appreciate and feel, understand in our very bones that, even in our spiritual behavior, we are an expression of earth forces. We are "the universe come to consciousness" (Meland 1934, 156).

For Meland religion will have a sustaining and consoling, but also and more important, a challenging and invigorating function. People who are in "vigorous psychic health" do not need "consolation, but discipline and spirited encouragement to live venturesomely, to respond to the *perilous open*" (Meland 1934, 163).

In this early period Meland develops his conception of God in terms of an alternation between two approaches to reality. One, called worship, is a contemplative or synthetic approach "involving deep emotional enjoyment of our relation to the total cosmic environment as well as loyal commitment to its demands and opportunities." The other, which is analytic, is a theoretical and experimental investigation of the world as well as practical adjustment to it. Although "the One and the Many constitute the same reality, each designates a distinct and characteristic approach to that reality" (Meland 1934, 175). Thus people will alternate between responding *appreciatively* to the significance of our surroundings and seeking to understand and use these realities. One of the very best statements of the unity of God as a theoretical notion and the plurality of experiences of the sacred is found in Meland's early, "Toward a Valid View of God," one of the gems of religious naturalism discovered in writing this history (Meland, 1931).

God will be a term we use in the synthetic, contemplative mood in which we respond appreciatively. In short, "God, as a religious concept, is a collective representation of certain sustaining relations having cosmic implications" (Meland 1934, 176). Analogously a minister or politician may refer to "my people" in public address. When the context changes to a pastoral or practical context, this phrase does not infer a single entity. "If the word God is a collective term meaning 'those most important conditions upon which human life depends,' it may be used for purposes of devotional address; but for occasions of practical adjustment and theoretical reflection the language of worship, including the collective term, would best be set aside and in its place empirical language used" (Meland 1934, 172). Here Meland finds a difference between his approach and that of Wieman. For Meland any term, such as the process of integration, the creative event, or God, used to designate that coordination of activities, "does not connote a singular, consistent behavior" (Meland 1934, 179). Here Meland is nearer to the pluralism of Dewey, except less reluctant to use the term "God," and less focused than Dewey on what Santayana called "the foreground of experience." One more point in understanding Meland, there can be no neat distinction between the activities of humans and the activities of God, since human activities can be part of the conditions on which human life depends (Meland 1934, 180).

A further corollary of this approach is that Meland defines the heart of religion to be an appreciative response. "What turns dogma, morals, and ritual into a religious response? Religion . . . is the reality-embracing element. . . . The distinctive religious dimension, then, is awareness and appreciation of reality. Religion is reality-centering" (Meland 1934, 185). Now this use of the term "Reality" is anathema to many postmoderns. However, this use of the term is not epistemological or designative. "Like the language of art, poetry, and friendship, the language of religion is suggestive, not descriptive or definitive. Its terms are employed not to describe the object of reference, but to vivify its total significance and to enhance emotional feeling for it" (Meland 1934, 186). Put succinctly, "religion is a fine art with cosmic content" (Meland 1934, xv). Many of us who drink deeply of Meland's waters believe that this appreciative response provides a powerful antidote to the truncation of religion to the rational and moral dimensions in liberal Protestantism and the consequent need to supply some depth to misguided and tasteless sentimentality. (See Meland 1953, 1–9; Meland 1955, 22–36.)

It is important for Meland that the appreciative response can be nurtured and trained. "Just as the capacity for appreciation in poetry, music and art increases with cultivation, so one's sensitivity in worship and religious living grows through discerning participation" (Meland 1934, 188).

Meland continued this line of thought in "Kinsmen of the Wild," an article in the *Sewanee Review* on "Religious Moods in Modern American Poetry" (Meland 1933, 443–453). Meland found four of these moods acknowledging our intimate relations with nature, that we are the child of earth. First there is "the mood of integrity, sheer unadorned, elemental honesty in seeing things and events as they exist and happen," exemplified in the poetry of Carl Sandburg (Meland 1933, 444). Then there is "the mood of adventure, agreeable to change, variety and indefinite openness to life" as discerned in Oppenheim's sonnet, *To the Perilous Open* (Meland 1933, 446). The third religious mood is "the readiness to meet death unafraid" (Meland 1933, 449). Here Meland quotes from Lew Sarett's *Let Me Go Down to Dust.*

> Let me go down to dust and dreams
> Gently . . .
> In such a manner as beseems . . . a child
> Of earth, a kinsman of the wild. (Sarett 1925, 16)

"Too long man has separated himself from the rest of nature, insisting that he is of different origin, hence of higher destiny. He has dreamed dreams of immortal blessedness. . . . Orienting one's emotions in the universe means essentially bringing one's self into accord with the spiritual outlook of the world of nature, an outlook shorn of pretentious claims to self-survival, but rich in recognition of social obligation and opportunity: obligation that is cosmic in depth, opportunity that is cosmic in breadth" (Meland 1933, 451–452). The final mood is a mood rich in fellow feeling for these "kinsmen of the wild." One of the reasons for the difficulty in achieving this mood is that we have attributed our vices to the vestiges of our supposed animal nature. Agreeing more with Samuel Alexander than with Shailer Mathews, we may be able to acknowledge our organic relations with animals. "In the spirit of fellow-feeling, we may help to integrate the life of the universe in a richer, cosmic fellowship." Then in language prescient of Aldo Leopold, Meland wrote: "The circle of fellowmen has widened. It has grown from tribal, national, to international scope. Is it conceivable that, to some extent, it might become more inter-creatural?" (Meland 1933, 453). For this fourth mood Meland refers to the "cosmic sensitiveness" of Edwin Markham's *Little Brothers of the Ground, The Fate of the Fur Folk,* Lew Sarett's *Four Little Foxes, To a Wild Goose Over Decoys,* Edna St. Vincent Millay's *Wild Swans, Buck in the Snow,* and the sketches of Carl Sandburg (Meland 1933, 453). (I am sure that were he alive today, Meland would be a fan of Mary Oliver.) Meland also devoted thirteen pages in *The Reawakening of the Christian Faith* to precursors in American poetry to the mood of theological disillusion that descended in the 1930s in the form of neo-orthodoxy and companions. He cited and quoted T. S. Eliot, Edwin Arlington Robinson, Robinson Jeffers, and Edna St. Vincent Millay (Meland 1949, 22–34).

Meland recognized that in his Mystical Naturalism he was "blood brother" to the Religious Humanist, yet he was concerned about the "anthropo-inflation" of the latter (Meland 1935). In an interview with Larry Axel, he reveals that part of his concern came from experiencing an arrogance and fundamentalist zeal conveyed by humanist classmates at Chicago (Meland 1980). Yet he felt that Eustace Haydon, a Religious Humanist leader, in his writing made an eloquent statement of Mystical Naturalism and showed an openness in personal contacts. For Meland worship, as an "expression of praise and gratitude toward the Sources of Being which sustain us," promotes an "expansive habit" of living that moves beyond humanism's man-centered orientation (Meland 1935, 73).

In 1936 and 1937, while teaching at Pomona College in California, Meland moved from his earlier thinking toward a concern with the Christian tradition, especially with the human need for redemption and the reality of resources of renewal. This turn was precipitated by his reading of Reinhold Niebuhr, Karl Barth, and Emil Brunner and his participation in the Oxford Conference on Church, Commnity, and State. There is great value in Meland's later work and he certainly never became neo-orthodox. Yet from the perspective of the twenty-first century it seems unfortunate that his early work has been nearly forgotten. In some sense the hiatus in the career of naturalism in religion is manifest in Meland's own career. (For an understanding of this turn in Meland, see Tyron Inbody's *The Constructive Theology of Bernard Meland* [Inbody 1995, 25–32]).

Meland's mature thought developed approximately at the time of his move to Chicago. A good place to begin is his notion of "appreciative awareness" or "sensitive awareness." (See Meland 1953, 82–87; Peden and Stone 1996, vol. II 224–230.) The stance indicated by these phrases is crucial to the work of William Dean and myself. Meland uses these phrases to speak of being more open to the full dimensions of the world than is possible when clarity and precision are dominant concerns. He did not deny the significance of clarity in both perception and thought but insisted that reality is more complex than can be captured by clear and distinct ideas. A radical empiricism, such as he advocated, will try to be open to these complexities instead of limiting its inquiries to the manageable. In his metaphor, there is a penumbra that surrounds the luminous area that we clearly know. Real experience overflows the boundaries of focused attention and abstract ideas. The effort to give full justice to this fringe is what Meland called appreciative awareness. It is not a special sense, but it can be nurtured. It draws on feelings or emotions and also on reflection on the nuances of the world.

There is a danger of obscurantism here, but the danger is no greater than that posed by the view that limits reality to what can be securely grasped. The way to counter the danger of obscurantism lies in the training and disciplining of the appreciative consciousness. Such training is often overlooked and is sadly neglected in education. Just as discrimination of wines can be improved, just as artistic taste can be informed, so awareness in all its dimensions can be trained. Many theories that either dismiss or glorify feelings ignore this possibility of educating perception.

What Meland is referring to is not a special experience, certainly not a special religious experience, but an experience of the joys and sorrows of life. Such an awareness is not a direct awareness of God, but an awareness of creativity and healing in our experience. We may call these events the workings of God, although sensitivity to these events is not a sufficient foundation for a religious epistemology, for there is none. However, without an awareness of such events, whether articulated in religious language or not, the phrases of religion ring hollow.

One of the most astute interpreters of Meland, Nancy Frankenberry, finds that "a gap exists between extralinguistic meaning and its linguistic expression," a gap that results in an epistemological impass for radical empiricism. "If it is the case that 'we live more deeply than we can think,' then we are at a loss to *describe* any awareness which surpasses language or thought without employing language in the very process and thus exhibiting the 'more' as intralinguistic after all" (Frankenberry 1987, 136–137). However, I suggest that "transaction" might be a better image than "gap." When we describe (linguistically) the taste of wine (which is extralinguistic), we are engaged in an interplay between language and that which lies beyond language, even though we use language to point to that which lies beyond language.

It would be misleading to overlook the social dimension of experience for Meland. He used the term "structure of experience" to indicate the way in which a culture organizes the thoughts, perceptions, and sensibilities of its members. As for whether such cultural structures prevent us from being in touch with the world, Meland had a sense that experience has a vector character. There are realities with which we have to deal. Culture structures experience, but it does not create experience from scratch (Meland 1962, 210–211; Meland 1976, 187; Peden and Stone 1996, II, 250–251).

Much of Meland's mature thought concerned what he called the New Vision in science and metaphysics, which he saw as replacing the Newtonian worldview. (This is adapted from Stone 1995; see also Meland 1937; Meland 1947, 49–56, 120–122; Meland 1962, 91–94, 116–127, 130–133, 145–164, 198–199, 290, 343.) We can speak of emergent levels, such as the physical world, life, personality, and spirit. This notion of emergence, which Meland derived especially from Samuel Alexander, Jan Christiaan Smuts and C. Lloyd Morgan, is similar to the viewpoint of Dewey and Sellars. It is a way to avoid both dualism and reductionism, allowing for the distinctively human within a naturalistic outlook. Meland stressed that the discontinuities between levels takes place within the continuities between them. The novel event is never reducible to its antecedents, yet it is never separated from its parts or lower levels. Like existentialism, this view provides for the reality of freedom. Unlike existentialism, it sees freedom and novelty as occurring with the continuities of structure. This enables Meland both to value the past and to be open to the future. The past has a tendency to live on, in part through the structure of experience. It is internally related to present events through duration. Grace and spirit can now be seen as transcending without being separate from personality. Thus a chief fault of liberal theology, its reduction of religion to the rational and moral, can be overcome and the traditional Christian language of Revelation, Redemption, and Spirit and the biblical images of Covenant and *Imago Dei* can be retrieved in the new imagery. Idealism no longer is needed to relate science and faith. The creative character of the world replaces the antithesis of humanity and nature that underlay both mechanism and idealism.

For religion this revolution in imagery means that the evolution of life is no longer a source of despair or a matter to be denounced but, rather, an anchoring of humans within the matrix of physical and biological nature. For Meland, this included rooting the spiritual in the psychophysical and the possibility of the creative advance of humans toward spiritual growth. (See the important articles by Dean and Ferré in Miller 1992; Dean 1992.)

A further aspect of this New Vision is the tentativeness of all human formulations. This tentative character is not a call to irrationalism, but a caution against dogmatism, against the premature enclosure of concrete realities within preestablished categories. The recovery of the sense of depth beyond the grasp of precise and clearly formulated thought did not mean an abandonment of reason and disciplined thought. It did mean a chastened and modest sense of the limitations of human powers of comprehension.

An important part of the background of this New Vision was the shift in worldview or formative imagery that changes in science foster, especially the rise of post-Newtonian physics (Meland 1962, 109–136). Sir Isaac Newton climaxed a process starting as early as Descartes, the fundamental notes of which were the orderliness of the world, conceived of as mechanical, and confidence in the power of the human mind to understand this order, especially confidence in precise and exact thought. Of course, this development also represented a barrier to belief in anything outside of the clearly conceived human orbit of meaning. Further, given the status of mathematical physics as the model of knowledge, truth became limited to what had universal application. Hence, historical religions and cultural traditions lost validity except for whatever could be found in the way of an apparent core of truths universal to all of them. In the later part of the nineteenth century, this formative imagery was transferred to the biological and human sciences. Behavioral scientists often kept to this Newtonian imagery, focusing on a rather limited sphere of inquiry. Finally, to complete this process, industrialization spread this imagery to all areas of culture.

Post-Newtonian physics played a major role in the development of a new formative imagery. Meland focused on such themes as the importance of relations and contexts, the possibility of discontinuity (quantum jumps), and the limitations of human knowledge (the uncertainty principle, and apparent validity of both the wave and the particle theories of the electron, the relativity of the observer, the loss of absolute time and space, and the discovery of the limitations of the physics of the day). Above all, the physical world was no longer seen as inert, mechanical, and easily comprehended within a deterministic outlook. Gestalt psychology fed into this imagery, which in his view crystallized into the process-relational worldview articulated most thoroughly by Whitehead. He always felt a kinship with Whitehead, although somewhat restive with what he termed the rationalistic excesses of some of the Whiteheadeans. Meland has influenced recent radical empiricist thinkers such as William Dean and myself.

Thus, Meland found the relation between science and religion to be at the level of worldview or basic imagery and further found that the new physics removed the major barriers that science had placed before religion. More positively, the new vision in science and metaphysics provided resources for a comprehension of the depths of the Christian tradition that had been denied or truncated in an earlier era when religion meant either a withdrawal from or the scientific spirit or else a trimming down of religious realities to their rational or moral dimensions. Although he wrote before Thomas Kuhn, Meland's understanding of science focused on the paradigm shift from mechanism to the New Vision.

Rather than trying to define God, Meland preferred to direct attention to such empirical or quasi-empirical notions as the creative and redemptive work of God. He was led by his generous empiricism to speak of God as the Ultimate Efficacy within relationships (Meland 1976, 151–152). Although we are continually sustained and nourished by this creative nexus of spirit, our occasions of conscious encounter with it are intermittent, and of short duration. Often these occasions are situations in which a sense of defeat and despair is resolved through forgiveness, love or friendship. Or there may be a sense of awareness in which the not-self is apprehended—as in I-Thou relations. Such occasions frequently are times of sorrow or joy. Note that the frequently interpersonal nature of such occasions, as well as the references to sorrow and joy, are the experiential anchors of Meland's empiricism. The key is that these are experiences in which the self comes to recognize its limits and receives a good beyond itself.

Although Meland on principle shied away from definitive articulation of a conception of God, there were two images that he used. (See Inbody 1995, chap. 6, esp. 186–189.) One is that God is "a sensitive nature within nature," brooding on, attempting to persuade, seeking to bring meaning out of brute force. In this Whiteheadean notion, the divine works as a lure, not as an efficient causal force. This is a repudiation of notions of God who acts miraculously to bring the rain or stop our enemies. We have hints that individual growth of character, the blossoming of care and beauty between people, even institutional creativity are called for and also empowered by the divine sensitivity at work. Meland wagers on the strength of patience, of gentleness, on the power of love and nurture, and a repudiation of arrogance and aggression. This is religious naturalism insofar as the divine creative and redemptive power is located within the world. It is a rejection of fossilized institutions and overbearing egotism. The divine forces of sensitivity are vulnerable and subject to defeat by egotism, misguided power, inertia, fatigue and disorder. Hence faith, in the sense of a psychic energy or cultural power, is never won without wrestling long and hard with the full acknowledgment of the powers of destruction. The real puzzle is not that there is evil, but that there is as much goodness as there is.

Meland's other image of God is a sensitive matrix of relations that nurtures and sustains us. This image is of a piece with his naturalism. Familial love, the nurturing web of friends, schools, community, and heritage are all part of this matrix. However, the door is left open for a "More" of nurturing forces that may not be disclosed by empirical analysis. Note that if there is any transcendence of divine powers it would be a discontinuity within continuity with the natural. The reality of such a matrix cannot be proved, but it can be discerned if experience is conceived broadly (Meland 1931; Meland 1933; Meland 1934, 144–157, 165–170).

In my judgment the use of these two images of God place Meland within the bounds of religious naturalism, despite the deliberate tentativeness of his assertions.

There is much that is omitted in this sketch of Meland's thought, including his historiography of liberal theology, an analysis of secularization, a Christology in emergent categories, and a view of the encounters between religions. He was one of the earliest theologians to use the term "myth." For those interested in reading Meland, his *Higher Education and the Human Spirit, The Realities of Faith, Fallible Forms and Symbols,* and *Essays in Constructive Theology* and the selections in Peden and Stone, *The Chicago School of Theology,* volume II are especially recommended (Meland, 1953, 1962, 1976, 1988; Peden and Stone 1996, vol. II). The essays by William Dean, Nancy Frankenberry, and Tyron Inbody in Randolph Crump Miller's *Empirical Theology* are helpful (Miller 1992). For Meland's analysis of secularization see Meland 1966.

Bernard Loomer

Loomer was Professor of Philosophy of Religion (1942–1965) and Dean (1945–1954) at the University of Chicago's Divinity School. Throughout his career he was an advocate of using Whitehead's philosophy to articulate Christian theology and, along with Charles Hartshorne and Bernard Meland, helped give rise to process theology in America, particularly through their students Schubert Ogden and John Cobb. At the end of his career Loomer taught at the Graduate Theological Union in Berkeley (1965–1977), where he developed a naturalistic theology expressed in a brief but seminal writing, "The Size of God" (Loomer, 1987). Loomer also wrote a seminal article on the distinction between unilateral and relational power, which may be the first statement of the distinction between power-over and power-with (Loomer 1976; Peden and Stone, 1996, II, 369–384).

Loomer notes that there has been a shift in perspective from the two worlds, this world and the next, of traditional thought to "the one evolved and relativized world of contemporary thought. This movement entails a revolution in our conception of the life of God and of our participation in it." This will be a transition "from a theology that maintains that resources for salvation ultimately derive from a transcendent God to an outlook that suggests that the graces for the living of a creative life emerge within the depths and immediacies of concrete experience. It is a transition from the wisdom of the sojourner . . . to the wisdom of the evolved earth-creature" (Loomer 1987, 21). The main thesis of this essay is that: "If the one world, the experienceable world with its possibilities, is all the reality accessible to us, . . . then it follows that the being of God must be identified in some sense with the being of the world and its creatures" (Loomer 1987, 22–23).

Loomer then sets up a dichotomy: "As an actuality or group of actualities God is then to be identified with a part or with the totality of the concrete, actual world, including its possibilities" (Loomer 1987, 23). *The Size of God* is an exploration of one of these options, "the alternative that God is to be identified with the totality of the world." He notes that this exploration requires courage, especially since this is "unfamiliar and traditionally forbidden territory" and the conclusions "appear to be so at odds with what has been accepted as true and adequate for so long." Such "courage and tentativity, along with humility, are inherent qualities of faith" (Loomer 1987, 23).

Loomer's naturalistic outlook is expressed in "basic empirical, methodological principles." These principles "do not have an independent justification; they are of a piece with the accompanying ontological stance. They are in fact the methodological expression of this ontology" (Loomer 1987, 23). The general empirical principle is that "knowledge is derived from and confirmed by physical experience" (Loomer 1987, 24). In elaborating this principle, Loomer, drawing on Whitehead, distinguishes between physical feeling and sense perception. By this distinction he separates himself from the older British empiricism that is based on sense experience. "The heights and depths of life, the unmanageable and efficacious undertows of existence, and the transformative energies of creative interchange are known first through our bodily feelings. Sense perception, by contrast, is an abstract version of physical experience. . . . It is a more specialized type of prehension that enables us to have relatively clear and distinct impressions of the more manageable features of our experience" (Loomer 1987, 24). It is significant that Loomer is able to articulate a theory of religious intuition on the basis of this empiricism. "An intuition in the perceptual sense is a physical experience with a modicum of conceptual interplay. The far-ranging insights of religious intuitions are derived from the fusion of physical and conceptual sensitivity to life-directive and life-transformative qualities and relationships" (Loomer 1987, 25).

The naturalistic outlook, according to Loomer, may be expressed in a positive and a negative assertion. "The disavowal of transcendental causes, principles, and explanations is the negative side of the assertion of the self-sufficiency of the world and of our descriptive analysis of it. . . . This naturalistic orientation can be restated in terms of a principle that is both methodological and ontological in scope: the reasons why things are the way they are and behave as they do are to be found within the things themselves and their relationships (including the factor of chance) to each other" (Loomer 1987, 25). Loomer elaborates this naturalistic outlook in terms of four topics: the web of life, the unity of the web, the concept of ambiguity, and the creative advance.

In explicating the concept of the web of life, Loomer stresses the importance of relationships at all levels. "Actualities are largely constituted by their relations." Indeed, "We create each other" (Loomer 1987, 31). This is not necessarily love. "Love does not create our essential interrelatedness. Love is an acknowledgment of it. We love because we are bound to each other, because we live and are fulfilled in, with, and through each other." By the same token, the interrelatedness of things is "exemplified as much in the mutual destructiveness of evil" as in "the mutual enrichment of a loving relationship" (Loomer, 1987, 33).

The "all-inclusive human web is the primordial covenant . . . to which all are called and all are chosen, and in whose service all covenants of lesser generality, both religious and secular, receive their justification." However, we are "coming to understand that the human community belongs to a larger web that includes all forms of terrestrial life" (Loomer 1987, 34). This idea of an extended web is a generalization of field theory and an expansion of our sense of community. It is "an imaginative extension of the sentence: 'Inasmuch as you have done it unto one of the least of these, you have done it unto me' " (Loomer 1987, 35).

The nature of the extended web of interconnected events seems to lie between two extremes. On the one extreme, there is the personal unity of an experiencing subject, which the world as a whole, approached empirically, appears to lack. The other extreme is that of an aggregation, but the world seems to be more unified than that. The tentative conclusion is that the universal web has the kind of unity which the term "web" suggests, that of a generalized enduring society. This idea of the world as a whole as an interconnected web does involve an imaginative leap of the imagination. While it goes beyond the limits of scientific evidence, yet it does have some support in scientific theory. It has "rootage in poetic insight, parapsychological phenomena, and in deep intuitions emanating from several religious traditions" (Loomer 1987, 36).

Here Loomer introduces the notion of religious intuition into his empirical outlook.

Evidence is a function of perception (and accessible data), and perception is a matter of sensitive discernment. Discernment is a variable, reflecting the inequality of sensitivity among observers. In order to obtain a discerning and penetrating "seeing," physical perception must be informed and prepared by appropriate and suggestive theory that guides our seeing, prefigures possible connections, and enlarges our receptivity concerning what may be presented to us. (Loomer 1987, 36)

At this point Loomer introduces the term "God." "In terms of this analysis, God as a wholeness is to be identified with the concrete, interconnected totality of this struggling, imperfect, unfinished, and evolving societal web" (Loomer 1987, 41). Why call this interconnected web of existence "God"? Why not simply refer to the world? Since "God is not an enduring concrete individual with a sustained subjective life, what is gained by this perhaps confusing, semantic identification?" (Loomer 1987, 42).

In our traditions the term 'God' is the symbol of ultimate values and meanings in all of their dimensions. It connotes an absolute claim on our loyalty. . . . It points the direction of a greatness of fulfillment. It signifies a richness of resources for the living of life at its depths. It suggests the enshrinement of our common and ecological life. It proclaims an adequate object of worship. It symbolizes a transcendent and inexhaustible meaning that forever eludes our grasp. The world is God because it is the source and preserver of meaning; because the creative advance of the world in its adventure is the supreme cause to be served; because even in our desecration of our space and time within it, the world is holy ground; and because it contains and yet enshrouds the ultimate mystery inherent within existence itself. (Loomer 1987, 42)

Loomer goes on to assert that anything unambiguous is an abstraction. Hence an ambiguous God is of greater stature than an unambiguous deity. "The aim in the first instance is not to seek and cherish ambiguity for its own sake. . . . The quest is for a living, dynamic, and active God—in short, a concrete God. . . . The concretely actual is ambiguous; only the highly abstract can be unambiguous" (Loomer 1987, 43).

Given Loomer's distinction between perfection as a bloodless abstraction and complexity as fullsome concreteness, the creative advance of the world is not a movement toward perfection, but toward greater stature, a movement which "involves the transformation of incompatibilities and contradictions into compatible contrasts within the unity of the web and within the lives of its members" (Loomer 1987, 51). Finally, Loomer ends his essay by the hint that the interconnected web of existence is growing toward a unity of experience. "The conception of the stature of God that is presupposed in this essay may be indicated by the speculative suggestion that the world is an interconnected web endeavoring to become a vast socialized unity of experience with its own processive subjectivity" (Loomer 1987, 51).

Ralph Burhoe

Our next naturalistic theologian is Ralph Burhoe. Trained in the natural sciences, he used his position as the first Executive Officer of the American Academy of Arts and Sciences to develop, in 1954, the Institute on Religion in an Age of Science. In 1964 he went to Meadville Theological School in Chicago to develop possibly the first theological teaching position using modern sciences as a prime resource. There he established the Center for Advanced Study in Religion and Science, now the Zygon Center for Religion and Science, and became the founding editor of *Zygon: Journal of Religion and Science.*

He believed that the wisdom of the ancient religious traditions about humans and their place in the world can be reinterpreted and placed on a firm footing by the findings of modern science. His central notion is that the evolutionary process is in fact what the ancient religions referred to as God, the judgment of God being the selective process of evolution. His discussion of God may be found especially in "The Concepts of God and Soul in a Scientific View of Human Purpose," in chapter 5 of his book *Toward a Scientific Theology.*

For Burhoe the two major elements of traditional religion are the concepts of God and soul, concepts whose loss represents the breakdown of once flourishing cultural systems and whose reinterpretation might help reverse the present cultural breakdown. These two symbols provide the motivation of long-term purpose, motivation that recent humanistic social philosophies lack.

The first of these two elements of religious belief "is that there is a system of reality or power sovereign over men individually" and collectively to which we must learn to adapt (Burhoe 1981, 116). This is the sovereign system that Burhoe claims the sciences understand more fully as the process of evolutionary selection. In other words, *god* denotes "the total sovereign system, which in scientific language may be said to be the total cosmic ecosystem including the details of local ecosystems on earth" (Burhoe 1981, 124). He uses the typographical devices of using quotation marks and italics to refer to these traditional concepts "to indicate that these terms are to be symbols that relate in some ways closely to some of their traditional meanings as well as to concepts of the contemporary sciences" (Burhoe 1981, 117).

William Bernhardt's Operational Theism: God as Dynamic Determinant

One of the clearest and most logical of theological writers, Bernhardt developed, in a series of articles, a variety of religious naturalism with contemporary relevance. Bernhardt was Professor of Philosophy of Religion at Iliff School of Theology in Denver from 1929 to 1964 and sometime Dean or Acting President. Known for his exchanges with Henry Nelson Wieman, his use of "the reality principle" and a "verifiable God-concept" is a powerful support for one side of a crucial debate in theology as to whether "sovereignty" or "goodness" is the prime character of God. (For a further discussion of this point see Stone 2004 and chapters 2 and 5 in this volume.) Bernhardt championed intellectual rigor in theology at a time when the use of reason was either downplayed by pragmatism among the liberals or more severely castigated by Reinhold Niebuhr and the neo-orthodox. He was an original metaphysician. He also stood for a rejection of wishful thinking in religious inquiry at the same time holding that religion had a crucial role to play in human life. His approach still has relevance today. (I have been helped in writing this by conversations with Charles Milligan of Iliff. For studies of him see articles by Brush, Milligan, Templin, and Tremmel in Peden and Axel 1989. See also Charles Milligan, "The Pantheistic Motif in American Religious Thought," Milligan 1987.)

There is an urgency to Bernhardt's thinking. "If Christianity is to serve the present generation, theologians will have to develop a conception of God adequate to the demands of the times." We face brutal realities and palliatives dressed up in traditional terminology will not suffice. "A conception of God adequate to these times must be based upon the actualities as we now understand them. . . . A conception of God based upon actualities requires the use of a methodology of thinking capable of dealing with them" (Bernhardt 1959a, 21).

He uses the term "Operationalism" to refer to the method of thinking that has been refined over the past 500 years and the term "Operational Theism" to the concept of God that utilizes this method.

Operationalism, as he explicates it, is "both a theory of meaning and a method of verification." First, "as a theory of meaning, Operationalism defines meanings in terms of relations and modalities." This is because "What can be known about existence or existents consists in their relations with one another and how they function as related (Modality)" (Bernhardt 1959a, 21).

As a method of investigation Operationalism involves clarification of language and propositions and a statement of the conditions under which the propositions are to be tested and the specification of the support that other well-established theories provide. In all of this, for Bernhardt, as our understanding of the natural world increases, we will change our notion of God.

We now turn to clarifying Bernhardt's conception of God and then move to his attempt at justifying it. Bernhardt uses a series of equivalent technical phrases: God is the "Directional Momentum" or "Dynamic Directionality" within the totality of the cosmic process. Earlier phrases that Bernhardt used are "Dynamic Determinant" or "Dominant Phase of the Existential Medium" (Bernhardt 1959a, 25–29; Bernhardt 1959b, 28–29, 42; Bernhardt 1942, 257; Bernhardt 1943b). Bernhardt's language is technical and abstract. But it repays careful reading.

Bernhardt makes three statements in explaining his concept of God. (Bernhardt 1959a, 29). The first is that God "is the religious name for the Directional Momentum operative" in all that exists (Bernhardt Winter 1959a, 25). The second is that the Directional Momentum in all processes may be considered as single or plural depending on whether each event or the totality of all events is considered. Third, God is the religious name for the directionality involved in temporal processes, including the human, which result in a culmination of the process.

1. God "is the religious name for the Directional momentum immanent in the episodes which together comprise the Existential Medium" (or all that exists) (Bernhardt Winter 1959a, 29). In his earlier writing he expressed this by saying that God is the Dominant Phase of the Existential Medium or that God should be conceived as Dynamic Determinant (Bernhardt 1942, 1943b).

    A parallel statement published a few months later uses the notion of dynamic directionality. "Directional momentum or dynamic directionality constitutes the core of all that lives," indeed, of existence at all levels (Bernhardt 1959b, 28). God is the religious name for the dynamic directionality that exhibits itself in the formation and destruction of suns, societies, and the origin and growth of persons

(Bernhardt Spring 1959b, 29). Examples of directional momentum include the warfare of grass with weeds and, on the human level, "commerce, industry, empire, scaling high peaks." Indeed, humanity "is a form of directional momentum." (Bernhardt 1959b, 28). These examples illustrate the radically naturalistic thrust of this view.

2. The dynamic directionality in all processes may be considered as single or plural depending on whether each event or the totality of all events is considered. "God is generically One but operationally many" (Bernhardt 1959a, 29). Bernhardt makes a distinction between generic and numeric otherness. Diamond *qua* diamond always has the characteristics of diamond. This is generic unity. But we always encounter specific, numerically distinct diamonds. "If we accept Directional Momentum as the basic category of Existence for Deity, we may conceive of God as one generically. At the experimental level, however, God as Directional Momentum is found in various episodes, and therefore must be viewed as numerically plural" (Bernhardt 1959a, 26).

    The statement, that "God is generically one and operationally many," could be taken to mean: (a) God is distinct from the world but operative within it (Calvin), (b) God is one process within the world (Wieman), or (c) God is a designation for one characteristic of the world (Samuel Alexander). The first option can be ruled out from the whole tenor of Bernhardt's work. Bernhardt is serious when he says that God "is the religious name for that *in our total environment* which makes possible religious values under the proper circumstances" (Bernhardt 1958b, 11 emphasis mine). I suggest that in terms of these three hermeneutical options, Bernhardt's statement that God is generically one and operationally many means that God is more like an abstract name for a characteristic of the world process and less like a unitary process within the totality of existence. I also suggest that the examples given of Directional Momentum plus the abstract nature of the generic unity of God indicate that this is a more radically naturalistic viewpoint than that of Wieman.

3. The third statement concerns the fact that episodes or events within the total process of existence tend to result on occasion in processes with a degree of temporal duration that result in what could be called culminations. "God's operations or activities function within episodes with directionality dominant over randomness. The outcomes of these activities appear in a persistent succession of culminations which are more or less temporary" (Bernhardt 1959a, 29). To use more

traditional language, God is the religious name for the directionality
involved in temporal processes, including the human, which results
in culminations of these process.

These three statements are couched in a metaphysical language
that Bernhardt developed, a language that may be described as a set of
empirical generalizations concerning the total cosmic process. (Here he
owes much to Smuts and Schopenhauer. Cp. Arthur Schopenhauer, *The
World as Will and Idea*, part IV; Jan Christiaan Smuts, *Holism and Evolution*.)
Bernhardt claims that this language is functionally equivalent to traditional
religious language, provided that this language is disciplined by the use
of the "reality principle," which would eliminate the humanization of
the world that traditional religions foster through a human-like God.
Thus the three metaphysical statements can be translated into traditional
religious language, but not without remainder, because the humanization
of the traditional language needs to be eliminated.

Involved in these notions is the idea that the Directional Momentum does not operate for human good except incidentally. Bernhardt has
referred to this as God's "disinteredness" (Bernhardt 1959b, 41–42) and
recognizes its echoes of Calvin. He cites the relative insignificance of
humans in relation to astronomical time and space as well as the fact that
the directional momentum that results in creation of some processes can
result in the destruction of others. The recognition of this is the acceptance of what he calls "the reality principle" in religion (Bernhardt 1959b,
25–29). In an earlier article he calls this "Pure Realism" or the "Dynamic"
as distinct from the "Agathonic" view of God (Bernhardt 1942). God is
dynamic rather than agathonic, fundamentally power rather than goodness.
In the agathonic conception of God (from the Greek *agathos* or "good")
God serves to promote human welfare. The agathonic idea violates the
reality principle. It is a failure to recognize human limitations.

As a consequence of this dynamic conception of God, Bernhardt
rejects using the term "creative" in reference to God (*contra* Wieman and
Kaufman). Creativity includes or alternates with destruction or disinte-
gration. "Creativity is a limited concept, applicable to specific phases of
Episodic Durationality, but hardly designative of God as the directionality
involved in all" (Bernhardt 1959b, 32).

Much of the thrust of Bernhardt's writing is an explicit challenge
to upholders of the agathonic notion of God as primarily productive of
good, including Henry Nelson Wieman for whom God is the source of
human good and Boston personalism.

When Bernhardt asks the question of whether his concept of can
be translated into traditional religious terms, he answers that "this is pos-

sible only to the extent that the humanizing of nature, or the centrality of human values can be surrendered." If Operational Theism is adopted, "it becomes necessary for humanity to accept a much more modest place in the nature of things, and to find values in more inclusive structures of existence. Theology will be based upon 'the reality principle,' or, perhaps we should say, assume a new Calvinistic form" (Bernhardt, 1959a, 33).

We turn now to the question of justifying this approach. Bernhardt derives this notion of God from his study of the function of religion (Bernhardt 1943a, 101–102; Bernhardt 1943b, 281–282). He and his students devoted considerable time to the study of the function of religion in human history (Bernhardt 1932; Bernhardt October 1943; Bernhardt, *A Functional Philosophy of Religion*). In his study of the shifting functions of religion in relation to the agricultural and medical practices of the Trobriand Islanders, the ancient Romans, and Midwestern American Methodists, he located a constant function. People no longer pray for crops or healing. That function has changed. But the constant function is that people use religion to relate to the unsatisfactory and nonmanipulable and thus inescapable features of existence with courage and hope (Bernhardt Oct. 1943, 281). In order to relate to these features, we need to orient ourselves to reality, not to wishful thinking. Hence we need a religion based on reality, not on the wishful thinking of the agathonic approach.

As just indicated, Bernhardt derives his notion of God from the function of religion elaborated in his *A Functional Philosophy of Religion*. He justifies this notion both in terms of its function and also, because this notion is of a piece with metaphysics conceived of as the organization of our knowledge of the all-pervasive aspects of the Existential Medium, a knowledge ultimately derived from empirical studies.

For Bernhardt God is a religious, not an essential metaphysical principle. "Yet if God is to be more than a satisfactory idea or poetic expression, the reality denoted or designated by the name must have metaphysical grounding" (Bernhardt 1958b, 11). Here we see the reality principle at work again.

What is metaphysics? Man, to use Bernhardt's pre-gender-inclusive language, "lives within some context, environment, or medium. The more inclusive medium within which he exists I normally speak of as the Existential Medium. As I am using the word metaphysics, it constitutes that study which focuses attention upon the Existential Medium as broadly defined" (Bernhardt 1958b, 11). The further distinction between metaphysics and other broad areas of study, such as astronomy, may be made thusly: "*The metaphysician is a processor rather than a producer of knowledge.* He examines the information or conclusions reached in specific fields to discover or determine what may be true of the universe conceived or envisioned as a whole. . . . As a processor of knowledge, the metaphysician is dependent upon those who investigate specialized fields or areas for his basic data. This suggests that metaphysics is concerned with *human knowledge*, with the results of empirical or experimental studies. There are no esoteric sources from which metaphysicians draw knowledge" (Bernhardt 1958b, 12 emphasis in original). Revelation, traditionally conceived, is not a source of metaphysical knowledge.

This does not mean that science is the exclusive source of metaphysics. Common sense can be a source of unsystematic empirical knowledge. Art and religion may also give us knowledge, although they contribute more to our knowledge of the ways we respond to their objective referents than to our knowledge of them.

Another feature of metaphysics is that analogies may play a useful role "if some rich key concept from a given field provides categories sufficiently inclusive to organize the available knowledge." However, the growth of knowledge "makes it increasingly difficult to find any one analogy capable of serving as mind, matter and organism did in the past" for Idealism, Materialism, or Organicism (Bernhardt 1958b, 13). It appears more likely that we can find the organizing analogies in an examination of various fields rather than just one.

A third feature of metaphysics is its inferential nature. There are at least three kinds of objects used in thinking. These may be called "epistemic objects." The first type are perceptual objects. These are subject to empirical investigation (including introspection, to a limited degree). Second are inferential or "heteroscopic" epistemic objects, which "refer to what may be inferred from the results of perceptual activities." For example, "one may *perceive* a vermiform appendix, but not organic evolution. It is an inference based upon insight and supported by evidence such as the appendix. . . . Heteroscopic epistemic objects consist in *ideas derived from the information obtained by perception and continuous with it*" (Bernhardt 1958b, 13, emphasis in original).

> We may use a term such as "heteroscopic" to designate realities like evolution, gravity, and historic events. Heteroscopic objects, therefore, are those which are not observable either through normal human senses or yet by means of such instruments as microscopes and telescopes. . . . (B)elief in their existence appears to be warranted by the nature and behavior of microscopic and macroscopic objects or events. (Bernhardt 1943a, 96)

The third type of epistemic objects are metascopic objects, which "refer to *realities believed to be of such nature that they cannot be perceived nor can they be inferred from what is perceived*" (Bernhardt 1958b, 13, emphasis Bernhardt's). Traditionally they were believed to be known through revelation, more recently often to be required by subjective needs. God is not a metascopic epistemic object, as often understood, for then we would have no basis on which to have any knowledge of God. Rather, God is a heteroscopic metaphysical object, an inference from and continuous with the objects of perception.

Bernhardt lists objectivity as a final feature of metaphysical thinking, a specific counter to pragmatism (specifically that of F. C. S. Schiller).

> Metaphysics as we conceive it is a serious attempt to conceptualize the all-pervasive characteristics, qualities, trends or tendencies discoverable in the Existential Medium. It must be based upon the most reasonable and accepted theories and be formulated as critically and honestly as possible. But it must be more than that. . . . Once it has been formulated as precisely and objectively as possible, then and only then should its implications for values be explored. We are here concerned with a metaphysical basis for value theory and religion. However, if this concern is permitted to control one's thinking from the beginning of the metaphysical quest, the result is apt to be what Schiller called it, a poem. (Bernhardt 1958b, 13–14)

Bernhardt is now ready to summarize his notion of metaphysics in the following formula.

> *Metaphysics may now be defined as the organization of knowledge of the all-pervasive characteristics, qualities, trends or tendencies of the Existential Medium in order to provide a framework for the understanding of man and that in which he exists.* Whereas a given metaphysical system may serve scientific and other uses, our interest is more limited. We seek to determine its relevance for religious values and God. If it fails when applied to scientific and other fields of thought, it fails also for religious values and God. *This is but to say that it must be an honest and adequate interpretation of all of the knowledge available to the metaphysician, no matter what his personal interests may be.* I do not recognize one test of honesty and adequacy in

science and another in metaphysics." (Bernhardt 1958b, 14, emphasis Bernhardt's)

The relevance of this metaphysics to the conceptions of God and religious values is that, "In an empirical theology, the conception of God must be related positively to what is known about the Existential Medium. Religious values must also find their place in the nature of things if they are to serve the values which religion prescribes" (Bernhardt 1958b, 36).

What does all this abstract theorizing mean practically for real life? This conception of God as Dynamic Determinant or Directional Momentum has a role in the reconstruction of life. In Bernhardt's view religion "is a complex form of individual and group behavior whereby persons are prepared intellectually and emotionally to meet the unsatisfactory and inescapable aspects of existence positively, i.e., with confidence, courage, and hope" (Bernhardt 1943b, 281). Religion has three aspects. The first is the human interests or values which this behavior is designed to provide or conserve. The second is the interpretation or reinterpretation of the situation. The third is the technique or overt behavior employed (Bernhardt 1943b, 280). In Bernhardt's technical language the concept of God functions in the second or reinterpretative phase in the creative reorganization of life in the face of the unsatisfactory and inescapable.

When Bernhardt elaborated the details of this creative reorganization of life in one of his last major articles, "The Reality Principle in Religion," it seems to have three aspects. It involves (1) trimming expectations by the adoption of the reality principle. This includes (2) a refusal to humanize either nature or the Directional Momentum, a refusal that in religious language could be called a recognition of the "disinterestedness of God." Yet this trimming of expectations is not a fatalism or quietism, for the third aspect of the creative reorganization of life is (3) a genuine, if chastened, activism, a "salvation by participation" to use Bernhardt's language (Bernhardt 1959b, 34).

The religious life that respects the reality principle will learn to acknowledge the "Disinteredness" or impartiality of God, what Bernhardt had earlier called the Dynamic, as distinct from the Agathonic, view of God. God as Directional Momentum can be traced in all movements of the universe. But we see that movements potentially come into conflict.

We may lament the destruction of one natural factor by another, but it can hardly be called evil in ordinary terms. This is the way directional momentum operates at this level. . . . There are no rational grounds for applying moral attributes, on human terms, to the divine. "Evil" and "good" are terms we apply to human ways of relating persons to one another and not to the more inclusive reality within which the divine operates. Any extension of these judgmental concepts beyond the human leads to confusion and frustration. (Bernhardt 1959b, 40)

This is Bernhardt's translation of Matt. 5:45 (God "makes his sun to rise on the evil and on the good and sends rain on the just and the unjust") into theo-philosophical terms.

This disinterestedness or impartiality of God provides a reliable setting for human living. The soul that sineth shall die. If you violate the conditions under which you must live, these conditions will cause you misery and, at the extreme, death. These facts are tragic only if we insist that we and our values are central to the cosmos. "We must accept the possibility that we are more or less 'incidental' to the scheme of things" (Bernhardt 1959b, 41).

Salvation by participation calls for some explication. The "creative reorganization of life in the presence of the unsatisfactory and inescapable factors in existence is made possible, in part, by placing oneself in situations where God becomes operatively effective in the process" (Bernhardt 1959b, 32). This is not done by withdrawal or denial of these unsatisfactory and inescapable factors. Rather one must place oneself where participation in the divine activities is possible. Salvation occurs when one

> accepts himself for what he is with all of his limitations and resources; when he takes his place in the life of his times, and when he opens himself to the healing which flows from a "companionable" interest in the place where he is, be it city, sea, or mountain. In terms of Operational Theism, God is operationally present in all phases of existence, including all that is. (Bernhardt 1959b, 35)

In showing how his operational theism is involved in the creative reorganization of life, Bernhardt deals with guilt, rejection, and estrangement. All three of these are different names for the same problem, a failure in relationship or participation. His solutions to this failure involve reestablishing participation. In the first place it may be that there are actions and motives in ourselves that hinder relationship and which we can revise. Again, we may have impossibly high standards and should move toward more flexible and realistic standards. Finally there are beauties in the natural world which bring satisfaction. In these experiences we are recipients as well as givers and these also involve participation.

If "religion consists of individual and group activity designed to effect creative reorganization of persons in the presence of unsatisfactory and inescapable conditions," this reorganization will be "done by reinterpreting the values or value-systems of the person or persons concerned and the relevant context." In this process Bernhardt finds that "Conceptions of God emerge from and are modified by continuous reinterpretations of the situational context made necessary by changing conditions and the growth of knowledge. From an Operational point of view, God is ideally an experienceable reality" (Bernhardt 1959b, 29).

Then the question becomes, where may God be experienced? Traditional answers have included language (Bible), the group (the church), and the divine majesty (Kant, Schleiermacher, Tillich). With his notion of "God as Directional Momentum," for Bernhardt God "is the religious name for that in oneself and the inclusive environment which makes creative reorganization of life in the presence of the unsatisfactory and inescapable facts of existence possible" (Bernhardt 1959b, 31). Thus, the locus of the experience of God will be where this creative reorganization of life occurs.

Bernhardt wishes to find a place for the use of the Bible. Ancient scriptures can be a source of wisdom for us today (Bernhardt 1959b, 39). (Bernhardt is focusing on the Bible, but his suggestions are applicable to religious traditions generally.) However, in line with the general approach of Bernhardt's Operational Theism, this wisdom needs to be "subjected to the test of operational efficiency." This is another way of saying that the ancient scriptures yield hypotheses that need to be "tested by their checkable consequences" (Bernhardt 1959b, 39).

The upshot of this view of God and salvation by participation is what I call a measured meliorism. We must learn to transform what we can and yet to live within limits. "Despite the fact that we are not pampered, and that we have to use our intelligence, initiative and courage if we are to live in this world, a satisfactory human existence is still possible" (Bernhardt 1959b, 42). Accepting the disinterestedness of God and the presence of the detrimental forces in our environment and ourselves, we should become active participants with others in the attempt to remold conditions so as to remove as many of the destructive forces as possible. In the process we may become humane, learning to respect and cooperate with others.

All of this, maintains Bernhardt, "may mean some serious reorganization in our theologies and philosophies of religion. If so, it will not be the first time in Christian history that this has been necessary. To this end it may be necessary that we take a long look at the possibility of using the reality principle in the religion we transmit to our children and grandchildren" (Bernhardt 1959b, 42).

There are a number of points where Bernhardt's philosophical theology has continuing relevance in today's world. The first is that he not merely claims the compatibility of science and religion, but shows how the very concept of God can have an empirical basis if we pay attention to what we mean by God. In the process Bernhardt's theology is an alternative not only to such older pragmatisms as that of Schiller, but also to many neo-pragmatisms such as that of Richard Rorty. The second is that salvation by participation can have excellent pastoral as well as theological implications. That this is in the Arminian tradition need not prevent a doctrine of grace if God is understood as the directional momentum in all processes. The third is that religion should respect the reality principle and not indulge in wishful thinking.

As a fourth point Bernhardt makes a contribution to a continuing theological debate, namely whether God's power or goodness is of primary importance, which is related to the question as to whether we should relate to God in awe or gratitude and imitation. Although this debate does go back at least to Aquinas and Ockham, and Jonathan Edwards, William Ellery Channing and Hosea Ballou, in contemporary form it continues in discussions between Charles Milligan, Donald Crosby, and William Dean on the one hand and Charley Hardwick on the other. Bernhardt's exchanges with Henry Nelson Wieman clearly places Bernhardt with Milligan, Crosby, and Dean (Dean 1994; Hardwick, 1996; Kaufman, 1993; Milligan 1991; see Milligan 1987; Milligan 1996).

Finally there is a fifth point of relevance, although Bernhardt hardly articulated it, since it was only beginning to be of significance in his time. This point is that theology needs to be beyond its restriction to the believing community, beyond the restriction of theology to the "ghetto" of a communal language game. In this Bernhardt is allied with theologians like Philip Hefner, Robert Neville, Jeffrey Stout, and Wentzel van Huyssteen as distinct from the communitarian restriction of Stanley Hauerwas, George Lindbeck, Alasdair MacIntyre, John Milbank, and Richard J. Neuhaus.

Mordecai Kaplan:
Jewish Reconstructionist

Mordecai Kaplan, New York Rabbi, Dean of the Teachers Institute of the Jewish Theological Seminary and teacher in its Rabbinical School, was the inspiration for Reconstructionist Judaism as well as the teacher of many of the leaders of Conservative Judaism. The editor of the *Reconstructionist*, he revised the Sabbath Prayer Book and was the first rabbi to perform the *bat misvat* ceremony for women. (For Kaplan's life see Mel Scult 1985.) For our purposes his essential writings are *The Meaning of God in Modern Jewish Religion*; chapters 10 and 11 of *The Future of the American Jew*; *Judaism Without Supernaturalism*, part one and chapters II through IV of *Dynamic Judaism* which is an anthology of his writings (Kaplan 1937, Kaplan 1948, Kaplan 1958, Kaplan 1985). Helpful studies are to be found in Jack J. Cohen's *Guides for an Age of Confusion*; Emanuel S. Goldsmith's "Mordecai M. Kaplan: His Interpretation of Judaism," in *Dynamic Judaism*; Emanuel S. Goldsmith "Salvational Zionism and Religious Naturalism in the Thought of Mordecai M. Kaplan," Delores Joan Rogers, *The American Empirical Movement in Theology*; Robert M. Seltzer's "Introduction: Kaplan and Jewish Modernity," in *The American Judaism* of *Mordecai M. Kaplan*, edited by Emanuel S. Goldsmith, Mel Scult, and Robert M. Seltzer; and Emanuel Goldsmith's "Mordecai M. Kaplan's Synthesis of Judaism and American Religious Naturalism" (Kaplan, 1985; Rogers, 1990; Goldsmith, Scult, and Seltzer 1990; Goldsmith 1990; Goldsmith 1993; for Wieman's treatment of Kaplan, see Wieman 1952).

Mordecai Kaplan was most interested in the dynamic vitality of the tradition of a specific people bound together by their religion. In this he differs from most other religious naturalists, except Jack Cohen. (Henry Levinson is deeply immersed in the Jewish tradition, but he does not attempt reconstruction as do Kaplan and Cohen.) On the other hand, many religious naturalists like Sellars, Wieman, Burhoe, Bernhardt, Kaufman, and myself to a certain extent, are interested in reconstructing a religious tradition, but these traditions are not as intimately bound up with a specific people. This reflects the fact that these naturalists have some connection (however attenuated in the case of Sellars) to a denominational Christianity requiring voluntary adhesion rather than Judaism as the religion of a people to whom one is born. *"We are faithful to Jewish religion, not because we have chosen it as the best of all religions, but because it is ours, the only religion we have, an inseparable part of our collective personality as a people"* (Kaplan 1948, 47, italics Kaplan's).

Thus Kaplan had a strong concern for the particularities of his tradition. "A living religion is not universal abstract truth but local and concrete experience, which is interpreted in terms of universal human interest" (Kaplan 1934, 201). More specifically, Judaism is a civilization. "As a civilization, Judaism . . . consists, therefore, of a continuing history, a common language and literature, folkways, mores, laws, ethical norms, and in addition, possesses a distinct social structure" (Kaplan 1948, 445.

See Kaplan 1934, 312 propositions under "D," and his comments on Jewish socialism, Kaplan 1948, 6–8).

A significant part of the intersection between a civilization and its religions are what Kaplan calls its *sancta*, "the events, the heroes, the writings, and the occasions signalized by a people as giving concreteness to the values deemed essential by the people to its existence" (Kaplan 1985, 42). "*These sancta, the attitude toward life that they imply and the specific observances that they inspire, together constitute the religion of a people.* . . . American civilization also has its *sancta*: Washington and Lincoln, the Constitution, the Declaration of Independence, Thanksgiving Day, the Fourth of July, and other national holidays, the Stars and Stripes. They, and what they imply, represent American religion. The American Jew sees no contradiction in reverencing both constellations of *sancta*. . . . The difference between Jewish religion and all others does not consist so much in the uniqueness of its conception of God, as in the uniqueness of its *sancta*" (Kaplan 1948, 46–47, italics in original. See also Kaplan 1948, 174 and Kaplan 1985, chapter II, "Jewish Peoplehood"). It is significant that the work of Kaplan that is the most theological of his better known works, *The Meaning of God in Modern Jewish Religion*, is constructed around the major festivals of the Jewish year (Kaplan 1962).

Kaplan is, of course, not a traditionalist, in the sense of dedication to the preservation of a tradition in a supposedly pristine form. He is a traditionalist in the sense that he is an appreciative student of the history of Jewish civilization focused on a living and critical reconstruction of it. He was, for instance, the one who introduced the practice of having a *bat mitzvah* for Jewish girls. As quoted in the opening mottoes of this book, for Kaplan, "Our responsibility to our forefathers is only to consult them, not to obey them" (Kaplan 1962, 98; that is only half of the quotation). Further study of Kaplan's approach to tradition would involve his Biblical hermeneutics and his attitude toward Torah. See *Dynamic Judaism*, Chapter IV "Torah in Our Day" for his general hermeneutics and Chapter V "Interpreting the Torah, the Prophets, and the Rabbis," for detailed examples of his hermeneutics (Kaplan 1985). See also Emanuel S. Goldsmith in *Dynamic Judaism*, 24–25 (Kaplan 1985). For his hermeneutics in practice note that he suggests that the biblical passages that stress the power of God (Kaplan's word is "force") over his goodness "contain more of what the Jewish religion as a whole deprecates than of what it accepts. Their significance for Jewish religion is as a corrective to certain abuses of faith, rather than as an affirmation of positive religious belief. Their inclusion in the biblical canon, therefore, does not invalidate the truth of our contention that *Jewish religion maintains the eventual triumph of justice over brute force, as the very essence of faith in God*"

(Kaplan 1948, 286; italics in original). It is clear that here Kaplan would side with Wieman rather than with Bernhardt and Crosby on the issue of power versus goodness in the object of religion, *while yet recognizing the importance of both passages in the biblical canon.*

In my judgment one of the keys to Kaplan's understanding of tradition is his discussion of the stages in the history of the Jewish religion and of human religions in general. For example, in *The Future of the American Jew* he posits three stages in the development of the conception of salvation, a development that will influence the notion of God. *"Progress in the truth and spirituality of the conception of the Power that brings about salvation reflects the progress in the understanding of what actually constitutes salvation"* (italics in original). In the earliest stage salvation "is conceived as the fulfillment of the elementary physical hungers, namely those for food, mating, shelter, and security." The second stage arises after the first quest has been fully individualized. Then the worshiper finds that "this world is not such as God had intended it to be when He created it. He allows it to exist only for a time, but will ultimately replace it with a better world, in which all the inequities of this world will be righted. There, man will attain eternal life of bliss, which is his salvation." In the third stage now being reached, humans discover that we do not need to postpone salvation, but that we may "change *this* world in conformity with" our heart's desires (Kaplan 1948, 175–176) An interesting study would be to compare Kaplan with Sellars, Haydon, and Rue on the stages of religion.

In chapter 11 of *The Future of the American Jew* Kaplan describes this stage as "spiritual religion." This stage will be compatible with freedom of conscience and thought. It will move from fear to the valuing of human thought and intelligence in both its logical and ethical dimensions. It will be less concerned with specific doctrines and rules and more with the discovery of a method of spiritual adjustment with universal application. It follows supernatural religion much as astronomy and chemistry replace astrology and alchemy. Supernatural religion focused on miracles, theophanies, and external authority, while spiritual religion is concerned with those needs of human nature that the idea of God, as the Power that makes for salvation, underlines as imperative and capable of being addressed.

The ideas of God which have been employed are "tentative ideas" by means of which people, *"in accordance with their limited experience and intellectual development, have endeavored to express their affirmative attitude toward life, despite all the hardships it may entail"* (Kaplan 1948, italics in original). Spiritual religion "takes for granted that the conception of God is subject to ever progressive approach to the truth in accordance with our widening experience, that the ideals upon which we set our hearts are in continual need of clarification and reinterpretation to meet the changing conditions of human life" (Kaplan 1948, 189). In words reminiscent of Wieman's that all human ideals stand in need of transformation, Kaplan writes that spiritual religion helps to refashion our "heart's desire in accord with the will of God as the Power that leads to salvation" (Kaplan 1948, 196).

Kaplan's naturalism can be seen in his revision of the concept of God. The two major texts here are *The Meaning of God in Modern Jewish Religion* (Kaplan 1937) and chapter 10 of *The Future of the American Jew* (Kaplan 1948). What we find examining these texts is two major types of statement about God: God as the power that makes for salvation, conceived as human flourishing with justice, and God as the sum of the natural processes within the world that makes for salvation so understood. The first type can be illustrated by the following: "We may state, therefore, that *belief in God is belief in the existence of a Power conducive to salvation which is the fulfillment of human destiny*" (Kaplan 1948, 172, italics in original). This is the more frequent type of expression and is found scattered throughout Kaplan's writings (e.g., Kaplan 1937, 324, 327; Kaplan 1948, 182). The second is most clearly naturalistic. It may be illustrated by the following: "*It is sufficient that God should mean to us the sum of the animating, organizing forces and relationships which are forever making a cosmos out of chaos. This is what we understand by God as the creative life of the universe.* Religion is the endeavor to invoke these animating and organizing forces and to get us to place ourselves in rapport with them" (Kaplan 1962, 76, italics in original. See also pp. 25–26, 226 and 306; Kaplan 1958, 202; Kaplan 1970, 10). The similarity to the language of Shailer Mathews is striking.

Kaplan is clear that these animating and organizing forces include some within us. There is not sharp dichotomy between inner and outer forces. He can refer, for example, to the "elements in the life about us, in our social heritage and in ourselves, that possess the quality of Godhood" (Kaplan 1962, 29).

It might appear that this notion of a sum of forces, which is a pluralistic notion, has polytheistic implications. But a sum has some degree of unity. This means that our life is not to be the pursuit of contradictory goals, as in dissipating sexual energy in ways detrimental to family life. Likewise other pleasures should not be pursued in ways "that do not engage the whole of our personality in harmony with its unitary purpose" (Kaplan 1962, 227).

In my reading of Kaplan the connection between these two notions, God as power and God as the sum of forces, comes when the pluralistic possibilities of the idea of a "sum" are restrained by conceiving of the Power conducive to salvation as a process. *"We suggest that God be thought of as the cosmic process that makes for man's life abundant or salvation"* (Kaplan 1948, 183, italics in original). A process is a way of thinking of a sum of forces in a more unified, as well as temporally spread, sense. Clearly Kaplan uses "process" to indicate that "God" is not to be conceived of in personal terms. Nothing would be lost if we substituted for the notion of God as a personal being "the one of 'process,' which, at least with the aid of science, most of us find quite understandable. Why, then, not conceive God as process rather than as some kind of identifiable entity?" (Kaplan 1948, 183. See also 193–194).

For Kaplan God conceived as *"the Power predisposing mankind to salvation"* is also understood as operating *"through the conditions which are essential to salvation"* (Kaplan 1948, 179, italics in original). For the Jewish people these conditions will include the *sancta*, whereby the ancient experiences of the will to live abundantly are reinterpreted and given a new life. "Thus, for example, freedom or liberation from all manner of bondage, is the central theme in the celebration of the Passover festival. By observing that festival, the Jew remembers freedom as an indispensable condition of salvation, conceived in terms that are objective, this-worldly and, simultaneously, spiritual and ethical" (Kaplan 1948, 180). The chapters in Kaplan's *The Meaning of God in Modern Jewish Religion* are organized around this idea, showing how the major Jewish holy days serve this function (Kaplan 1962). He starts with Sabbath reminding Jews of "God as the Power that Makes for Salvation" (the title of chapter II) and Rosh Hashanah reminding Jews of "God as the Power that Makes for Social Regeneration" (chapter III). In similar fashion Yom Kippur brings to mind "God as the Power that Makes for the Regeneration of Human Nature" (chapter IV), Sukkot "God as the Power that Makes for Cooperation (chapter VI), Passover "God as the Power that Makes for Freedom (chapter VIII), and Shabout "God as the Power that Makes for Righteousness—Not Ourselves (chapter IX).

Kaplan addresses head-on the issue of worshiping or praying to a cosmic process. The answer "depends on what experiences we choose to identify as indicative of godhood. God as the Power, transcending ourselves, that makes for salvation, also inheres in all the forces of our minds and wills. As such, *God functions not only in our own bodies, but also in our relationships to one another and to the environment in which we live. By becoming aware of those forces and relationships, we induce them to function most efficiently. The purpose of worship and prayer is to produce such awareness*" (Kaplan 1948, 183–184, italics in original). Kaplan realizes that this seems as if prayer is merely talking to oneself. "Since God is immanent in man, then there must be something in the individual human being which is part of God, in the same way as the light which enters the human eye is part of the sun" (Kaplan 1948, 184). Here Kaplan asserts the importance of reason and conscience. The human self consists of actualized and potential parts. "The potential part represents the operation of those universal forces in the environment with which the individual must cooperate to achieve his maximum. That part operates as truth, when, as reason, it elicits from man the knowledge of reality. It operates as goodness, when, as conscience, it elicits love" (Kaplan 1948, 184). To continue, "Whenever man reasons or consults his conscience, he is engaged in a dialogue. So, also, when he prays. Then that part of him which is the actualized element in him addresses itself to that part which is potential. It is then that one's entire personality is implicated. When one's personality is entire, it necessarily includes something of the divine which transcends it" (Kaplan 1948, 184–185). It appears that "transcends" here means the lure of the potential, not the incursion of something beyond the natural. "All thinking—and prayer is a form of thought—is essentially a dialogue between our purely egocentric self and our self as representing a process that goes beyond us" (Kaplan 1956, 105).

Kaplan will even apply the adjective "personal" to God, in a modified sense. "A God who makes a difference in one's personal life should be designated as a personal God" (Kaplan 1956, 104). To put it succinctly, God as personal does not mean that God has personal characteristics, but that God is the creative process by which we become persons.

> If we believe in God as the totality of the influences in the universe which make for our becoming fully human, we must understand by personality that in us in which all those influences are brought to focus. Personality, understood in that sense, and not merely in the sense of the sum total of our mental life, is the manifestation or revelation of the divine. God is thus personal to us, the very ground of our personality. In this sense it is possible to believe in a personal God. (Kaplan 1956, 104–105)

Furthermore Kaplan wishes to dissociate the conception of God as Power conducive to salvation from indiscriminate power. From early days Jews, for example, learned to think that "godhead was not synonymous with might, but rather with justice to the oppressed and downtrodden"

(Kaplan 1962, 364). He brings this theme down to the present. *"Just as in olden times the Jews countered the imperialism of might with the imperialism of the spirit, so should they at present counter the nationalism of might with the nationalism of the spirit"* (Kaplan 1962, 365, italics in original). The Jew should challenge the nationalism and patriotism that is a "camouflage for the domination of the privileged classes," and champion a nationalism "based upon social justice and equitable opportunity for all" (Kaplan 1962, 365–366).

There is a passage in Kaplan that is troubling for a naturalistic reading of his work. In a paragraph in which he draws a parallel between God, viewed as a process, and the soul, he writes: "what is distinctive about the God-process is that it is superfactual and superexperiential . . . *the God-process is 'trans-natural.' . . . The soul-process, too, is superfactual, superexperiential and trans-natural"* (Kaplan 1948, 183, italics in original). There is no further explication of the meaning of these terms, except one. "Transnaturalism is that extension of naturalism which takes into account much that mechanistic or materialistic or positivist science is incapable of dealing with. Transnaturalism reaches out into the domain where mind, personality, purpose, ideals, values, and meanings dwell. It treats of the good and the true" (Kaplan 1958, 10; I owe this reference to Emanel S. Goldsmith). In my judgment the preponderance of the writings of Kaplan, including the immediate context of the troubling passage, calls for a strictly naturalistic reading consistent with the criteria proposed for naturalism in this history of religious naturalism. For example, in this same passage Kaplan adds, "Were one to add 'supernatural,' the whole point of this approach would be missed, since the term 'supernatural' implies miracle or suspension of natural law" (Kaplan 1948, 183). Possibly the following will succeed as an interpretation of this passage. A key sentence is the following: "As cosmic process, God is more than a physical, chemical, biological, psychological, or even social process. God includes them all" (Kaplan 1948, 183). By "superfactual, superexperential and trans-natural" Kaplan is referring to all of these natural processes together, or at least the aspect of them leading toward human fulfillment. He is probably also referring to these processes in so far as they are responded to religiously, not merely empirically. He has in mind an "all-inclusive view" that is more than empirical in the strict sense, yet which does not abandon the naturalistic framework. "Spiritual religion would indicate wherein the empirical and scientific approach is not enough. *Neither the remedy of an evil nor the solution of a problem can dispense with that all-inclusive view of reality which it is the main purpose of true religion to uncover for our inner eye"* (Kaplan 1948, 194). In a move similar to that of Shailer Mathews, when Kaplan writes "God is more than" a natural process, he refers to the togetherness of these natural processes together with their being viewed religiously. If this reading is correct, Kaplan remains a naturalist despite his problematic language in this passage. (Note that Kaplan's notion of the supernatural is narrower than the one utilized in this volume. Process theologians generally and also Paul Tillich, for example, do not speak of God as interfering in the natural order, yet they do not have a naturalistic notion of God in the way defined in this history.)

Jack Cohen:
Jewish Naturalist

Some of Kaplan's ideas were continued in a systematic form in Jack Cohen's readable *The Case for Religious Naturalism* (Cohen 1958). Cohen taught philosophy of religion at the Jewish Theological Seminary and the Hebrew University of Jerusalem. His book is devoted to a naturalistic reconstruction of religion, particularly Jewish religion. His argument against traditional religion includes the "existence of multiple systems of revelation, with their rival claims to absolute truth, together with the evidence advanced by natural and social science" (Cohen 1958, xvi). His definition of naturalism is "the disposition to believe that any phenomenon can be explained by appeal to general laws confirmable either by observation or by inference from observation." The naturalist "would deny that there is a realm of meaning 'beyond' the process of life manifest to human investigation." Of course, "this is not to say that everything that happens is the universe is necessarily explainable. Only extreme arrogance would lead men to believe they possessed the potentiality of omniscience. All the naturalist insists upon is that man has only one instrument of knowledge, his reason, and than any knowledge or 'vision' purportedly received from sources beyond 'nature' are products of that same rational faculty" (Cohen 1958, 21–22). Like Wieman's functional transcendence and my own minimal transcendence, he does have a naturalistic notion of transcendence, which "is a necessary category of all human thinking; but it in no way requires going beyond nature" (Cohen 1958, 23). Here he refers to the imaginative vision which searches for ever more inclusive frameworks of explanation, the source of intellectual, moral, and spiritual challenge. In this outlook, "God is that quality of the universe, expressed in its order and its openness to purpose, which man is constantly discovering and upon which he relies to give meaning to his life. God . . . may conceivably be a lot more. . . . Surely in all this there is enough transcendence to evoke the feeling of awe and sublimity in any man" (Cohen 1958,

130). Cohen also approaches Kaufman's notion of God as relativizer. "A mature religion would invoke the God-idea not to justify its own ethical position but to check any pretensions to ethical certainty. . . . No man, therefore, who believes in God can legitimately absolutize any of his practices or beliefs, not even his ethical values" (Cohen 1958, 134–135). Further exploration of Jack Cohen should explore his *Guides for an Age of Confusion* and *Major Philosophers of Jewish Prayer in the Twentieth Century*. (I owe these two references to Emanuel Goldsmith.)

Other Early Religious Naturalists: Bateson, Einstein, and Phenix

Gregory Bateson

Cultural anthropologist, therapist and speculative generalist, Gregory Bateson has come up with very suggestive insights. (See *A Sacred Unity*, 265–270, 299–306 [Bateson 1991]; *Angels Fear*, chapters I, V, VII, VIII, XIII, XIV, XVI, and XVII [Bateson and Bateson 1987]; Charleton, *Mind, Beauty and the Sacred: An Introduction to the Thought of Gregory Bateson*.) His style is difficult, mixing anecdotes with technical language drawn from anthropology, cybernetic theory, and cultural history. But his insights concerning the function of religion and the nature of the sacred are worth attending to. Bateson clearly rejects a separate, anthropomorphic deity along with the Cartesian dualism which he finds so dominant (Bateson and Bateson 1987, 6). Positively religion and the sacred are attempts to refer to the larger whole of which humans are an integral part (Bateson 1991, 299–300; Bateson and Bateson 1987, 8). An important insight that he hints at is that language appropriate to an organized whole is of a higher logical type than that used by a speaker within the whole and cannot be spoken without destroying the connection with the whole. The information of some processes in a system, if communicated, would destroy the working of the system. This necessary noncommunication, like the noncommunication of acquired characteristics to DNA or lack awareness of one's own processes of perception, is formally similar to the fact that the direct communication of religious rites will destroy their sacred character. This is also related to the fact that the awareness of the sacred can be so easily manipulated and thus destroyed (Bateson and Bateson 1987, 85–87; Bateson 1991, 267–268, 301–302). Any view of the whole of which we are a part needs to have a sense of its beauty and its terrible aspect. Ecological destruction will have terrible repercussions from the greater whole.

Albert Einstein

One writer who views elicited discussion in the popular press in his life-time was the physicist Albert Einstein whose scattered views on religion might fall within our definition of religions naturalism. Einstein definitely rejected any notion of a personal God. He held that genuine religiosity involved both a striving after rational knowledge of the natural world and a humility about achieving it (Jammer 1999, 95, 117, 121–122). He espoused a "cosmic religious feeling," admired Spinoza's *amor Dei intellectualis*, and spoke of the wonder of Nature and the harmony of the universe (Jammer 1999, 78–80, 97, 117, 121–122). "My views are near to those of Spinoza: admiration for the beauty of and belief in the logical simplicity of the order and harmony which we can grasp humbly and only imperfectly" (Einstein 1947 in Jammer 1999, 138–139). Einstein was a determinist, thus differing from some naturalists (Jammer 1999, 80 and elsewhere). He separated morality and religion (Jammer 1999, 135). The possible difficulty of including him among the religious naturalists comes out in his reference to "the existence of a spirit vastly superior to that of men," and the phrase, "The divine reveals itself in the physical world" (Einstein 1936 in Jammer 1999, 93 and Einstein quoted in Rosenkranz 1998, 80 in Jammer 1999, 151).

Philip Phenix

In 1954 Philip Phenix, an educational theorist who taught philosophy at Teachers College, Columbia University, published his *Intelligible Religion*. In it he explores the experiences of change, dependence, order, value, and imperfection and suggests that "God is the name applied to a set of definite and intelligible *aspects* of the world" (Phenix 1954, 99–100). Here he stands, if not self-consciously, in the tradition of Ames and Mathews. (For a fuller treatment of Phenix, see Stone 1992, 66–69.) Indeed, I have a fondness for Phenix because he is one of the few writers who explicitly uses the term "minimal" in his approach, which he terms a "minimum view" of the experiences of these aspects. This approach is made clear in the following, "The infinite God or the perfect God might with a minimum of speculation be taken simply as a symbol of the limitless wealth of possibilities inherent in existence" (Phenix 1954, 87–88).

Chapter Three

Analyzing the Issues

Controversies in Early Religious Naturalism

From the 1920s to the 1950s there were a number of published exchanges between exponents of what we are calling the religious naturalists. These exchanges represent important differences that continue to shape discussion. Some readers who admire harmony may see these points of disagreement as questions which should be resolved. Others, including myself, view these as continuing issues, grappling with which can be sources of continuing creativity.

The major topics and writers of these discussions can be named as: the meaning of naturalism (Santayana and Dewey), the relationship between human good and the object of religious orientation (Bernhardt and Wieman), the unity of the object of religious orientation (Dewey and Wieman), the theistic question within naturalism (naturalistic theists and religious humanists), and the nature of empirical inquiry (Wieman and Meland).

The Meaning of Naturalism

In 1925 George Santayana reviewed Dewey's *Experience and Nature* in the *Journal of Philosophy*. Dewey replied early in 1927 (Santayana 1925, 367–384; Dewey 1984, 73–81; Shaw 1995, 74–77). For Santayana naturalism asserts that all causes and conditions are material. Nature, for Santayana, is the great background of human life, and we should not view it as it appears from the perspective of the human foreground. He saw Dewey as the latest way of making the human foreground to be dominant, whereby nature has only the values it receives from human valuation. To humanize nature as Dewey has done is to misunderstand it. Values do not disclose nature, but rather reveal human interests. A genuine naturalism must not adopt a privileged viewpoint. Dewey's naturalism is "half-hearted and short-winded. It is . . . [a] specious kind of naturalism" (Santayana 1925, 375).

Dewey continued the banter, replying that Santayana's naturalism was "broken-backed," that is, disrupts the continuity of experience by a bifurcation between nature and humanity (Dewey 1984, 74). (Actually Santayana's bifurcation was not between nature and humanity, but between the real and the ideal or, in his later writings, between matter and spirit.)

Three separate issues appear to be involved here. One is the relation of human ideals to material conditions. Is there a bifurcation between ideals and material conditions as Santayana maintained, or is there a basic continuity between them as Dewy held? Later discussion among naturalists has tended to agree with Dewey. A second is the issue of the foreground. Santayana maintained that Dewey focused on the human enterprise, ignoring the immense background of the natural world. Dewey held that he was not denying the reality of this background, but rather focusing attention on the problems of humanity without denying this background (Dewey 1984, 76). At this point it must be noted that there continues a strong interest among many naturalists in the non-human world. This problem of the foreground and background is related to another issue, not made explicit in this exchange. This question is whether the religious orientation is primarily a matter of dedication and striving and whether the object of the religious orientation should be conceived of in those terms. For Dewey, in *A Common Faith*, religion has a moral cast, while Santayana could appreciate a wide range of religious responses, as is born out not only in his *Reason in Religion*, but also in his little jewel on Spinoza (George Santayana, "Ultimate Religion," in Santayana 1936).

The Moral Determinacy of God

A second exchange took place in the *Journal of Religion* in 1943 and 1944 between Henry Nelson Wieman and William Bernhardt. (See Bernhardt 1942, 1959a, 1959b; Wieman 1943a, 1943b, Jan. 1944; see also Shaw 1995, chap. 5.) Marvin Shaw, in *Nature's Grace*, points out that this exchange grew out of correspondence between Bernhardt and Wieman. Shaw suggests that three questions were involved in these exchanges: Is God to be understood primarily as the source of value for humans or as the creative power at work in the entire universe, is God immanent or transcendent, and is God perceived or inferred? (Shaw 1995, 88).

Wieman's best known book refers to God through its title as *The Source of Human Good.* Bernhardt calls this an "Agathonic" view of God (from the Greek *agathos* or "good"). He contrasts it with his own "Dynamic" or "Pure Realism" view of God, so called because *dynamis* or "power," not goodness, is the chief category for understanding God. This debate is cast in terms of what Shaw calls "naturalistic theism," that is, assuming the appropriateness of God-language, the debate concerns the nature of the God. In more recent discussion, this debate is not limited to those who use theistic language. In the section in chapter 5 on power and goodness in the object of the religious orientation, I refer to the axiological ambiguity (Bernhardt) or determinacy (Wieman) of that toward which our religious attitude is directed, whether called God, Nature, or experiences of the sacred, and show that this debate is still very much with us. Charles Milligan, William Dean, Donald Crosby, and Thomas Berry and Brian Swimme would line up with Bernhardt, although not necessarily using the term "God." Charley Hardwick, and myself (until recently) would agree with Wieman, again not necessarily using theistic language. In that section I point out that Sharon Welch has changed her position on this issue, while Karl Peters and Gordon Kaufman have managed to produce a nuanced and balanced view.

The second question Shaw finds in the exchange between Bernhardt and Wieman is whether the divine is immanent within or transcendent over nature. It seems as if this question is settled in favor of immanence for religious naturalists. However, the present writer finds that the concepts of "relative" or "situational and continuing transcendence" point to important questions as we seek to understand our experiences of the sacred within a naturalistic framework. These are issues which I have sought to explore in my writings on "the minimalist model of transcendence." (See Stone 1992, chap. 1.)

The third question in the Bernhardt-Wieman exchange, whether God is inferred or perceived, may seem like scholastic triviality. Actually, from within a naturalistic orientation, it points to an important issue.

For Bernhardt God is the object of inference (at least in philosophy of religion). For Wieman God is perceived, but he labored long in refining his definition that relates the term "God" to perception. This is part of his empirical methodology. If God is defined as the process of integration within human life or as the creative good, then we know what to look for as we perceive. (See *inter alia*, Wieman, 1987, 34.)

My suggestion is that the religious life involves a transaction with or orientation toward events or aspects of the world that can be called "sacred" and for which I use the theoretical term "relative transcendence." These aspects or occasions are perceived, but more important, they are *appreciated*. Perception and evaluation are seldom separated, certainly not within the religious transaction. The use of the term "appreciation" also helps point out that agreement in appreciation is possible, but not necessary, thus avoiding the necessity of agreement among trained observers that is desired in empirical inquiry. Furthermore, it is granted that a tradition, religious or otherwise, may shape appreciation, but to be shaped is not the same as to be determined. The fact that my own appreciation has been shaped by the various faith traditions in which I share or study, by Henry David Thoreau, John Muir, Aldo Leopold, and Delores LaChapelle as well as by Dewey, Ames, Wieman, and Meland, does not mean that I appreciate only what I have been trained to do. Influence and training is not the same as bias or distortion (Stone, 1992, 122).

The Unity of God

In an exchange between John Dewey and Henry Nelson Wieman in *The Christian Century* in 1933 and 1934, the ideas of both thinkers were clarified. (Dewey's *A Common Faith*, which appeared in 1934, was based on the Terry Lectures at Yale given in the same year.) Dewey stressed the plurality of the "factors in experience that generate and support our idea of the good as an end to be striven for," while Wieman stressed their unity.

In *The Christian Century*, Dewey asserted:

> There are in existence conditions and forces which, apart from human desire and intent, bring about enjoyed and enjoyable goods. . . . Does this admitted fact throw any light whatsoever upon the *unity and singleness* of the forces and factors which make for good? (Dewey 1933a, 196, italics mine)

The word "God" is used to designate a multitude of factors and forces that are brought together simply with respect to their coincidence in producing one undesigned effect—the furtherance of good in human life. This is a rejection of Wieman's conception of God, understood by Dewey to be the "hypostatization" of the "experience of things, persons, causes, found to be good and worth cherishing, into a single objective existence, *a* God."

Furthermore, while some people get an added ecstasy from the concentration of emotion that this unification can bring, this emotion gives no added validity to the idea of God as a unified being. Indeed, a life lived without this concept is not only legitimate, but may even be saner for many people.

Those who choose *distribution* of objects of devotion, service and affection rather than hypostatic concentration are wholly within their intellectual and moral rights. . . . For the great majority of persons this is much the saner course to follow. (Dewey 1933a, 196, italics in original)

In his third contribution to the exchange Dewey reiterated his point. Dewey points out that in *A Common Faith* he had referred to "many different natural forces and conditions which generate and sustain our ideal ends. The *unification*" of these forces and conditions in the concept of God "is the work of human imagination and will" (Dewey 1934b, 1551, italics in original).

Wieman emphasized the unity of these forces. This is still within the naturalistic outlook, since God as the unity of these forces is conceived of as within the totality of natural forces. At times Wieman's language stressed this unity. In *The Issues of Life*, published a few years before this exchange with Dewey, he wrote that God "is that *one particular* order of nature, both existent and possible, which includes and mediates the greatest value that is to be achieved" (Wieman, 1930, 164, italics mine). In *The Source of Human Good* he refers to "a single, total event continuously recurrent in human existence" (Wieman 1946, 65). At other times he suggests that this is a complex unity. Bernard Loomer's image of a "web" might suggest the type of unity Wieman is aiming at. "Now then, is that wealth of reality we call God one or many? It is both. From the standpoint of practical efficiency and scientific analysis, it is many. From the standpoint of loving devotion it is one. The same is true of Mr. Jones or my home or anything else." However, the important aspect is the unity. "It is the oneness, not the manyness, of God that is most important. This is so because it is the unity, the organic connectedness, of the conditions which constitute the good" (Wieman 1933, 727).

Dewey made clear that these natural conditions and forces are not objects of love or adoration. These forces can be aided by human effort and they do not demand love or adoration.

The important thing is the fact . . . that certain objective forces, of a great variety of kinds, actually promote human wellbeing, that the efficacy of these forces is increased by human attention to and care for the working of these forces. . . . That which *makes* for good, whether it be singular or collective, demands care, attention, watchfulness. . . . But there is nothing . . . to demand love and adoration. (Dewey 1933b, 395)

The task that Dewey leaves the contemporary religious naturalist is to clarify what is to go in the place of love and adoration, which seem to require a personal object and a submissive attitude. For example, some current religious naturalists speak of a sense of mystery, awe or wonder. Also, the issue of the unity or plurality of the object of the religious orientation needs to be addressed. The present writer is among the most pluralistic of religious naturalists.

The Legitimacy of the Term "God"

Another question at issue in earlier religious naturalism was the debate between religious humanists and what we may call naturalistic theists concerning the legitimacy of belief in God within a naturalistic framework. The following are naturalists who continued to use theistic language: George Burman Foster, Shailer Mathews, Frederick May Eliot, William Bernhardt, Henry Nelson Wieman, Bernard Loomer, and Ralph Wendell Burhoe.

Although G. B. Foster spoke of the death of the supernatural God, at least in his 1909 publication *The Function of Religion in Man's Struggle for Existence*, he continued to use the term "God." One of his key statements is that "the word God is a symbol to designate the universe in its ideal-achieving capacity" (Foster 1909, 109; Peden & Stone 1996, I, 52). For a discussion of Foster's interpreters, see my "The Line between Religious Naturalism and Humanism: G. B. Foster and A. E. Haydon," Stone 1999). His other key statement is that just as we have developed an immanent notion of the soul or mind, so too we can and should develop an analogous immanent notion of God (Foster 1909, 20–22; Peden & Stone 1996, I, 45–46).

Shailer Mathews, Dean of the Divinity School at Chicago, thought theism was an important alternative to humanism. He always thought of himself as standing within the Christian tradition, however much revision it needed. I have always read his definition of God in his later writings as belonging within the naturalistic framework. One version in *Is God Emeritus?* reads: "While the term *God* was assumed to imply a personal existence, *it was in reality an anthropomorphic conception of those personality-producing activities of the universe with which humanity is organically united*" (Mathews 1940, 34; Peden & Stone 1996, I, 152, italics in original; see Mathews 1931). In reading the last essay in his earlier *Contributions of Science to Religion*, there seems to be some ambiguity concerning his naturalism that was later resolved (Shailer Mathews 1924). I suggest this was a transitional writing.

Another theistic naturalist was Frederick May Eliot, Unitarian Pastor in St. Paul and later President of the American Unitarian Association, 1937–1958. In *Towards Belief in God* Eliot equated his belief in God with "belief in the reality and significance of three great experiences," the moral imperative, a rational order behind the mystery, and darkness of life, and the "insight which tells me that I am not an accidental collocation of atoms but that I am a child of the universe and heir to all its glories" (Eliot 1928, 93–94).

There is an important difference between the philosophy of language of Dietrich and Eliot. Dietrich wished to drop God-language as being more honest than the liberal's equivocation. For Eliot religion is found in depths which lie too deep for words, but gestures, including gestures in words, can give expression to them.

When it comes to the term "God," Eliot is quite deliberate. The word "God" is "the simplest and the most familiar of all the symbolic forms by which belief in the purposefulness of the universe can be expressed." Eliot grants that some people are unwilling to use the term "because it has meant such very different things to different people, and they are afraid of being constantly misunderstood" (Eliot 1928, 107). Remember that John Dietrich, the humanist, was preaching across the river in Minneapolis. Eliot thinks the advantages of using the term outweigh the difficulties.

When I use the word "God," writes Eliot, "I am using a symbol for the reality that I believe exists behind the deepest convictions of my own mind and heart," convictions which he has described in terms of "the moral law, the rational nature of the universe, the kinship of my life with the universe, and the element of purposefulness." Furthermore, his conviction is that there is a reality behind these experiences and the term "God" can be used to summarize and symbolize the reality of these convictions and "their authority over my life" (Eliot 1928, 108). Eliot grants that it is possible to find some different word than "God," such as Julian Huxley's phrase "sacred reality." However, there are practical difficulties. "It is obviously cumbersome, and unfamiliar, and awkward. Furthermore, it lacks the connotations which grow up about a word through long use in certain definite circumstances, and for this reason it lacks the emotional quality which a religious symbol needs" (Eliot 1928, 109–110).

Henry Nelson Wieman was probably the most influential theistic naturalist. He was brought to the Divinity School at Chicago to counter the influence of the humanist A. Eustace Haydon. It is quite clear that Wieman, although a religious naturalist, clearly utilized the concept of God, at least until he left the Divinity School. (See Wieman, 1930, chapter VI; Daniel Day Williams, "Wieman as a Christian Theologian," sec. II, in Bretall 1963.)

Bernard Loomer identified God with the "concrete, interconnected totality" of the world as a whole. He explicitly asks: "Why deify this interconnected web of existence by calling it 'God'? Why not simply refer to the world and to the processes of life?" Especially since "God is not an enduring concrete individual with a sustained subjective life, what is gained by this perhaps confusing, semantic identification?" His answer is reminiscent of Eliot.

> In our traditions the term 'God' is the symbol of ultimate values and meanings in all of their dimensions. It connotes an absolute claim on our loyalty. It bespeaks a primacy of trust, and a priority within the ordering of our commitments. It points the direction of a greatness of fulfillment. It signifies a richness of resources for the living of life at its depths. (Bernard Loomer, 1987, 41–42)

Ralph Wendell Burhoe was another theistic naturalist. For Burhoe God was equivalent to the process of evolution, biological, and cultural. The process whereby new species and individuals and new cultural forms were developed was seen as the creativity of God in traditional religious language. Somewhat like Bernhardt, the process whereby species, individuals, and cultural forms were destroyed was seen as the judgment of God in traditional religious language.

The issue as to whether to use the term "God" within a naturalistic framework continues today. Donald Crosby and Karl Peters, for example, stand at opposite sides of this issue. It is significant that Peters draws explicitly upon the resources of both Wieman and Burhoe. For my own comments on the term, see *The Minimalist Vision of Transcendence*, 18–21. I draw on Loomer, but with a greater reticence to use theistic language.

On the topic of God I find that religious naturalists tend to fall into four groups: (1) those who think of God as the totality of the universe considered religiously, (2) those who conceive of God as the creative process within the universe, (3) those who think of God as the sum of human ideals, and (4) those who do not speak of God yet still can be called religious. In the first belong Spinoza, Samuel Alexander, George Burman Foster, Frederick May Eliot, and the later Bernard Loomer. In the second group belong, among others, Shailer Mathews, Henry Nelson Wieman, Ralph Wendell Burhoe, Karl Peters, and also, I would claim, William Dean. Some humanists fall into the third group. The fourth includes Usrula Goodenough, Donald Crosby, Willem Drees, and my-self. The first two groups might be called naturalistic theists, following Marvin Shaw's description of the Chicago naturalists and Karl Peters self-designation (Shaw 1995, 13–31; Peters 2002, vii).

The Nature of Empirical Inquiry in Religion

The final controversy within earlier religious naturalism which we wish to examine concerns the nature of empirical inquiry in religion. The key figures are Wieman and Bernard Meland. Wieman had been Meland's much-respected teacher at Chicago in the late 1920s. Wieman made a powerful impression on several people (Meland 1962, 109–111). He came bringing a sense of the reality and objectivity of God in naturalistic terms but with a sense that God is more than our conceptions of God. Some of the faculty, especially Shailer Mathews, had been inclined toward a "conceptual theism" in which God is our conception of the personality-producing forces in the universe and Wieman's thought challenged the incipient subjectivity of this. (Actually I have always thought that this charge of subjectivity is overblown. I always felt that Mathews stressed "in the universe.") Further, with the Whiteheadean categories of his early days, Wieman brought a metaphysical dimension to the discussion at the Divinity School, which had been dominated by the sociohistori-cal approach of Mathews, G. B. Smith, and Shirley Jackson Case. The irony is that this metaphysical emphasis was later forsaken by Wieman, but taken up at Chicago by Hartshorne, Loomer and, to some extent, by Daniel Day Williams.

When Meland started teaching the two worked together, on *American Philosophies of Religion.* Within a common commitment to what they termed empirical religious naturalism, they began to discover their differences. As Meland put it, they agreed to go their separate ways, Wieman to develop a science of religion focusing on the manageable aspects of experience, Meland on the unmanageable. Meland wrote a number of papers and pages on Wieman, becoming a friendly critic of Wieman's attempt to articulate the depths of faith within a precise and objective language.

Wieman and Meland were colleagues briefly at Chicago in the 1940s. After that, Meland continued to teach Wieman to his students, although Wieman's last books did not loom large in Meland's scholarship. Meland's criticism of Wieman was laregly a one-way street.

For Wieman everyday and scientific empirical inquiry are the standard for religious inquiry. There is only one method of separating truth from falsehood, and religious inquiry is a subset of this method.

He distinguishes four phases of empirical inquiry: (1) the emergence of a hypothesis, (2) the specification of this insight in precise and unambiguous language, (3) the elaboration of observable consequences through tracing the logical implications of the hypothesis, and (4) testing the hypothesis through the observation (or lack) of the predicted consequences. Note the significance of specification for prediction and testing. "Seeking to specify as accurately as possible is what we understand science to be" (Wieman 1987, 34).

On this model of empirical inquiry, once the hypothesis and the observable consequences have been specified, there should be agreement among competent observers. Wieman cites as an instance of the lack of agreement among observers the biblical interpretation of Carnell, Tillich, Barth, and Bultmann. One might expect that Wieman might welcome this as an opportunity for creative interchange. But, there is no creative interchange because, according to Wieman, "there is no agreement on the principles of inquiry nor on what to seek when they seek Christ" (Wieman 1987, 61). It is clear that Wieman demands definitional agreement on the specifics of what is to be observed and observational agreement on what is observed. (For my critique of the naïvité of this type of demand, see Stone 1992, 151–153.)

Meland has an alternative to Wieman's notion of empirical inquiry. Meland calls his approach, following William James, "radical empiricism." A good way to begin understanding this is to examine his concept of appreciative awareness. By this phrase he is trying to denote a way of apprehending fuller aspects of experience than is usually available to our thinking. This way is "holistic and appreciative, aiming at opening one's conscious awareness to the full impact of the concrete occurrence. It is very much like allowing one's visual powers to accommodate themselves to the enveloping darkness until, in their more receptive response . . . one begins to see into the darkness and to detect in it the subtleties of relationships and tendencies which has eluded one" (Meland 1969b, 292).

Rational thought, with its drive toward clarity and precision, is often held up as the ideal of thinking. Meland however points out that much of the world is too complex to fit into our clear and distinct ideas. He does not deny the idea of clarity and precision, but wishes to point to the aspects of experience that overflow their boundaries. A radical empiricism recognizes these complexities instead of restricting its view of the world to a truncated version, manageable but lacking in concrete fullness.

Appreciative awareness is what Meland calls this discernment of the penumbra of complexity and concreteness surrounding the area of luminous clarity. This awareness is not a special faculty. It is the attempt to be more fully aware. It uses emotion, not to lose objectivity, but to perceive more fully, as in the empathetic understanding of a person or culture. The insights thus gained must often be communicated in poetry, images, metaphors and myth rather than in analytic language.

We must be careful to avoid obscurantism here. Meland insists that appreciative awareness needs to be trained, disciplined, and criticized.

Appreciative awareness or sensitive discernment allows us to avoid the dichotomy between the rational and the moral approaches to religion, both of which, in Meland's view, suffer from the attempt to reduce reality to its manageable aspects. Meland's critique of the history of liberal theology is a development of this insight. Here Meland follows Schleiermacher's concern to move beyond the reduction of religion to its rational (orthodoxy and Hegel) and moral (Kant) dimensions. The question today is whether this move can be made within the limits of a naturalistic outlook. I believe that it can.

Appreciative awareness includes a sensitivity to past evaluations and sensitivities in one's culture. Meland calls the network of these valuations a communal structure of experience. At this point, religious naturalism needs to learn to have an appreciative appropriation of the religious heritage of humanity, especially the tradition of one's own community. Santayana, Haydon and Meland began this task, which is why their thinking is so much richer than that of, say, Dietrich or Wieman. Dean, Kaufman and others continue this task to this day. Chapter 4 of my own *The Minimalist Vision of Transcendence*, "A Generous Empiricism," is an attempt to develop Meland's radical empiricism (Stone 1992, 111–168, especially 111–114. For my criticism of Wieman's lack of historical awareness, see 151–155).

Toward a Naturalistic Concept of "Soul" or "Spirit"

At least five early religious naturalists developed a naturalistic conception of "soul," "spirit, or "mind," including Santayana, Foster, John Dewey, Meland, and Burhoe. We could also reflect on Aristotle, Spinoza, Samuel Alexander, J. Christiaan Smuts, C. Lloyd Morgan, and Roy Wood Sellars.

For Santayana *spirit* is one of several key categories developed in his later writings (Santayana 1923, chap. xxvi; Santayana 1942). Its function as the act of awareness or attention serves to anchor his conception of the spiritual life, a conception which has been seen by various interpreters as detached observation (Stroh 1968, 229–230) or comic faith (Levinson 1992, 205–248).

Foster uses a naturalistic concept of *soul* as a fairly common notion to start an analogous concept of God. He gives a brief historical treatment of the concept to illustrate how we got there and then proposes that we likewise develop a nonanimistic concept of God (Foster 1909, 20–22; Peden and Stone 1996, I, 45–46).

Dewey has a concept of *mind* as an emergent, as the product of communication. It is one part of his systematic presentation in *Experience and Nature*. *Soul* seems to be a parallel concept, but more of an afterthought for Dewey (Dewey 1925, 191–225).

For Meland *spirit* is the next emergent level above *mind*. It is a part of emergent thinking, part of the New Vision in science and metaphysics, although the concept is not as central in his later writings. (See Dean 1986; Dean 1988; 1991; Frankenberry 1987; Inbody 1995; Meland 1948, 75–90; Meland 1953, 137, 161–168; Meland 1955, 160–175; Meland 1962, 130–131, 225–227; Stone 1995; and the articles by Dean, Fankenberry and Inbody in Miller 1992.)

For Burhoe *soul* is not as central in his essays as the concept of God, there being only one chapter of his book devoted to it, but the notion is important culturally as providing motivation for living in the face of despair (Burhoe 1981, 113–150).

Finally, we may ask what we can do with these three concepts of mind, spirit, and soul in a naturalistic framework. All three of them can be anchored in an emergent worldview, as Dewey and Meland indicate. They could also be revised in scientific terminology serving cultural functions as Burhoe indicates. Definitely the old animism has to go.

Whether any of these terms can be retrieved will in part be a judgment as to how likely their reinterpretation will be misunderstood as a continuation of older ideas. The concept of *mind* seems most viable. *Spirit* is more problematic, but I think that Meland provides a clue. It may be also that we need a term for our orientation toward ultimate questions of meaning. *Soul* would seem like a good candidate, but it may contain too much of the older animism to be any longer useful. Ours is not a time of total semantic confusion, but any of the old terms must be used gingerly, if at all.

Interlude

Religious Naturalism in Literature

Besides the philosophers, theologians, and scientists that occupy most of this book, we should at least briefly refer to poets and nature writers. (Mention of poets is made elsewhere in this volume in chaps. 2 and 5.)

The poem by Wordsworth, *Lines Composed a Few Miles Above Tintern Abbey,* is close to religious naturalism. It has the well-known passage:

> *And I have felt a presence . . . Of something far more deeply*
>   *interfused,*
> *Whose dwelling is the light of setting suns, And the round ocean,*
>   *and the living air,*
> *And the blue sky, and in the mind of man.* (William
>   Wordsworth, 1947, 308)

Thoreau is a wellspring of resource for religious naturalistic reflection. Besides *Walden,* his exploration of the wild summit of Mount Ktaadn is a vastly different encounter with nature than many people remember from his more famous book (Thoreau 1988). Max Oelschlaeger stresses the importance of this event in Thoreau's development (Oelschlaeger 1991, 133–171). Thoreau's *Journals* are a rich resource, especially volume 4 of 1851–1852 (Thoreau 1992). Also of great value for religious naturalism is the recently published last manuscript of Thoreau on "The Dispersion of Seeds" in which he writes, "I have great faith in a seed. Convince me that you have a seed there, and I am prepared to expect wonders" (Thoreau 1993, iii). One of the most helpful of the books on Thoreau is Laura Dassow Walls, *Seeing New Worlds: Henry David Thoreau and Nineteenth-Century Natural Science* (Walls 1995).

John Muir is also an important source for religious naturalist re-
flection. For helpful studies, see chapter 6 of Oelschlaeger's *The Idea of
Wilderness*, Michael P. Cohen's *The Pathless Way: John Muir and American
Wilderness* and Catherine Albanese's *Nature Religion in America*, pp. 95–105
(Oelschlaeger 1991; Cohen 1984; Albanese 1990).

In the mid-twentieth century D. H. Lawrence moved toward religious naturalism. Recently Delores LaChapelle, herself an important
religious naturalist, has explored Lawrence along these lines in her *D.
H. Lawrence: Future Primitive* (LaChapelle 1996).

One of the clearest expressions of religious naturalism in poetry
is found in the work of Robinson Jeffers. (Helpful studies of Jeffers are
found in Max Oelschlaeger 1991, 245–261; James Karman 1987, 51–129
and Robert Ian Scott 1986.) In "The Double Axe" we find these lines:

> And as to love: love God. He is rock, earth and water, and
> The beast and stars; and the night that contains them.
>   (Jeffers 1977, §45, part II)

This view is part of a view that Jeffers calls "Inhumanism," which
involves "a shifting of emphasis and significance from man to not-man." This
view "provides magnificence for the religious instinct" (Jeffers 1977, xxi).
This view turns toward the beauty of a world that transcends humanity.

The beauty of things is not harnessed to human eyes and the little
active minds:

> It is absolute. It is not for human titillation, though it
>   serves that.
> It is the life of things, and the nature of God
>   (Jeffers 1977, 113).

In "The Answer," a poem which contains some of his most famous
lines, Jeffers proclaims the significance of the universe and the insignificance of humanity if viewed apart from this whole.

> A severed hand is an ugly thing, and man disseered from
>   the earth . . .
> Often appears atrociously ugly. Integrity is wholeness, the
>   greatest beauty is
> Organic wholeness, the wholeness of life and things, the
>   divine beauty of the universe.
> Love that, not man apart from that. (Jeffers 1959, 594)

Gary Snyder's poetry and essays are a rich resource for religious naturalism. The essays "Good, Wild, Sacred" and "Survival and Sacrament" from *The Practice of the Wild* are very significant (Snyder 1990; see also *A Place in Space* [Snyder 1995] and *No Nature: New and Selected Poems* [Snyder 1992]).

One of the clearest expressions of religious naturalism in recent literature is found in Alice Walker's *The Color Purple*. The turning point in the empowerment of Celie, the main character, comes when her friend and lover unfolds her vision of the divine (Walker 1982, 164–168). Through the words of Shug, Walker first demolishes the oppressive male, white God and the suppression of all who buy into it. Then there is an unambiguous declaration that "I believe that God is everything. . . . Everything that is or ever was or ever will be." Immediately there is a strong feeling of identification with everything, especially with the healing power of the natural world. "My first step from the old white man was trees. Then air. Then birds. Then other people. But one day . . . it come to me: that feeling of being part of everything, not separate at all. I knew that if I cut a tree, my arm would bleed" (Walker 1982, 167). Then there is a paean to sensuous joys. Of sexual feeling, "God loves all them feelings. That's some of the best stuff God did. . . . I think it pisses God off if you walk by the color purple in a field somewhere and don't notice it." The language is anthropomorphic here, but the emphasis is on the sacral character of the natural world and its healing power. "Next to any little scrub of a bush in my yard, Mr. _____'s evil sort of shrink. But not altogether. Still, it is like Shug say. You have to git man off your eyeball, before you can see anything a'tall." The defense against the screening of nature by anthropomorphic projections is a tactic of rejection and replacement. "Whenever you trying to pray, and man plop himself on the other end of it, tell him to get lost, say Shug. Conjure up flowers, wind, water, a big rock" (Walker 1982, 167–168).

There are two religious naturalist strains in African American writings. One is an appreciation of the natural world, as represented by Walker. (See Johnson and Bowker 2004; Kimberly Smith 2004, Kimberly Smith 2005, esp. her footnote 3 for further references.) The other is the humanist reaching for justice, which we have discussed earlier.

Max Oelschlaeger's *The Idea of Wilderness* is both an important study of American nature writers (Thoreau, Muir, Leopold, Jeffers, and Snyder) and a history of attitudes toward nature from the Paleolithic to the romantics and gives an overview of recent environmental thinking (Oelschlaeger 1991). J. Ronald Engel's *Sacred Sands* is one of the best histories of people respecting a sacred place, the Indiana Dunes (Engel 1983).

Recently many religious naturalists have been drawing inspiration from the poetry of Mary Oliver. Like Snyder she writes of the particularity and concreteness of the nonhuman world. She writes of learning to love our only world and of wild love for the morning sun ("Starfish" and "The Sun," in Oliver 1992, 113, 50; see also "The Summer Day" and "Morning in a New Land," Oliver 1992, 94, 251).

It is truly difficult to know where to stop in mentioning nature writers. Annie Dillard's *Pilgrim at Tinker Creek* is well known, as are the writings of John Burroughs, Loren Eiseley, Barry Lopez, Diane Ackerman, and Leslie Marmon Silko. This will have to suffice. But it is important to remember that religious naturalism need not be expressed in discursive writing, which is the burden of this book. The Earth Charter should also be mentioned.

As to whether religious attitudes of a naturalistic character can be found in the visual arts or music, I am not clear. There can be a transcendence of the ordinary for both artist and appreciator, but to call this religious might be to stretch the term beyond all usefulness. On the other hand, the transport or mildly ecstatic experience I have when moved by Brahms, Miles Davis, T. S. Eliot, Sophocles, or Cézanne may perhaps aptly be characterized as religious. Paul Tillich pointed out that the work of van Gogh, Picasso's *Guernica*, and the post–World War II German expressionist painters broke up the surface of objects and opened up the depths (for Tillich's treatment of art see J. L. Adams, 1965, 65–115). *Depth* was his favorite metaphor for the power of being that underlies all finite things, and such downward-directed language is helpful in shaping the evocative language which a naturalistic outlook needs to employ at times. Although Tillich said that he was moving beyond both naturalism and supernaturalism, in my judgment his notion of the ground of being or the unconditional also moves beyond the ontological reticence which I consider naturalism to advocate (Tillich, 1957, 5–10). Having said that, I do resonate with his move beyond supernaturalism. This is also why I have felt a kinship with Augustine's neo-Platonism and with Philip Hefner's Lutheran sense of the divine as a *presence* within things.

When I think of religious values within a naturalistic framework in the visual arts, my mind turns to Chinese landscapes and the Hudson River school, Rothko, Georgia O'Keeffe, and Agnes Martin. I also think of the persistent appreciative explorations of one particular place, such as Mount Sainte-Victoire by Cézanne, the Massif Central by Monet, and Prout's Neck by Winslow Homer. And salt marshes by Martin Johnson Heade. A full treatment of this would take us into the history of park design, the varieties of gardening tradition, architecture, and the relation of Pueblo Indian dwellings to their natural context.

Part Two

The Rebirth of
Religious Naturalism

In my reading of the history of religious naturalism, there was a forty-one
year hiatus in major publications in religious naturalism from 1946 to
1987. Henry Nelson Wieman's *The Source of Human Good* was published
in 1946. He left the Divinity School of the University of Chicago the
following year and with this his major role in a graduate center of liberal
Protestant graduate study. *The Source of Human Good* was the last major
writing in religious naturalism until Loomer's "The Size of God" was
presented at the American Academy of Religion in 1978 and 1979 and
then published in 1987 ("Preface" by Larry Axel and William Dean in
Loomer 1987, vii). One exception was the lone appearance of an article
titled "Religious Naturalism" by Wieman (Wieman 1958). One might
look at the public presentation of *The Size of God* as a transition point
and its joint publication as the beginning of the rebirth of religious
naturalism. The following decade saw a fluorescence of religious naturalistic writings.

Wieman continued to teach and write, but his writings, such as
Man's Ultimate Commitment, minimized references to God or the Creative
Event as functionally transcendent (Wieman, 1958). Thus, even though
these later writings are still valuable, especially his analysis of "creative
interchange," his contributions to the stream of writings in explicit religious naturalism came to an end.

The Size of God, together with "S-I-Z-E Is the Measure," formed a
major turning point in Loomer's theology, from a paradigmatic process
theology with God as the supreme exemplar of metaphysical categories
(and thus not within the criteria of religious naturalism as sketched in our

Introduction) to a full-blown naturalistic theism that uses the term "God" to apply to the whole universe in its concrete actuality (Loomer 1974).

What caused the hiatus in religious naturalism in mid-century? One can speculate with a feeling of relative certainty. In philosophical circles there was a loss of interest in philosophic naturalism. In part this was due to the rise of logical positivism and, later, analytic philosophy and its virtual stranglehold over the programs at the more prestigious Eastern Division of the American Philosophical Association. Even when philosophers held naturalistic presuppositions, the times were not conducive to the articulation of comprehensive world views, naturalistic or otherwise, as a serious philosophical task. (See Danto 1967, 450.)

Theologically, liberal Protestant graduate schools became focused on neo-orthodoxy and its American cousins, the Niebuhr brothers and Paul Tillich, and, later on, process theology. Even the University of Chicago's Divinity School, where Wieman had represented an explicit and vocal naturalistic outlook, shifted its focus to process theism with the work of Charles Hartshorne and Daniel D. Williams for a period, and Dean Bernard Loomer. Even Bernard Meland, whose early writings represent a clear expression of religious naturalism, had passed to a more ambiguous form of naturalism by the time he joined Chicago's faculty in 1945 (See Inbody 1995, 25–32).

What led to the rebirth of religious naturalism is harder to discern. In part it was a matter of the expansion of religious studies departments in colleges and universities in the United States as a place for graduate students to get jobs without having to worry about confessional concerns. In part it was a loss of the dominance of the concerns of neo-orthodoxy and companions as setting the agenda for theological thinking. Indeed, the so-called death of God theologies in the late 1960s signified that the foundations of religious thinking had been placed in question.

In addition four specific institutional homes opened their doors to explicit religious naturalistic concerns, historical or constructive.

First was the establishment of the *American Journal of Theology and Philosophy* with its first issue in 1980. Core people around this journal started the Highlands Institute for American Religious and Philosophical Thought (HIARPT) in 1987, which brought together scholars who were sympathetic with naturalistic themes. Religious naturalism was probably always a minority position within HIARPT and the contributors to the *AJTP*, but both were places where religious naturalists could appear publicly and receive valuable criticism. It is significant that both HIARPT and *AJTP* explicitly added "naturalism in American theology and philosophy" to their list of interests.

Second was the foundation of the Institute on Religion in an Age of Science (IRAS) in 1954 and its journal *Zygon: Journal of Religion and Science* in 1966. Starting about 2000 there have been a number of presentations at IRAS conferences at Star Island and articles in *Zygon* that are explicitly religious naturalistic in orientation.

Third, starting about 1990 there was a long-standing program unit in the American Academy of Religion, "Empiricism in American Religious Thought," later "Pragmatism and Empiricism in American Religious Thought." Again there was some occasion for discussion of religious naturalism, although again, religious naturalists were not the dominant figures.

Fourth, Charley Earp, a widely read amateur theologian, started a religious naturalism e-mail discussion group, a venture which helped spin off an IRAS religious naturalism e-mail group.

These four settings helped give religious naturalists a place for public discussion and criticism. As of this writing Rabbi David Oler is exploring being religious without belief in the supernatural and a Unitarian Universalist Religious Naturalist group is being organized.

Our approach shall now change slightly. Analysis will take precedence over the exposition of individuals. Thus a given thinker may now appear in more than one chapter.

Chapter Four

Sources of Religious Insight

In researching this history of religious naturalism, as well as to develop my own practice and reflection, I have discerned six main types of what could be called *data* for religious inquiry or sources of religious insight: experiences of grace (or judgment), imperatives for justice, the natural world, science, religious traditions, and literature.

Experiences of Grace and Obligation

This section will deal with experiences of grace and obligation as sources of religious insight in the writings of recent religious naturalists: Charley Hardwick, William Jones, Sharon Welch, and myself.

Experiences of Grace

JEROME A. STONE. I have elaborated a version of religious naturalism in my *The Minimalist Vision of Transcendence*. Starting with experiences of apparently transcendent resources and imperatives, I have developed a conceptual scheme for understanding these experiences within a naturalistic framework. According to this minimalist model, *the transcendent refers to creative powers and also felt norms that are relatively or situationally transcendent*, that is, transcendent to a specific situation as perceived yet naturalistically conceived as immanent within the world. Within the limits of this naturalistic outlook, the transcendent dimension of powers and norms is understood as a collection of situation transcending creative powers and continually compelling norms. They are "relatively transcendent" to situations within the world yet are within the world as realities and relevant possibilities beyond a situation as perceived. Further, this minimalist model makes a distinction between relatively transcendent resources and relatively transcendent lures or challenges of values, such as the drive for truth, significant aesthetic form, authentic selfhood, and justice, which are never reached but only approximated. Thus they function as continually challenging imperatives. (The influence of Tillich's theology of culture can be seen here; Stone 1992, 77–81; Tillich 1963, 262–265; Tillich 1969, 171–177.)

Although I place a heavy emphasis on the significance of particular experiences, I recognize an interplay between theory and experience. While perceived experience can give rise to and modify theoretical concepts, theory also guides and focuses perception. Thus my conceptual framework concerning relatively transcendent challenging norms and creative powers arises from my experiences and at the same time offers a map for exploring experience further.

First, the relative transcendence of continually challenging norms is illustrated by four types of relatively transcendent challenges: the drives toward truth, beauty, self-hood, and justice. These types furnish paradigms of relative normative transcendence but do not exhaust the variety of the search for values. These relative but continually challenging goals are the naturalistic analogue to the social critique of the Hebrew prophets, the drive toward wisdom for the Confucians, the value of the utopian vision as criticism from Plato onward, and the smashing of idols from Augustine through Luther and Calvin and the radicals of the Protestant Reformation to the hermeneutics of suspicion of Kierkegaard, Marx, Nietzsche, and Freud, and the powerful social and psychological analyses of Henry Nelson Wieman, Reinhold Niebuhr, Paul Tillich, and Langdon Gilkey.

These four types of the drive toward the relative transcendence of continually challenging norms are regulative ideals. The struggles for truth, beauty, selfhood, and justice are toward possibilities relatively transcendent to our present attainments and thus are regulative, not constitutive, ideals. They do not represent a transcendent realm of the already attained or a realm ontologically superior to our present approximations to them. These norms remain continually challenging norms no matter how far we have come in their direction.

Second, the other pole of occasions of relative transcendence are those moments in which we experience creative resources in our environment that are transcendent to our situation as presently perceived. For example, openness to healing or restorative powers of medicine, counseling, or pedagogy means a readiness to receive creative and recreative powers relatively transcendent to our present situation and yet located within the world.

In *The Minimalist Vision of Transcendence* I have given analyses of courage in the face of finitude, courage to act in an opportune moment, and courage as an answer to despair. In this analysis I have stressed that such courage is not merely the result of choice and resolution but often also includes a receptivity to unexpected resources from outside of the perceived situation. Courage may come from the unexpected power of an antidepressant or from the encouraging word of a friend. The occasions of the experience of these situationally transcendent resources are naturalistic analogues to the moments of experiencing gifts of divine empowerment (Stone 1992, 35–37, 106–108).

To summarize, I urge us to be open to norms and resources that are beyond our narrowly perceived present situation yet are not resident in a different realm. The transcendent element in these experiences refers to the continually challenging aspect of these norms that elude definitive attainment and to the situation-transcending aspect of these resources that elude our present perception of the situation in which we find ourselves. These two types of transcendence are naturalistically conceived in that the norms do not reside in a transcendent realm but are imaginatively conceived by humans within history and the resources do not intervene from a supernatural realm, but arise from within this world beyond our situation as perceived. Thus we have this-worldly or relative transcendence.

This element of transcendence is why this can be called a *religious* naturalism. All of the paradigm cases of religions point to a dimension beyond this life as perceived or values as attained. This form of naturalism, while not recognizing any supernatural realm, does maintain an openness to relative transcendence naturalistically conceived. This openness is sufficiently similar to the standard forms of religion that it is legitimate to call this, by analogy, a religious naturalism.

Finally, within the limits of what I call my minimalist approach, no claim is made that these norms or resources are unified. Norms may conflict and resources be in opposition. This is a radically pluralistic naturalism.

Recently I have articulated a simplified version of this minimalism in a theory of the sacred: (1) as a quality of events or processes of overriding importance, (2) not within our control, and (3) to be treated with respect. However, I insist, as a counter to fanaticism and superstition, that the sacred is not to be walled off from questioning, criticism, and rational-empirical inquiry. (For my intellectual autobiography, see Stone 2002b.)

CHARLEY HARDWICK. In *Events of Grace*, Charley Hardwick, Professor of Philosophy and Religious Studies at American University in Washington,

DC, expounds a Christian theology of grace within a naturalism that asserts that only physical entities exist. (Hardwick 1996. My exposition is drawn from my article, Stone 1996b. I have criticisms of Hardwick in this article. This entire issue of the *American Journal of Theology and Philosophy* is devoted to expositions and critiques of Hardwick and his replies.)

Hardwick finds four basic features in naturalism which he urges theologians to affirm: (1) only the world of nature is real, (2) this world requires no sufficient reason beyond itself to account for its origin, (3) nature as a whole is understandable without appeal to any kind of intelligence or purposive agent, and (4) every natural event is itself a product of other natural events (Hardwick 1996, 5–6; adapted from Rem Edwards 1972, 133–141). The implication of these theses are denials: (1) that God is personal, (2) that some form of cosmic teleology is true, and (3) that there is a cosmic conservation of value (Hardwick 1996, 7–8).

Hardwick's physicalism asserts that while nothing exists except mathematical-physical entities, yet nonphysical things, specifically emergent properties, such as consciousness and intention are real, though there are corresponding occurrences at the level of physics. Thus there is explanatory and semantic autonomy among domains other than physics, including theology.

God-language is nonreferential and God cannot be an entity. Yet we can affirm "God exists." This is a meta-assertion, a nonreferential assertion that expresses the theistic valuational stance. Drawing on a tradition including Paul, Luther, and Bultmann, Hardwick sees the heart of the Christian life as God's gift of faith as openness to the future and liberation from inauthentic to authentic existence. This gift is what is expressed in the nonreferential metaassertion that "God exists." This assertion articulates a "seeing-as," specifically, it expresses the gift of openness to the future. The Christian valuational stance is openness to the future, the move from bondage to liberation, transformation from inauthentic to authentic existence. "God" means the giftedness of this move, the fact that this transformation is not of ourselves but comes to us. God language is not required for this transformation, but does provide the best account of it. It is these experiences of transformation or grace that Hardwick calls "Events of Grace."

Experiences of Obligation

SHARON WELCH. Sharon Welch, Provost of Meadville Lombard Theological School, has been reflecting on how to work for social justice under conditions of finitude with limited knowledge about the consequences of our actions and no assurance about their success. In particular, how do people of relative privilege work with people of less privilege and different ideas? Her thinking about the theological dimension of social action falls into two periods.

In both periods the divine is not a separate entity. In her earlier period the divine is a characteristic of relationships or of the capacity or power to enter into right relationships with other people, with nature and with ourselves. "I argue that the divine *is* that relational power, and that it is neither necessary nor liberating to posit a substance or ground that exists outside of relational power. . . . I would argue that grace is not the manifestation of the divine in our lives, the gift of a separate or foundational being; but that grace is all there is or need be of the divine" (Welch 2000, 173–175, italics in original). It is quite clear that this is a theology of radical immanence. There is no separate divine entity. Rather than God-language, she uses "divine" as an adjective to refer to grace or the power of relations.

What then is the function of the divine? I detect at least three threads here. One is that divine refers to the unexpected healing of relationships. Grace is "a power that lifts us to a larger self and a deeper joy as it leads us to accept blame and begin the long process of reparation and re-creation." Grace is "the gift of being loved and loving that enables work for justice. The connotations of grace are many . . . grace is a power or an intensity of relationship that is more than we can predict or produce solely by our own volition." Grace connotes a surplus, a joy of loving and being loved, of amazing changes in the lives of people (Welch 2000, 174). "Divinity, or grace, is the resilient, fragile, healing power of finitude itself" (Welch 2000, 178).

Another function of the divine is as the compassion and anger needed to nurture and protect. This power of compassion and anger is holy (Welch 2000, 173).

A third function of the divine is as a focus of respect, orientation, and worship. "Divinity then connotes a quality of relationships, lives, events, and natural processes that are worthy of worship, that provide orientation, focus, and guidance to our lives" (Welch 2000, 176). "The terms *holy* and *divine* . . . denote the quality of being worthy of honor, love, respect, and affirmation." Innumerable processes and actions are divine, including "work for justice, love, creativity itself, the web of life, joy, and beauty." By calling these divine, "we affirm that these aspects of human existence are worthy of worship." Attentiveness to these "provides energy, focus, and a challenging reorientation of our lives" (Welch 2000, 178–179, italics in original).

In her later writing Welch is even more reticent to use traditional religious language. She is aware of the limits to our knowledge of the consequences of our actions, to the limits of our resources, and to the moral ambiguity of our deeds. She is very aware of how religious people can be cruel and destructive. For her religion's power is in "the collective support of meaning and commitment." This communal solace, joy, and challenge is not unambiguously good.

> Religious experience, while most certainly real and compel-ling, is fundamentally amoral. Belonging to a religious group, feeling connected to other people and to the sacred, can as easily fuel campaigns of genocide and coercion as movements of compassion and social transformation. Slave owners and abolitionists, participants in the Civil Rights movement and members of the Ku Klux Klan, alike drew comfort and chal-lenge from their religious beliefs and their participation in religious communities. (Welch 1999, 127)

She now speaks of the wellspring of moral action as arising from such things as gratitude, joy, mourning, and rage. Acts of persistence, resistance, and transformation spring from a reservoir of vitality and joy in life. They come from gratitude and the affirmation of this life in which there is suffering and moral failure, where we make mistakes and where we love people who will die. This is still an attitude of openness to resources of grace and healing as in her earlier writing, but the religious language is no longer used, even tenuously.

Spirituality has power and value, and yet is fraught with danger. What is needed is an ironic spirituality that recognizes our limits and failures and finds joy in our successes. We need to be ironic and com-mitted, suspicious and celebrative simultaneously (Welch 1999, 128 and 156, n. 25).

WILLIAM JONES. William Jones, Professor of Religion Emeritus and former Director of Black Studies at Florida State University, develops his thinking within the context of Black resistance and liberation in the post–Civil Rights era in America. Specifically he is attempting to open a place for Black humanism by engaging in a polemic against the Black theologians who identify Black religion with Black theism and who see the Black church as the major institutional vehicle for the struggle for Black liberation. (Along the way, Jones develops what he calls a "hu-manocentric theism," to indicate the concern for human issues that he says that Black religion and theology should focus on. It is somewhat akin to much process theology. As I read him, this view is not Jones's own view, but he presents it as a compromise position with which Black theologians should be able to agree. However, some critics have failed to see that this is not the position with which he identifies himself [Jones 1978, 230; Jones 1998, 185–202; Pinn 1995, 17, 111, 145]).

Jones's opening move in his constructive statement of Black humanism is "to formulate a definition of religion that can accommodate humanism" (Jones 1978, 227). He does this by defining the essence of religion as soteriology, and then showing that humanism is a way of salvation. Jones cites Winston King's definition that the purpose of religion is "to convince men that they need salvation and then to offer them a way to achieve it" (Winston King, *Introduction to Religion* 1954, 286).

> Religion, I contend, reduces ultimately to a way of salvation. Its basic purpose is soteriological. . . . In this sense, religion is like the medical enterprise: its activity is always preventive or corrective. That is to say, the raison d'être for religion is the conviction that something is radically wrong with man; something essential to man or his condition must be replaced or supplemented, or special precautions must be taken to prevent the occurrence of the unwanted condition that demands correction. (Jones 1978, 227–228)

The next step in the position elaborated by Jones is to articulate the prescriptive principle of his variety of humanism.

> That principle for me is *the functional ultimacy of man.* This is another way of describing Protagoras's epigram, "Man is the measure of all things," and Kierkegaard's principle of truth as subjectivity. Humanism tends to affirm the functional ultimacy of man relative to values, history, and/or soteriology. (Jones 1978, 230, italics in original)

In 1998 Jones words this as *the functional authority of wo/man.* He further explicates this by saying that "choosing without absolute guides is the given condition of humankind, the inevitable expression of our finitude" (Jones, 1998, 213). I take it that Jones uses the term functional ultimacy as distinct from ontological ultimacy, the liberation of Black people and indeed of all humans functioning as ultimacy (Jones 1998, 243, n.2).

This notion of functional ultimacy, not ontological but ultimate none the less, in William Jones is the reason why I include him within the wide category of religious naturalism. It is clear from the writings of Jones that the condition from which he wishes his humanism to liberate us is economic, social, political, gender, and, above all, racist oppression and that humanism is a call, not merely to announce, but to struggle for liberation from all forms of oppression.

JEROME STONE. The heart of my ethical and social writings is to be found in "The Ethics of Openness," chapter 3 of *The Minimalist Vision of Transcendence*. My earlier thinking here was shaped by my peripheral involvement with the local African-American struggle. After *The Minimalist Vision* there was shift of focus to the environmental struggle, due in part to a shift of residence and teaching responsibility. My environmental writings are treated elsewhere in this study. However, both the Black and the environmental concerns are lifelong, the former since 1967 and latter since 1971.

The drive toward the realization of personal and social ideals lies at one half of the heart of my "minimal model of transcendence," as *the ideal aspect of transcendence*, as distinct from *the real aspect of transcendence*. "The ideal part of the transcendent, defined minimally, is the *set* of all continually challenging ideals *insofar as* they are worthy of pursuit" (Stone 1992, 16, italics in original). In elaborating on this I make four comments: (1) as this is a set or collection, there is a plurality of values with the possibility of conflict between them, (2) they are transcendent insofar as they continually challenge us to new attainment, (3) these ideals may be destructive and are generally ambiguous, their "transcendence" referring only to their constructive aspect, and (4) while some ideals may make us complacent, these ideals are potentially revolutionary. (I would now add "or transformative.") The first comment suggests conflict between values without an eschatological unification. The second represents my attempt to have a minimalist, this-worldly, naturalistic version of ideal transcendence. The third aligns me with Wieman against the later Loomer and Dean paralleling the distinction between the goodness and the power of the ontological absolute (Stone 2004). The fourth indicates my attempt to have a basis for prophetic protest against the norms and values of any culture. My naturalization of ideas from Tillich and Niebuhr is why I have felt a kinship with James Luther Adams since I started reading him seriously in 1996. (For how my notion of continually challenging ideals relates to Charles Hartshorne, Schubert Ogden, Bernard Lonergan, Emerich Coreth, Charles Winquist, and above all Paul Tillich, see Stone 1992, 77–82).

My version of the categorical imperative follows easily, when the need to be critical is added to balance the drive toward openness: "Thus the basic moral principle of this philosophy is that we should be critically open to situationally transcendent resources and committed to challenging ideals. In short, *we should adopt and continually nurture a stance of critical openness and commitment*" (Stone 1992, 83, italics in original). The rest of my moral philosophy is elaboration on this principle.

The first point of elaboration, which is my notion of appreciation, based on Bernard Meland's notion of appreciative or sensitive awareness, is discussed elsewhere (Stone 1992, 112–114). Mention can also be made of William James's essay "On a Certain Blindness in Human Beings" and to Charlene Haddock Seigfried's use of the same (James 1983, 132–149; Siegfried 1996, 222–223).

The second aspect of inner-worldly transcendence, the ideal aspect of transcendence, is expressed in the drive toward concern for the universal community of all beings. This is the naturalistic version of the theocentric drive toward loyalty to the Lord of all being. (In *The Minimalist Vision of Transcendence* I trace the roots of this concept in H. Richard Niebuhr's concept of radical monotheism, especially in the drive toward universal intent in science and democracy and G. H. Mead's concept of the generalized other, Josiah Royce's concept of loyalty to loyalty or to the Beloved Community, and Jonathan Edward's notion of True Virtue as Benevolence to Being in general. When writing that book I had not yet considered Michael Polanyi's notion of science as an attempt to speak with universal intent. See Stone 1992, 87–97.)

Another implication concerns care for others. To act "in accordance with a discernment of worth and openness to ideal transcendence implies not only a willingness to refrain from harming others because of their intrinsic worth as persons, but also a positive degree of respect, defense, care and nurture." This means being "ready to listen, to respect, to accept the other's intrinsic worth as a person and to appraise the other's merit impartially. No specific directives follow from the principle of discernment of worth, but some directions do." We are to be open to the divine, however this-worldly understood. Also we are to care for others in the universal community with a prudent care, since we are not to waste ourselves foolishly. This will be a self-regarding care, for we ourselves are a part of the universal community. Furthermore respect for our own worth protects our weaker brothers and sisters who may be more ready to lay down the burden of responsible selfhood. "It will be a critical care, since it is all too easy to find a false fulfillment in life by abnegating ourselves for another, by following any messiah who calls." Yet "it will be a care which is ready, at the appropriate time, to sacrifice ourselves" (Stone 1992, 98). When I wrote this I had not yet read feminist literature on the issues of care and selfhood. I had been working on the philosophical notion of a right to defend someone else's rights.

The call for a lifestyle of service is rather out of fashion in a consumer-oriented culture. While there are no directives, there is a direction.

There is a sense of humor without self-deprecation, of lightness about one's own importance coupled with a sense of dedication, a balancing of Confucian *yang* with Daoist *yin*. The imperative of this vocation cannot be demonstrated, but it can perhaps be apprehended, especially through historical and living exemplars. It is probably true that this is easier to apprehend when one's basic needs are met. Since first outlining these thoughts the danger of this talk for those who have a weak sense of selfhood has become very insistent to me, but danger is part of the human condition. (For further treatment of this see "Care for Sisters and Brothers" and "The Persuasiveness of a Life of Care" [Stone 1992, 97–99, 104]. For the dangers of this approach, see the powerful and important *Proverbs of Ashes: Violence, Redemptive Suffering, and the Search for What Saves Us* by Rita Nakashima Brock and Rebecca Ann Parker [Boston: Beacon Press, 2001]). It has also become very clear that there can easily be a condescension, an arrogance, to a vocation of service. That this weakness is not just a middle-class White problem can be seen in Alain Locke's criticism of some Black American's note of cultural superiority concerning Africa (Locke 1924, 37–40, cited in Lewis 2000, 120).

Mention of paradigms and the danger of a martyr complex suggest that this vocation of service is a naturalized version, somewhat attenuated, of the *imitatio Christi*. "It is better to recognize the Christian roots of [my formulation of] this imperative, with a touch of irony, rather than mistakenly claim the universal validity of this imperative and the . . . hardheartedness of anyone who refuses to accept it" (Stone 1992, 100). However, the lifestyle of prudent care should have significance to those guided by other paradigms, although the accents may be different. (For a discussion of how this notion of a vocation of service fits in with other ethical traditions and for how it is possible within a naturalistic framework to engage in "an autonomous appropriation of religious traditions," see Stone 1992, 99–104 and the section on "The Hermeneutics of Religious Traditions" in Stone 2003b, 783–800).

An important part of the metaphysical reticence of my naturalism is an insistence on a plurality of values. You can't have your cake and eat it, too, unless you bake two cakes, but then you've used time and energy to bake two cakes rather than do something else. Nor is there an ontological or eschatological realm where all goods can be achieved. There is no Big Rock Candy Mountain. Choices and trade-offs must be made, and priorities set. Liberty and security, maximal employment and control of inflation are different ends. The ideal aspect of transcendence has a regulative and perhaps even an emotional and devotional function, but that is no substitute for sensitive and critical decision making in concrete situations.

Another aspect of my ethics, learned from wrestling with Tillich as well as concrete problems of life, is the necessity to avoid both despair at the enormity of our problems and fanaticism of assuming that we have the answers. The answer is courage, which comes not from deciding to have it, but from an openness to situationally transcendent resources of renewal and to correction (see Stone 1992, 106–108; Paul Tillich 1952). Sharon Welch has some very helpful things to say along these lines. See *A Feminist Ethics of Risk*, Rev. ed. (Minneapolis: Fortress Press, 2000) and *Sweet Dreams in America: Making Ethics and Spirituality Work* (New York: Routledge, 1999).

There are two resources which I have found in my minimalist version of religious naturalism for my struggle for resistance and which may be of help for those struggling for liberation. One is that openness to continually transcendent values is a challenge to the status quo and its ideological justifications. This-worldly orientations often lack a prophetic or critical rejection of the status quo and the notion of openness to the ideal aspect of transcendence is an attempt to correct this. The other is that openness to resources of renewal which are outside of a situation as perceived can be a source of courage in the face of despair and the apathy of discouragement. Besides this an attitude of openness can loosen up the rigidity and seriousness that can infect the struggle for justice.

Nature as a Source of Religious Insight

This section seeks to explore the use of the natural world, including humans, by some recent religious naturalists as a source of two relatively different types of religious insight. Delores LaChapelle, Gary Snyder, and myself find nature as appreciated as a source of religious insight, while Brian Swimme and Thomas Berry, Michael Cavanaugh, Ursula Goodenough, Karl Peters, and Connie Barlow find nature as scientifically studied a source of religious insight. This is a matter of emphasis, since all of these writers have both appreciation and scientific understanding, but the difference of emphasis is clear.

Nature as Appreciated

DELORES LACHAPELLE. Deep ecologist, rock climber, deep powder skier, and recoverer of neolithic, Daoist, and native American earth rituals, Delores LaChapelle is a pioneer in breaking down old ways of thinking.

LaChapelle recognizes the difficulty of defining the term "sacred." As an approximation, her sense of the sacred can be indicated by saying that it involves an awareness of the movements of the many intertwined processes of the world. This awareness is often blocked by a focused attention on a task at hand. It is often experienced in moments of reverie and play and by children. It is a gift or presence and cannot be forced or induced. However, we can place ourselves in a receptive openness to its presence by appropriate rituals, festivals, or the rhythmic movements of Tai Chi.

For her the use of the term "sacred" suggests "profane" as its opposite. However, this often involves a boundary around sacred times, actions, or places that cuts off the sacred character of the ordinary and closes the openness to this character.

One significant aspect of LaChapelle's treatment of the sacred is her discussion of sacred sex. (See "Sacred Sex," chapter 15 of LaChapelle 1988 and her book on D. H. Lawrence, LaChapelle 1996.) Drawing upon both primal traditions and Daoist writings, she speaks of sexual activity (at least ideally) as atunement. It is not the expression of the ego's feelings, but a sharing within the larger context of the world.

Also of significance is LaChapelle's discussion of sacred land. (See "Sacred Land," chapter 13 of LaChapelle 1988 and LaChapelle and Bourque 1985.) Her theory and practice of rituals draws on and leads further to sensitivity to the trans-human world. She especially draws on rituals of North American plains Indians, particularly the Shawnee. Of particular importance is that sensitivity to and healing of this trans-human world is not simply a human accomplishment. Rather, something akin to the Christian idea of grace, the rocks, trees and wetlands enlist us in their process.

GARY SNYDER. The sources of Gary Snyder's religious naturalism can be traced in the events of his life. He grew up in the rural northwest of the United States and worked as a young man in the logging industry. During the period of the Beat writers he was a poet in San Francisco. Several years were spent in Japan as a student of Zen and Chinese poetry. In the past few decades he has been learning with his family to live lightly on the land in the foothills of northern California.

Snyder has always been observant of the nonhuman world. "From a very early age I found myself standing in awe before the natural world. I felt gratitude, wonder, and a sense of protection, especially as I began to see the hills being bulldozed for roads, and the forest of the Pacific Northwest magically float away on logging trucks" (Snyder 1995, 126–127).

He especially pays attention to the traits of a bioregion. Traveling by car, he carefully notes changes in the landscape. Driving in northern

California from Yuba River canyon to Crescent City, he observes transitions through four different bioregions (Snyder 1995, 219–221).

Even for a careful observer like Snyder, it may be years before he observes a certain tree.

> After twenty years of walking right past it on my way to chores in the meadow, I actually paid attention to a certain gnarly canyon live oak one day. Or maybe it was willing to show itself to me. . . . But the years spent working around that oak in that meadow and not really noticing it were not wasted. Knowing names and habits, cutting some brush here, getting firewood there, watching for when the fall mushrooms bulge out are skills that are of themselves delightful and essential. And they also prepare one for suddenly meeting the oak. (Snyder 1995, 263)

In his reflections on primal ways, Snyder has devoted attention to sacred land.

> For people of an old culture. . . . [c]ertain places are perceived to be of high spiritual density because of plant or animal habitat intensities, or associations with legend, or connections with human totemic ancestry, or because of geomorphological anomaly, or some combination of qualities. . . . *Sacred* refers to that which helps take us (not only human beings) out of our little selves into the whole mountains-and-rivers mandala universe. (Snyder 1990, 93–94)

The purpose of such transport is to return to what seems like the ordinary universe and to realize that it is of a piece with these special places and that a revivification of the apparently ordinary is possible. The trick is to listen to the land. It is not we who consecrate it, such as by making wilderness areas. Rather the land teaches us, if we let it.

> There is no rush about calling things sacred. I think we should be patient, and give the land a lot of time to tell us or the people of the future. The cry of a Flicker, the funny urgent chatter of a Gray Squirrel, the acorn whack on a barn roof—are signs enough. (Snyder 1990, 96)

Among the places where Snyder has learned the sacral quality of land are areas in the Australian outback were he was taught by tribal elders, among the Ainu in Japan, Shinto shrines, and American wilderness areas. The radical nature of this attention to the possibility that land might be sacred becomes clear when you think about the difficulty the American judicial system has in recognizing that land could be sacred to our native peoples. Reflection on these matters helps one realize that all of the models of civilization are not automatically acceptable. This does not mean that we should reject all of cililization, even if we could. It does mean that we are to work joyfully and with difficulty toward a new "future primitive."

JEROME STONE. In my environmental writings I stress two points and often a third. First I have a duality of the real and the ideal in my conception of transcendence within this world. Following this I develop a notion of appreciative awareness of the real aspect of transcendence and a notion of the drive of ideal transcendence toward the universal community of all beings. When appropriate I show how these two are enhanced by a third notion, the sacred quality of places.

Openness to the real aspect of transcendence naturalistically conceived "involves receptivity, including at times a disciplined and active awareness, to the creative or divine qualities emerging in a situation. This receptivity to surpassing qualities is a discernment of worth, an appreciative awareness" (Stone 1993b, 199; see also Stone 1992, 111–127). Here I have learned much from Bernard Meland (Meland 1934, 144–157; Meland 1933, 139–149; Meland 1953, chaps. I and VI; Meland 1969, 292; Meland 1988 43, 73). The phrase "discernment of worth" is an attempt to bridge the dichotomy of judgments of fact and judgments of value, with an emphasis on the objective pole so as to counteract the notion that apprcciation is arbitrary or privatc. The term "worth" also suggests that the value overflows its description in language and invites further exploration. Here I am agreeing with Aldo Leopold, J. Baird Callicott, and Eugene Hargrove that we need a land aesthetic (Leopold 1953, 280–295; Callicott 1989, 239–248; Hargrove 1989, 79–94). Here I am also developing a point similar to Karen Warren's "loving perception" and John Rodman's emphasis on the need for a change in perception (Warren 1990, 134–138; Rodman 1983, 167). We need not only both disciplined and spontaneous perceptions, but poems, stories and, as LaChapelle urges, to dance and learn new rituals (LaChapelle 1985, 247–250 and LaChapelle 1988).

Part of my second point is that "an appreciative empiricism and its recognition of the continuing lure of challenging ideals" provides "a general direction toward widening the sphere of moral consideration and toward including groups [species], networks, [eco]systems, and webs of relationships in this sphere. What religious naturalism can also do is to combine the abstraction of 'the community of all being' with a particular affection for very specific ponds, crane marshes, and *Calypso borealis* and draba flowers. . . . We need to bring the thinness of essays on nature back to the thickness of essays on Walden grounded in woodchucks, hoeing beans and thawing sandbanks" (Stone 1993b, 199).

The ideal aspect of inner-worldly transcendence can, with a nod to Jonathan Edwards, Josiah Royce, and H. Richard Niebuhr, be termed "loyalty to the universal community." This loyalty "involves a lifestyle of care for others, of respect, defense, and nurture. It will be an orientation ready . . . to learn from all creatures. . . . This is an open-ended and indefinite responsibility to protect and nurture" (Stone 1993b, 199).

When my audience is not likely to be put off by religious language, I refer also to the sacredness and resacralization of nature (Stone 1998 and 1995). "If we can go to special places, built by humans, which are designated as sacred, surely we can go to special places, shaped naturally, which are recognized as sacred. Indeed, the human and the natural can cooperate, as when tradition or an act of consecration acknowledge[s] the sacred place. There is a strong monotheistic tradition of cutting down the sacred groves. What we need is to realize that to have a sense of sacred place is not tree worship, in the sense of confusing the one Creator with a plant, but is rather the acknowledgment of the awesome, of the overriding and overwhelming" (Stone 1997, 431).

There is an ethical imperative dwelling here. "When the sacred is recognized there is a very strong motive to preserve, even defend it. For this reason the recognition and also the nurture of these experiences have a key place in the recovery of an appreciative stance towards the special places of the world" (Stone 1997, 431).

The danger of idolatry must be recognized. The Nazis sacralized blood and soil. However, this is an abuse of veneration, not a reason to desist from it.

Nature as Object of Scientific Inquiry

This section examines the work of world religions scholar Thomas Berry and physicist Brian Swimme, biotheologian Michael Cavanaugh, biologist Ursula Goodenough, theologian Karl Peters, and writer Connie Barlow, most of whom have been involved, in varying degree, in the discussions of the Institue on Religion in an Age of Science (IRAS). For all six the sciences are crucial in shaping their worldview. All of them depend on the literature of the sciences and Goodenough adds to this her own work in microbiology. It is important to note that the writers in this section devote much attention to topics in what theologians call "theological anthropology" (such as human freedom and our relation to other creatures). This is in part because most of them have been involved in the IRAS community and are readers of *Zygon*, which over the years has drawn attention to the wide variety of the ways in which the methods and findings of the sciences impact our understandings of the world.

We shall frequently employ a fourfold analysis, clarifying, for each writer, the *data* (Which sciences are used?), the *method* (How are they used?), the *principle of coherence* (How is science related to religion, philosophy, or other modes of inquiry?), and the *conclusion* (What do the sciences show us?).

THOMAS BERRY AND BRIAN SWIMME. For Berry and Swimme the *data* are the major results of scientific cosmology, including astrophysics and quantum theory, evolutionary biology, archaeology, and human history.

The first element of their *method* is to recognize that there is an evolving yet relatively consistent scientific picture which shows that the entire universe is a history which can be a narrative and, following this recognition, to articulate this narrative. The second element in their method is to combine precisely worded empirical generalizations with poetic metaphor. An example of such self-conscious use of emotionally charged language is their statement that "instant by instant the universe creates itself as a bonded community" or referring to carbon as the "thinking element" or "the element of life," abandoning univocal for analogical language (Swimme and Berry, 1992, 35–36; see Swimme 1984, 64–66, 77–79).

They achieve *coherence* between religious insights and scientific discoveries by such melding of empirical generalizations and poetic metaphor in a grand narrative. The cosmic scale of this narrative unites us with the mythic stance of primal peoples at the same time that its scientific underpinnings provide a new element in the history of world views and help prevent naïve romanticism. This narrative, cosmic yet inclusive of each person, helps bridge scientific inquiry and religious wisdoms. In fact, this universal creative process is sacred and, if the divine is regarded as transcendent, the universe becomes the primary revelation of the divine.

The *conclusion* of Berry and Swimme is that we can restore, in a contemporary fashion, some degree of the lost intimacy between humans and the rest of the world. This notion is part of their larger conclusion that affirms the interconnectedness, with perhaps varying degrees of relevance and intimacy, of all parts of the universe. This interconnectedness combines with the sense of historical narrative. The grasp of the significance of this irreversible, temporal dimension is a new element in human understanding, even though it has roots in the Abrahamic outlooks. When the threads of interconnectedness and historicity are woven together, what is perhaps the nodal point of their tapestry is created, namely that humans are an integral part of the ongoing universe-process, indeed, that humans are the universe-process become self-conscious. Hence they can say that "the mathematical formulations of the scientists are the way in which the multiform universe deepens its self-understanding" (Swimme and Berry 1992, 40). This sense of interconnectedness, of cosmic narrative, and immersion of humans in the universe process results in an appreciative yet critical transformation of the modern Western outlook, a new understanding able to meet the current ecological crisis. (Berry's *Evening Thoughts* is a brief summary of his ideas with a helpful intellectual biography by Mary Evelyn Tucker; Berry 2006; see also Berry 1988.)

MICHAEL CAVANAUGH. Cavanaugh organizes the data of science along the major lines of Christian theology. These topics are set within the framework of a discussion of the growth of belief systems. For each of these areas his *data* are distilled from a wide ranging literature concerning brain evolution, prehuman evolution, and paleoanthropology.

In his *method* Cavanaugh can be perceived first as striving toward balance and rejecting unbalanced views, not by polemics so much as by introducing alternative views. The balance is between biological, cultural, and individual factors and also between sameness and difference among humans as individuals, humans and primates, and humans and other animals. One might also mention balance between rational and nonrational factors in the development of beliefs and between disposition and separate actions.

A second aspect of Cavanaugh's method is that he systematically works through major topics of Christian theology in the light of scientific research: "free will," God, morality, sin, and salvation, conceived naturalistically as abundant life.

We may illustrate his *conclusions* with the topic of the neurobiology of choice. Evolution has resulted in complex neural pathways with variability and feedback loops. "Freewill" and "choice" are concepts which attempt to point to the complexity of curiosity, the interplay of the analytic and the intuitive, the role of culture in decision making, and the necessity of choosing between conflicting motivations. As judgment and choice evolved, they gained in flexibility. Evolution did not produce a unified organism, but rather a menu of potential behaviors. Thus evolution produces conflicting tendencies within both groups and individuals, for example, the dual drives toward sexual fidelity and promiscuity.

Another significant topic is morality. The evolutionary function of morality is survival, by helping us know what to expect from each other and thus avoiding energy waste and by solidifying the group. Every society has a morality, although the details differ. However, close examination will show that morality is not as relative as first appears. Further, religious bodies have an important role in the cultural evolution of morality. They should stop trying to declare what morality is and start research on what it should be in the light of changing biological and sociological discoveries. For example, are there biological underpinnings of homosexuality? What are the acceptable methods of birth control when exploding populations lead to starvation? Are there biological roots to fidelity and promiscuity, honesty and deceit, altruism and aggression? He is not promoting reductionism, but encouraging scientifically informed discussion so that decisions will be better informed and more credible. Religious bodies have the potential to consider long-range consequences of decisions apart from concern with power and prestige.

For Cavanaugh belief systems can be revised and institutions and individuals have the responsibility to change them in the light of scientific insight and moral sensitivity. God may be conceived as a key concept in the belief system of many people. He asserts that the concept may be retained, given its social and psychological importance. It is important to understand the changes that have occurred in the concept, especially in the Bible and church tradition, areas considered sacrosanct by some. An understanding of these changes will encourage further change. "God" is "a word summarizing our deep psychological experience, including not only love and truth but also patience, joy, peace, and justice" (Cavanaugh 1996, 132).

Ursula Goodenough. Professor of Biology at Washington University and past-president of the American Society of Cell Biology, Ursula Goodenough is the author of a best-selling textbook on genetics. Her major writing as a religious naturalist is *The Sacred Depths of Nature* (Goodenough 1998).

For Goodenough the *data* comprise the existence of the universe as a whole and the fact of our existence within it and also the major steps in the evolution of life and of humans.

Her *method* is a three step process of *scientific inquiry* giving rise to *disciplined deliberation* on her deeply felt responses to it culminating in an *artistically crafted expression* incorporating gems from the world's cultures all wrought in her own poesis. Her method could also be seen as a two-part approach, articulating a response to the universe as a whole and our existence within it, her "covenant with Mystery" and also a rich set of

"Reflections" at the end of each chapter on specific stages in evolution such as the development of enzyme cascades, speciation, or the regulation of gene expression. These reflections are combined with carefully chosen selections from poems, hymns, and meditations from a variety of cultures and religious traditions.

Goodenough has given much thought to *how* science and religion *cohere*. She points out that the religion/science dialogue is often perceived as a venture in theological reconstruction, a cycle of challenge from science and response from the adherents of the faith (Goodenough 2000). Rather than such a reconstruction, she conceives of her task as exploring the religious potential of the scientific understanding of Nature, a task made easier by the emergence in recent decades of a coherent scientific cosmology and account of evolution. Such a task is a poiesis, a making or crafting of religious material. No one person, of course, constructs a religion. But unless individuals "offer contributions, there will be no 'stuff' available to cohere into new religious orientations in future times" (Goodenough 2000b, 562). The collective nature of this project can alleviate our uneasiness in engaging in it.

A viable religious orientation, she claims, will come from the integration of theology and spirituality. Scientific cosmology "is not inherently a proposition that calls for belief. . . . Where the scientific accounts evoke our belief statements, then, is in the realm of our acceptance of their findings and our capacity to walk humbly and with gratitude in their presence. . . . Religiopoiesis, in the end, is centrally engaged in finding ways to tell a story in ways that convey meaning and motivation" (Goodenough 2000b, 565).

Her *conclusion* finds that religions address two basic concerns: "How Things Are and Which Things Matter." These become articulated as a Cosmology and a Morality. "The role of religion is to integrate the Cosmology and the Morality, to render the cosmological narrative so rich and compelling that it elicits our allegiance and our commitment to its emergent moral understandings" (Goodenough 1998, xiv). We need a planetary ethics, a shared cosmology and a shared morality to orient our global projects, to mitigate the fear and greed that presently operate. Her agenda "is to outline the foundations for such a planetary ethic, an ethic that would make no claim to supplant existing traditions but would seek to coexist with them." Such a global tradition needs to start "with a shared world view—a culture-independent, globally accepted consensus as to how things are" (Goodenough 1998, xv–xvi). From her perspective our scientific account of Nature, the Epic of Evolution, is the one story that has the potential to unite us, because it happens to be true. A cosmology works as a religious cosmology only if it resonates, if it makes the listener feel religious. The scientific account of how things are and came to be is likely, at first encounter, to elicit alienation, anomie, and nihilism. She does not articulate the global ethic, but suggests that the scientific account can elicit gratitude and reverence and help us acknowledge an "imperative that life continue" (Goodenough 1998, xvii).

There are two aspects to her religious orientation. First, she affirms that the opportunity to develop personal beliefs in response to ultimate questions, such as "why is there anything at all," is important for humans. Even though her beliefs are naturalistic, she does not dismiss these questions as meaningless nor treat them as simply scientific questions. Her own response is "to articulate a covenant with Mystery." She speaks of responses of gratitude that our planet is "perfect for human habitation" and "astonishingly beautiful" and of reverence in the face of the vast lengths of time, the enormous improbability and the splendid diversity of it all (Goodenough 1998, 167–168). Her naturalism is explicit in her profession that this "complexity and awareness and intent and beauty" plus her ability to apprehend it serve as the source of ultimate meaning and value, requiring no further justification, no Creator (Goodenough 1998, 171). These attitudes she sees as giving rise to action to further the continuance of life, including human life.

Goodenough also has a series of reflections on the religious significance of the stages in evolution. For example, "it was the invention of death, the invention of the germ/soma dichotomy, that made possible the existence of our brains," which can face the prospect of our own death (Goodenough 1998, 149). These reflections include meditation on "assent," on deference toward diversity of species, on the nature of human distinctiveness amidst other species, and the subtle difference between cosmic mystery and a sense of immanence.

Since *The Sacred Depths of Nature*, Goodenough has been exploring several innovative lines of thought. One of these is the concept of *mindful reverence*. In collaboration with philosopher Paul Woodruff, she explores four virtues—courage, fairmindedness, humaneness, and reverence, especially the last (Goodenough and Woodruff 2001; see Woodruff 2001). The virtues are capacities developed in the process of evolution, capacities which can be cultivated. To be mindful as developed here is more than awareness in the classic Buddhist sense, it is scientifically informed consideration. But it is also more than learning scientific facts, it is living in consideration of them. To be mindful of our place in the scheme of things is more than knowledge, it is consideration. The cultivation of such a scientifically informed reverence (capacity for awe and respect) in ourselves and our children is at the heart of religious education for religious naturalists.

Goodenough has also been exploring the metaphor of "horizontal transcendence" to explain her views (Goodenough 2001). The aesthetics of the usual notion of transcendence, "vertical transcendence," involves a striving for order, coherence, beauty, and purpose. The aesthetics of horizontal transcendence is about participation, attunement and delight with the immediate, ongoing, unpredictable. The sacralization of nature requires the location of the sacred not above but within messy contingency. Drawing on Michael Kalton, she suggests that the spirituality of horizontal transcendence requires identification not merely with the nonhuman living, but also with the inanimate, "the massive mysticism of stone," to use Robinson Jeffers's phrase (Kalton 2000, 199). The reward of vertical transcendence is unification with a purposeful Creator. The reward of horizontal transcendence is homecoming. The ethics of vertical transcendence is fitting into an ideal scheme. The ethics of horizontal transcendence is responding appropriately to our situation. "An ethical approach to nature must be anchored both in deep attunement and deep knowledge" (Goodenough 2001, 29). Our children must have a chance to play in the woods and to be taught, with wonder, gratitude, and respect, at their mother's knees that the trees are genetically scripted

Goodenough suggests that as we mature we find it easier to grasp after vertical transcendence. In her usual irenic stance, she affirms that it is possible to have both kinds of transcendence. We can be thrilled with our passion for vertical transcendence, for order, coherence, beauty, and purpose, "not because it represents the highest achievement in our world, but because we are blessed to have it" (Goodenough 2001, 30).

GOODENOUGH AND DEACON. Recently Ursula Goodenough and Terrence Deacon have been attempting to specify the concept of *emergence* in detail and to articulate its religious significance (Goodenough and Deacon 2006). In their shorthand wording, emergence refers to the generation of "something else from nothing but."

While recognizing that some physicists suggest that emergence starts at the subatomic level, Goodenough and Deacon begin their story at the molecular level, beginning with Stuart Kauffman's concept of "autocatalytic cycles," cyclical chemical systems that generate catalysts that produce amplification effects in the process of forming new molecules.

Deacon suggests the formation of hypothetical entities called *autocells* as a stage between autocatalytic cycles and life. Autocells display some of the features of life by means of thermodynamics and morphodynamics alone and result in what he calls *teleodynamics* (Deacon 2006, Goodenough and Deacon 2006). Among the features of life which autocells possess are substrate acquisition, self-replication, natural selection, and end-directedness without, however, having a separate coding mechanism to specify these features. Some autocells develop such a coding mechanism and become semiotic systems and achieve a degree of autonomy from specific configurations of matter and energy. Eventually, with the addition of a metabolism that provides the materials and energy to maintain them in a nonequilibrium state, these entities can be said to be alive.

With life genes encode proteins that fold into shapes that give rise to cell organization and behavior, metabolism and energy transduction, and communication between cells. These are emergent properties, the outcome of thermodynamics, morphodynamics, and teleodynamics. Especially important is the emergence of the *regulation of gene expression* and the subsequent evolution in the temporal pattern of gene expression. New kinds of multicelluler organisms result from using familiar protein families in novel patters of combination.

Skipping rapidly over the development of nervous systems, humans have new traits—symbolic languages, cultural transmission, and an autobiographical self—that are "something else" emergent from "nothing but" ancient protein families displayed in novel patterns and sequences. "Biologically we are just another ape; mentally we are a whole new phylum" (Deacon 1998). Human evolution entails the coevolution of brain, symbolic language, and culture.

The knowledge of the details of this evolution have no impact on our experience as self-aware beings, anymore than our understanding oxytocin affects our experience of romance. One of the beauties of the emergentist approach is that it suggests that our experience does not involve awareness of its underlying processes, which is just what we would expect from an emergent property. The experience of the soul as immaterial is a reflection of the way emergence distances each new level from its underlying details.

Goodenough and Deacon go on to suggest religious *responses* to this perspective. Both are "religious nontheists," which makes them of interest to religious naturalists.

They suggest that the *interpretive response* will be that the universe does not require a Creator. Rather than a Purpose deriving from a Creator, living beings can be understood as following trajectories made possible by the conditions and opportunities of our universe and planet and its ecological processes. They realize this is not for everyone. The idea of a self-creative universe will generate angst and anomie for some, excitement and orientation for others.

Further, the contingency of the processes of the history of the universe will be understood, not as "accidental and fortuitous," but as meaning "dependent" on the context of the previous processes and the opportunities thus generated. Thus evolution is not about randomness, although variation is random. Rather the emergent paths taken are contingent and, in a sense, anticipated.

Humans are understood in exciting new ways. Human consciousness epitomizes the logic of emergence, the creation of something else from nothing but. "To be human is to know what it feels like to be evolution happening" (Deacon 2001).

Goodenough and Deacon suggest that one *spiritual response* to emergentism will be a re-enchantment of the universe whenever we take its continuous coming into being into awareness and a re-enchantment of our lives when we realize that we also are continually transcending ourselves. Another spiritual response will be reverence, a deconstruction of hubris and a recognition that our context is vastly larger and more important than our selves. Further, the emergentist outlook can inspire our stammering gratitude for the creative universe, this astonishing whole to which we owe our lives. Deacon centers his notion of spirituality, much like Goodenough's notion of "horizontal transcendence," on a sense of connectedness with the world. He also refers, like Karl Peters, to an extended self beyond the space and time of our bodies, for the consequences of our lives ramify in all directions through all time. He suggests this as an improvement over the usual self-centered spirituality focusing on saving an immortal soul.

The *moral response* to emergentism will rest on seeing humans, not as distinctive in their moral capacities, but as expanding the prosocial capabilities of primates. Primates, of course, are capable of antisocial behavior, but in this respect also humans demonstrate a continuity with them, particularly when subjected to prolonged stress.

Finally our moral response to an emergent understanding is an expansion of our care past family, troop, and tribe to the entire human species to conserving ecosystems and sustaining biodiversity. Ecomorality flows effortlessly from emergentism, asking for our continuing participation in celebrating and protecting the matrix from which we have been birthed.

KARL PETERS. For Peters the *data* are certain concepts from science: first, those dealing with the twofold creative process of variation and selection in evolution, nonequilibrium thermodynamics, and cosmology and, second, the results of brain research and research from evolutionary psychology, primatology, and clinical psychology dealing with human emotional conflicts and their harmonization.

The approach Peters takes to *coherence* can be illustrated first by his metaphor of the two maps. Peters draws equally from evolutionary biology and some of the world's religious classics, as well as from his struggles to understand and relate constructively to some major losses in his life. His metaphor is that scientific and religious views are like two maps of the same area (like street and subway maps) that coincide in certain features (such as subway stations). Maps can be accurate, but are always partial. He illustrates this idea of two maps of the same area by showing that the traditional biblical terms for the basic twofold evolutionary pattern of variation and selection are Spirit (fluctuation) and Word or Logos (the law that selects some variations for survival) (Peters 2002, 53–58).

The second aspect of his approach to coherence is that insights can be gained from both science and religion that will help give us a sense of meaning and motivation. He develops the concept of a "big self," the cultural, biological, and physical streams of information which, for a time, intersect with our phenomenal selves but which extend long before and after this self. Our participation in the creativity of these streams is a source of responsibility, meaning, and motivation for us (Peters 2002, 68–82). Peters addresses the pervasiveness, indeed, necessity of suffering in life. To live requires eating, which is to kill. And the flourishing of new species sometimes requires the destruction of other species. His understanding is clarified with the help of the philosopher Holmes Rolston III, whose work is grounded on the science of ecology (Peters 2002, 106–112). Peters uses the image of a dance to illustrate how one can find meaning in participation in life without needing an overall *telos*. He points out that this image of the dance is informed by neo-Darwinian evolutionary theory (Peters 2002, 46, 49–50). One of the problems which Peters addresses is the motivation to act for the greater good. Geneticist Richard Dawkins and psychologist Donald Campbell, as well as philosopher-theologian Ralph Burhoc, scnsc thc limits of our biological nature in motivating us in this direction and suggest that additional motivation can come from culture. Peters agrees with Campbell and Burhoe that religion can be a major part of a culture-based motive for altruism. Of course all of this stays within the limits of his science-inspired naturalistic outlook.

Peters draws two major *conclusions* from the sciences. First, running like a thread throughout his thought is his concept of cosmic, biological, historical, and personal creativity as a twofold process of variation and selection which is, of course, an extrapolation of Darwin's idea of natural selection. He also uses Ilya Prigogine's work in nonequilibrium thermodynamics, which shows how random disturbances of certain systems lead to the formation of new structures. Also astrophysicist Eric Chaisson suggests how this dual pattern of chance fluctuation and natural law can be applied to the origin of galaxies. Peters uses this discussion to illustration his contention that the creative process in the universe can be seen as the twofold pattern of variation and selection and that we do not need the concept of a transcendent creator in order to have creativity.

A second major conclusion is the evolutionary basis for the conflict of human emotions with a person. Peters starts with ideas from evolutionary psychologists, summarized by Robert Wright, concerning the adaptive advantage of certain emotions and behaviors. These concepts are brought to the study of humans by placing them in the context of primatology by Franz de Waal and by Richard Wrangham and Dale Peterson. Another line of research, the model of the three part brain developed by Paul MacLean and Victor John is added. The internal dynamics of the model of human personality by family therapist Richard C. Schwartz brings another perspective (Peters 2002, 93–94). The problem of harmonizing these conflicts is addressed by Peters through the idea of "being in self," delineated by the clinical psychologist Richard Schwartz, and the concept of the "core self," developed in the brain research of Antonio Damasio (Peters 2002, 97–99). An important book on naturalist spirituality is his *Spiritual Transformations* (Peters 2008).

CONNIE BARLOW. The topic of Connie Barlow's *Green Space, Green Time* concerns ideas "that might improve the human-to-Earth bond" (Barlow 1997, 11). She explores "the way of science." There are other ways to infuse ecological concern with the vision of the sacred: reform of monotheism, the way of the primal traditions, the way of transcendence (Daoism and Buddhism), and the way of immersion through direct contact with nature. The appeal of each of these paths to eco-religious experience will vary with each individual, but familiarity with the path of science will enrich the journey on each path. Barlow's construal of the way of science draws on the biological sciences, specifically evolutionary biology, conservation biology, ecology, and geophysiology. Other sciences such as quantum physics, chaos theory, or the complexity sciences might be used. Barlow's method in the central four chapters is to report conversations with leading exponents of divergent views in these four branches of biology. We will focus on the first and last chapters, but much of the joy in reading this book comes from the conversations.

Barlow's concern is with meaning, with how an understanding of these four sciences can affect our moods, our commitments, and our sense of our roles on Earth and in the cosmos. Barlow, like Spretnak, strives to avoid the excesses of a postmodernist view. Science may not be able to tell us what it all means, but it is an important base for meaning-making today. The meaning drawn from science by each person who takes this route is constructed, but is not an arbitrary product of the imagination. Despite the subjectivity, meaning-making is not just fabrication. "It is a response to, a declaration of relationship with, Earth and the cosmos." To find meaning in the cosmos is as legitimate as to find beauty in a landscape. People have different responses, but to be fully human is to have some sort of response. "Some interpretations may be more plausible than others. Some may be more useful. Some may provide us with a greater zest for living and acting with commitment" (Barlow 1997, 17–19).

Barlow stresses the openness of science to revision. Of course, this means that we may have to revise our worldviews from time to time. Science does not provide us with an unchanging foundation.

One move which Barlow makes is to suggest that all life forms find the world meaningful. "Meaning emerges with life" (Barlow 1997, 225). In this way meaning is not merely a matter of subjectivity, as both modernist and postmodernist can so easily affirm. So even to find the world meaningless is itself an interpretative act and does not provide an anchor for that assertion. Furthermore, meaning should not be limited to purpose. The universe may not have a purpose, but it is still meaningful.

Those who take the way of science do not usually have explicitly formulated ultimate beliefs, but in the process of writing her book Barlow came to realize that she had a strong commitment to four ultimates. Slightly condensing her words, a credo emerges: "The evolutionary epic is my creation story, and 1) the pageant of life, 2) the diversity of life, 3) the integrity of bioregions, and 4) this self-renewing planet are evolution's great achievement" (Barlow 1997, 236–237).

Barlow stresses that this is a cosmologically based value system. It is derivative of the scientific creation story which she had rendered. This story is not identical with the scientific story, but it attempts to be faithful to it. "The epic that dances in my soul is a retelling of the strictly scientific story" on a par with the mythic narratives that motivate cultures. "It is poetic, awesome, inspiring, accessible to my level of understanding, and deeply meaningful" (Barlow 1997, 237). She recognizes that not everyone who accepts the scientific portrayal of the history of the universe (including Stephen Jay Gould and John Maynard Smith) grounds their value system on this story.

This four-part credo is anchored in four ultimate values: the pageant of life, the diversity of life, bioregionalism, and Gaia. In a clear affirmation of religious naturalism, she declares: the transcendent source of these values is "this self-enriching cosmos" (Barlow 1997, 237). These values function in a way that is analogous to, if not identical with, what we normally call religious. That is, they are sources of overriding trust and gratitude and call forth an overriding responsibility and obligation.

The credo is not intended to generate an interhuman ethics. While the credo is anthropogenic, it is not anthropocentric. Yet to pursue these four ultimate values is not to turn our back on human needs, for ecological health promotes reduction of human-to-human tension.

This credo gives a pluralistic richness which offers a range of approaches to the nuances of specific questions that emerge in the world. "For emotional wholeness as well as practical use in formulating (or justifying) my opinions on a range of environmental issues, I need and want them all" (Barlow 1997, 240). Hopefully future generations of children will be presented with "joyful, science-based cosmologies that nurture green value systems—well before children are exposed to the sadness of human-caused extinction and environmental desecration" (Barlow 1997, 240–241).

Having affirmed the sacredness of the pageant of life, biodiversity, bioregionalism, and Gaia, Barlow puts bite into these credos by applying them to real life issues, the reintroduction of the Mexican gray wolf into the Gila region and to the lamentable but inescapable problem of ecological triage (How shall we apply our limited conservation funds and attention? For whom are we willing to sacrifice some of our wealth and comfort?). The importance of the plurality of her ultimates is especially clear in these sections.

We are painfully aware of our ecological destructiveness, but "low species self-esteem" will not help (Barlow 1997, 213). We need a positive role to play while we lighten our ecological footprint. Underlying a sense of such a role will be a grounding image of our place in the world. She suggests multiple root metaphors for our relation to other beings: community, communion, and conversation (implying spontaneity and mutual creativity). Citing Berry and Swimme, she suggests for our self-image that "We are celebrants of the universe story. . . . We *are* the universe celebrating itself. Here the expanded self and joyful expression merge." It is in humans that life has "roused into awe-struck wonder of immensely diverse ways of being" (Barlow 1997, 271). Gaia awakened and aware is in our flesh. The meaning of life for us meaning-makers is to make meaning.

Some issues confront us. One is that "if you hang your star on a new idea in science, and it turns out not to be true, then you're left without a star" (Barlow 1997, 272, quoting Dick Holland, Harvard professor of geochemistry). So it is a crucial question as to how to find meaning in science, when scientific ideas are subject to revision. Barlow says that we must learn to live "with a book of revelation that comes with the promise of errata sheets" (Barlow 1997, 281). Barlow's answer rests in part on her view that there is a difference between speculative theories and well-established ones and that when an old paradigms dies there is a fresh one, already well developed, ready to take its place.

The second issue was articulated by John Maynard Smith, evolutionary biologist who warns against using science to develop myths, for it could lead to bad science. Drawing on earth system scientist Tyler Volk, Barlow suggests that the story behind all of the stories is "an equal celebration of the universe and celebration of the human mind discovering how to know about the universe" (Barlow 1997, 292). This is a continuing story, happening right now and in the future and we have a responsibility for that future. We are living in the midst of the evolutionary epic and in the story of science. So we need to celebrate, in personal devotion and public ritual, the story of the changing story.

The Hermeneutics of Religious Traditions

A third source of religious insight for some religious naturalists is religious traditions, usually crystallized in written texts, either from the writer's own faith community or else from the world's religions. We shall explore how a number of religious naturalists engage in the hermeneutics of religious traditions: William Dean, Jerome Stone, Willem Drees, Michael Cavanaugh, Karl Peters, Henry Levinson, and Charles Milligan. They are all addressing the question of whether anything of value can be recovered of these traditions from within a naturalistic framework. This concern is one difference, at least of emphasis, between some religious naturalists and many religious humanists. Little previous attention has been paid to this aspect of religious naturalism. Others, such as Gordon Kaufman, could also be treated.

WILLIAM DEAN. William Dean is a developer of a revisionist approach to theology, rooted in the American experience. I count Dean as a religious naturalist because his notion of God as a continually revised social construction seems to place him there, although his recent concern with mystery and "the irony of atheism" probably points to a conceptualization of experience with which many naturalists might not agree. (See Dean 2002, 87–110, 199–202.)

Dean is one of the religious naturalists most acquainted with writings in Biblical interpretation. In my reading Dean uses Scriptural interpretation not only as a source for his ideas but also to strengthen his arguments for some readers by pointing out that his ideas are in line with the Bible, once nearly forgotten dimensions of it are recalled. I find

Dean exploring three themes in Scripture. (See Dean 2002 104–108, 129–134, 161d–165.)

The first theme is historicist. Within the Jewish and Christian scriptures there is a continual revisioning of the God-human relation (Dean 1986, 2–5, 116–117; Dean 1988, 34–42; Dean 2002, 128–132). Dean has a number of Biblical interpreters that he appeals to, but he most frequently refers to the historians of traditions within the biblical text, Gerhard von Rad and Douglas A. Knight and the sociologists of Hebrew history Norman Gottwald and Robin Scroggs. This is part of the historicist approach Dean learned from the Chicago tradition and elsewhere, especially from Shirley Jackson Case and Shailer Mathews. A second theme is the moral ambiguity of God, that God is the source of both good and evil (Dean 1994, 144–145, Dean 2002 161–165). The interpreters that Dean refers to most often for this theme are James Crenshaw and Judith Plaskow. The third theme is God as creator, lord, and perhaps redeemer of the natural world (Dean 1994, 65–67). The interpreters Dean refers to for this third theme are Van Rad and James Santmire. Dean does not stress this theme as much, possibly because it is a less-well-developed theme in his total writing. These themes are often ignored by readers of the Bible but they are central to Dean's outlook.

JEROME STONE. I urge that there is much to be learned from the religious traditions. My terms are "appropriation," "dialogue," "exploration," "transaction," "listening," and "learning" (Stone 1992, 99–103; Stone 1997, 21–27, 421–436; Stone 2003a, 792–798). In my earliest published treatment in *The Minimalist Vision of Transcendence* it would seem to be a minor aspect of the total exposition of my minimalist philosophy of religion. But the entire book is implicitly an exercise in the hermeneutics of retrieval of the Western monotheistic tradition from within a naturalistic framework. The explicit discussion has three foci: (1) world religions as illustrative of the triadic schema (this-worldly transcendence with real and ideal aspects) of the minimalist model of transcendence, (2) Jesus as paradigm of a life of service and care, and (3) how this lifestyle relates to lifestyles advocated by other religious traditions.

I use the notion of an "autonomous appropriation of tradition," and separate the original meaning of a classic and its current significance. This is not looking down a well twenty centuries deep and seeing our own reflection. Rather it is a dialogue between the tradition (as faithfully reconstructed as possible, albeit from our perspective) and our own viewpoint, requiring the autonomy and integrity of our own viewpoint and the challenge of the tradition.

Reflection on religious tradition has long been a philosophical task, since the time of Plato. Friedrich Schelling, Josiah Royce, Paul Ricoeur, and Hans-Georg Gadamer were stimulus for me in developing what I call the hermeneutical task of the philosophy of religion (Stone 1992, 231 notes 30, 34, 35, 37, 40).

In *The Minimalist Vision of Transcendence* I engage in dialogue with Hindu, Buddhist, Confucian, Mohist, West African, and Muslim ethics on an ethics of prudent care. Convergences are found, many going beyond the no-harm principle and speaking of care for the oppressed. There are also differences in historical roots (which need to be examined in order to attain responsible autonomy, because they are not merely husks of an essential kernel), in the degree of universality of moral concern, and whether there is a priority of concern for those close at hand.

In a later article I focus on appropriating indigenous traditions, as a result of teaching African, and native American (Lakota, Dineh, Hopi) ways and a growing interest in retrievals of paganism by some figures in women's spirituality (Stone 1997). A new note in this article concerns the identification and removal of obstacles that prevent appropriating insights from the older ways. This means that the hermeneut-learner has a responsibility to remove unnecessary hindrances to appropriation, perhaps leaving some hindrances as points of divergence. The entire article concerns identifying and removing the obstacles in relation to what are often dismissed as "primitive" religions. The obstacles include using outmoded categories, polytheism, superstition, female and animal deities, and others. Addressing these hindrances includes pointing out the frequent exaggeration of the difference between modern Western and older ways, rethinking the superiority of humans, and to realize that the early ways are not simply prescientific. I also suggest rethinking gender, ritual, embodidness, sacred places, and using multiple images of time. Another new note is that I raise the question of whether appropriation is possible or respectful. My answer is that appropriation will always involve a shift in meaning and that respect is a matter of intention and how it is done.

Recently my language shifts from "appropriation" to the less im-perialistic "exploration" and "learning" (Stone 2003a). I elaborate on four functions that religion could perform in our moral life: challenge, specificity, empowerment, and values beyond morality, such as relating to moral failure (Stone 2003a, 792). When traditions are explored attention should be paid to this complex of functions. I also point out that the hermeneutical task has been undertaken by naturalists, including Spinoza, Santayana, Freud, George Herman Randall, Eustace Haydon, Marvin Shaw, Loyal Rue, and Charley Hardwick My focus in this article is on the polarity of works and grace, or self-power and other-power in the large religions. Four hermeneutical principles are elaborated: (1) more than one tradition should be explored, while trying to avoid dilettantism, (2) the counterpoint of divergences within a tradition is significant, (3) original expression and later elaborations are both important, and (4) the process should eventuate in a dialogue or transaction with the possibility of change in the interpreter (Stone 2003a, 795–796).

WILLEM DREES. Willem Drees, former executive director of the All European Academies of Science, is currently Professor of Religion, Ethics and Encyclopedia of Religion at the University of Leiden in the Netherlands. His view may be summarized in terms of (1) his nonreductive ontological naturalism, (2) his focus on the significance of limit questions, and (3) on the critical appropriation of the wisdom in the variety of religious traditions (Drees 1996, 274).

1. For Drees naturalism is a worldview that takes the natural sciences as its major guide for understanding the world. "Such a naturalism is not formally implied by the sciences, since other logically coherent constructions may be possible, but it is a view of the world that stays as close as possible to mainstream consolidated science" (Drees 1998, 619). Science is, of course, fallible. "Nonetheless, consolidated science is the most reliable source of insights available" (Drees, 2000, 854).

This naturalism rests on certain assumptions. (a) "The natural world is the whole of reality that we know of and interact with." There is "no supernatural or spiritual realm distinct from the natural world" that "shows up *within* our natural world, not even in the mental life of humans." (b) "Our natural world is a unity in the sense that all entities are made up of the same constituents." (c) "Physics offers us the best available description of these constituents and thus of the natural world" at its most basic and detailed level of analysis." (d) Nevertheless, "the description and explanation of phenomena may require concepts which do not belong to the vocabulary of fundamental physics, especially if such phenomena involve complex arrangements of constituent particles or extensive interactions with a specific environment" (Drees 1996, 12, 14, 16). Money exists only as paper, metals, or electronic signals. Yet it is not practicable to deal with economic processes in terms of the physics of money. Music exists as embodied patterns and processes in discs and instruments, but to study music you need not study physics. Pain as studied in physiological, but that does not mean that the pain is not real (Drees 1997, 530–531).

This is a naturalism which does not seek to degrade humans. A naturalist view does not mean that we devalue humans, but that we upgrade our view of reality. "This seems to be lost sight of by opponents of a naturalist view who fear that human dignity would be lost. It is also neglected by some ardent supporters of a naturalist view, who claim that the loss of human dignity is a fact" (Drees 1996, 249).

This also means that religion and science are not partners in the intellectual quest. The religion and science project is not symmetrical, as is often assumed by people trying to build bridges or trace parallels between the two. Rather our religious views of the world must be consistent with the sciences, at least with consolidated science, not vice versa (Drees 2000, 854).

2. Limit-questions are crucial in his naturalism. These questions are raised by human reflection but cannot be answered by science. "These are questions regarding the universe as a whole and regarding the most fundamental constituents of, or structures in reality." These questions include "the question of existence ('Why is there something rather than nothing?') and of structure ('Why this structure rather than another one, or none at all?')" (Drees 1996, 267).

For Drees naturalism does not dismiss these limit-questions as meaningless, nor does it imply one particular answer to such questions. Further, Drees hints a function to these questions. "The persistence of questions, even if one accepts a naturalist view informed by the natural sciences, may lead some to a sense of gratitude and wonder about the existence of our world" (Drees 1996, 271). One of the values of religious traditions is in nurturing these questions. "Even though earlier answers have lost their credibility and questions may have changed their appearance, humans can still be wondering persons, contemplating questions that transcend our current answers. Religious traditions offer answers to such questions, but—more importantly, in my view—they are thereby also ways of posing such questions, and thus ways of nourishing sensitivity to such questions." Maintaining a "speculative openness" is one function of limit-questions. Another is that of relativizing the particular religious traditions (Drees, 1996, 280).

For Drees naturalism does not rule out theism of a certain kind, a somewhat different definition of naturalism than employed in this book. "Religious views of reality which do not assume that a transcendent realm shows up *within* the natural world, but which understand the *natural world as a whole* as a creation which is dependent upon a transcendent creator . . . are consistent with the naturalism articulated here" (Drees 1996, 18). He suggests that such theistic assertions could be made by using a distinction between primary and secondary causes or by distinguishing between temporal processes within the world and timeless dependence of the world on God. "The divine can be identified with the prime cause or ground of the web of natural causes" (Drees 1997, 526).

3. The evolutionary naturalist view of religion, while denying reference to one or more transcendent realities, stresses the functional role of religious traditions (Drees 1996, 250–251). The functions of religion include helping us cope with things we do not understand or control. In addition there is the prophetic function of challenging unjust situations (Drees 2002, 51). Seen from an evolutionary perspective, humans have been endowed with the ability of imagination, of rethinking our situation from a different angle. This gives rise to the regulative ideal of an impartial view transcending all our perspectival views. "That such a point of view is inaccessible is beneficial because this protects us from fanaticism. . . . When considered in relation to the radical concept of divine transcendence, all regulative ideals as they arise in particular religious traditions are relativized" (Drees, 1997, 539–540).

Religious traditions are complex entities evoking a way of life, that is, a conception of moral and spiritual good life oriented by an ultimate ideal plus forms of worship and certain claims about historical events, ultimate destiny, or authoritative commandments which are supposed to justify the way of life (Drees 1996, 276–277).

Just as we have a native language and belong to an ethnic group, but consider other languages to be adequate and beautiful and other people worthy of interest, so Drees acknowledges his rootage in a liberal Protestant form of Christianity influenced by the European Enlightenment at the same time granting other traditions initial respect.

He has found much of value in this tradition, "in most of its parables and in some of its hymns, in a few of its representatives and in many articulations of ideals of justice nourished by it" (Drees 1996, 277). A part of the liberal Protestant tradition that Drees cherishes is an appropriation of Jesus. Drees uses the phrase, the faith *of* Jesus not *in* Jesus (Drees 2002, 91). Jesus is in part a prophet. Here he cites the Parable of the Good Samaritan, stressing the succor of the Samaritan despite the ethnic conflict (Drees 2002, 53). Jesus also is a person who extends an invitation to the outcast, stressing solidarity with the poor and the weak, the inclusion of strangers, love of the enemy, and forgiving those who persecuted him (Drees 2002, 91). Thus Jesus performed a dual role of fostering both protest and solidarity (Drees 2002, 88, 91). Other favorite aspects of the tradition for Drees include the Ten Commandments and the prophets protesting against injustice (Drees 1997, 537).

The variety of religious traditions should be cherished by naturalism. The longevity of some religious traditions, especially when seen from an evolutionary perspective focusing on their functions, "implies that surviving traditions embody well-winnowed practical wisdom that deserves attention, though . . . not necessarily uncritical allegiance" (Drees 1997, 537). However, no tradition is beyond critical scrutiny or development. Reasons for rejecting or modifying elements of a tradition include: (a) changing circumstances, including population growth, our increased power over the environment, and the global scope of confrontation; (b) changing moral and spiritual sensitivity ("for example with respect to conflicts between ethnic or religious groups, slavery, or cruelty to animals," and relations between men and women); and (c) changes in the cognitive credibility of parts of a tradition (Drees, 1996, 278; Drees 1997, 538).

Religious traditions, even if modified, should be kept alive. "They are useful and powerful, not only for unreflective moments and persons, but also for reflective and well informed persons." We are not merely rational beings. Much religious metaphor and ritual help us address reality "in a way which confronts us with ideals . . . or an ultimate comforting presence" (Drees, 1996, 278–279).

In addition there is much in the religious traditions by way of "stories, poetry, gestures, examples and songs" that cannot be replaced by explicit and univocal statements without losing much (Drees 2002, 90). Likewise myths have "the power to evoke emotions and attitudes, the power to trigger us into action." Myths are not literal descriptions of what happened. As with all aspects of religious traditions, we have to take responsibility for our use of myths, analyzing them and investigating whether what they evoke is for good or for evil (Drees 2002, 76).

Religious traditions reflect on our individual and social behavior in a way that promotes "a quietistic acceptance or an activist rejection of social inequalities" (Drees 1996, 282). In either fashion they give us a sense of transcendence with respect to our present situation.

Another way to say this is to suggest that "evolution has endowed us with the capacity for imagination, for reconsidering our situation from a different perspective. This capacity has as its limit the regulative ideal of an impartial view transcending all our perspectival views" protecting us from fanaticism. The concept of divine transcendence relativises all the regulative ideals of the particular religious traditions. This parallels the role of "the capacity for moral deliberation and for epistemologically more advanced forms of testing beliefs" (Drees 1996, 282).

One implication of the critical appreciation of religious traditions by Drees is his view of theology. Theology is not knowledge of God nor the study of religions as human phenomena. Theologies are "interpretations of existence with the help of particular religious heritages," interpretations in "which normative and factual elements are combined" (Drees 2002, 59).

Another consequence of Drees's appreciation of the wisdom and power of religious traditions is that he rejects a view which would set up naturalism as an alternative to the diversity of traditions. That is, there should be no new religion of naturalism (Drees 1997, 537).

Drees suggests that religious naturalism itself needs to become a tradition, a way of life, though not a new religion: "If *religious* naturalism is to be viable, it will have to become a *thick* naturalism, like a culture with all the idiosyncratic elements that make for a rich life, allowing for a decent amount of coping with the vicissitudes of life, with stories that support values and motivate humans" (Drees 2000, 855, italics in original). In his own sketch of the tradition of religious naturalism Drees refers to Spinoza, Santayana, Dewey, Kaplan Wieman, and Burhoe. Drees is clear that there are varieties of dialects in this tradition, from the sober and analytical to the ecstatic and evocative, from poetry to systematic elaborations, from viewing the object of religious orientation as morally ambivalent to seeing this object as primarily valuational.

For Drees the two approaches to religion, reflection on limit questions about the world as a whole and the critical appropriation of particular religious traditions, complement each other and can be brought together in a larger worldview (Drees 1997, 539). The cosmological approach focusing on limit questions is at home with "a mystical form of religion," issuing in gratitude and wonder centering on "a sense of unity and belonging" and dependence on something that surpasses our world. The functional approach offers opportunity for a prophetic form of religion contrasting what is and what is believed ought to be.

MICHAEL CAVANAUGH. Michael Cavanaugh, past president of the Institute on Religion in an Age of Science and a lawyer by profession, is one of the most creative amateur theologians of our age. His *Biotheology* is a rethinking of Christian beliefs in the light of recent studies in evolutionary theory, primatology, and brain research. Cavanaugh develops a theory of Scripture. A glance at his bibliography under "Biblical References" indicates a wide acquaintance with the Bible (Cavanaugh 1996, 287). His definition of scripture is that it is *"any set of writings embodying the main concepts of a culture's theological imagination, distilled over time"* (Cavanaugh 1996, 79, italics in original). Note that this definition prescinds from issues of validity and divine origin, hence allowing an exploration of one or more scriptures from a naturalistic perspective. As a function of culture, scripture can serve both the normal conservative tendency of culture and yet also help to institutionalize new ideas. While it can "thwart innovation," its "brilliant prophetic passages can also inflame the imagination to forcefully overcome culture's lethargy" (Cavanaugh 1996, 81).

Cavanaugh's views of Scripture apply to scriptures of any tradition, although his focus is on the Bible. For him the Bible is an excellent repository of truth about human nature and valid moral recommendations mixed with other material. Hence he provides a categorization of biblical material using biological science as the touchstone. These four types are: "a) Innate behaviors codified by scripture into cultural universals, which arise out of our biological commonality; b) Scriptural concepts that are biologically based but variable within the human population; c) Culturally relative scripture; and d) Errors in scripture" (Cavanaugh 1996, 82). Placement of specific items of scripture within these categories has varying degrees of probability. Prohibition against murder clearly and against incest probably fall within the first. The frequency of adultery suggests that the prohibition here may not fall within the first type. The fact that alcoholism and other tendencies may be a matter of genetic variability illustrates that prohibitions against these tendencies may call for variability in application. Rules permitting the ill-treatment of women illustrate the third category. The recognition that there are likely to be cultural variables within any scripture frees us to apply scripture appropriately. Cavanaugh's cultural conservatism is expressed at this point of seeming radicalism, suggesting that we should honor scripture as a record of past understanding and continue to accept most scripture as valid. We should "listen carefully to priestly voices supporting tradition, and also to prophetic voices trying to make a case for cultural relativity" (Cavanaugh 1996, 83). As for the fourth type, errors in Scripture, Cavanaugh suggests that they are more likely to occur in matters of science rather than personal morality, since our ability to measure and observe has changed since scripture was written, while our human nature has not changed much. However, scripture may also contain errors in morality, such as its permitting racism and slavery and perhaps war. We definitely need to recognize that people will apply this four-way categorization in different ways, some placing abortion in the first, others in the third. Above all it is clear that scripture is to be carefully evaluated in the light of scientific, especially evolutionary and genetic, understanding.

Cavanaugh is quite clear that the concepts and imperatives in any scripture can become fossilized. Writing can "freeze" an idea. The idolatry of concepts is the pathological possibility of scripture. The way to guard against this pathology is to be ready to modify our concepts. We should do this without cynicism, for scripture contains much truth.

This task is possible because the drive to modify concepts has a biological basis in humans. Further we can trace the development of ideas within scripture itself.

KARL PETERS. The key hermeneutical concept of Peters is his notion that the scientific and religious views are like two maps of the same area (like a street and a subway map) that coincide in certain features (such as subway stations). He illustrates this by showing that the traditional Biblical terms for the twofold creative pattern of variation and selection are Spirit and Word. Spirit corresponds to the scientific term "fluctuation," drawn from nonequilibrium thermodynamics and Word or Logos corresponds to the law that selects some variations for survival (Peters 2002, 53–58).

From an overall point of view the main task of Peters is the hermeneutical one of relating religious and scientific worldviews. From a more detailed viewpoint, references to the Bible and to classic texts in the world religions are scattered throughout his *Dancing with the Sacred.* The biblical texts are drawn mostly from the Christian writings, especially the synoptic gospels. His use of these texts seems partly generative of insights, partly illustrative of insights developed independently of the texts. This is not a criticism, given the creativity of his over all approach. See especially his use of the end of Mark's Gospel (Peters 2002, 117–118).

His use of texts from Hinduism, Buddhism, and Daoism is similar to that of his use of Biblical material. The texts used would be familiar to a student of world religions. Like the use of Biblical material, it is difficult to separate his use of the texts to generate ideas and to illustrate them. What is important is that no religious tradition is privileged. The predominance of material from the Bible is appropriate given his roots in the Western tradition and the probable background of most readers. Peters also uses material from Thomas à Kempis and Thich Nhat Hanh. He also uses poetry (used as hymns in his faith community) and excerpts from Nikos Kazantzakis as illustrations of his reflections.

HENRY LEVINSON. Professor of Philosophy at the University of North Carolina at Greensboro and writer of works on William James and George Santayana, Henry Levinson has been developing what he calls a "festive naturalism" or a "festive American Jewish naturalism." This naturalism will "involve accepting suffering, absurdity, evil, and death for what they are, and doing what we can to block or alleviate them. It will include finding—and perhaps being surprised by—joy in the precious light of day and in the restorative calm of night on this magnificent earth, and in the love of family and friends and in our responsibility to greater communities" (Levinson 2001, 10).

The center of his Festive Jewish American Naturalism he describes as a "deep concern for establishing conditions of joy and responsibility," while idolatrous concern for "existential authenticity, theological worship, or hegemonic stories about the one and only meaning of history or the one and only purpose of existence" give him "the heebeegeebees [*sic*], for the fanaticisms they can muster, and the giggles, for the sick jokes they can provide" (Levinson 2004, 38).

The humor here, the serious with a sense of pathos, is characteristic not only of Levinson the man but also is of a piece with his sense of festivity. The "comic," for Levinson,

> takes joy as seriously as it does meanness. Comedy, as I under-stand it, doesn't blink when it encounters suffering, absurdity, and evil. To the contrary, it insists on highlighting them. But it doesn't lend these things any romantic grandeur. Instead, it finds ways to celebrate "passing joys and victories in the world." Rather than revealing, or pretending to reveal, ways to triumph *over* finitude in some fantasy world of transcendent and eternal bliss, comic vision makes suffering, absurdity, and evil mean and tries to find festive ways to cope with them, ways geared to foster "more joyful life in a lasting world." (Levinson 2004, 40)

At the heart of this festive naturalism is the effort "to celebrate joy without transcendence, responsibility without theology or existentialism, science without scientism, coherence and clarity without essentialism, inquiry without foundationalism, reason without representationalism, chance without chaos, sufficiency without certainty and, all the way up through wit's end, the love of life in the consciousness of impotence" (Levinson 2004, 39). This means that Levinson will not attempt to pro-vide arguments to persuade people of his viewpoint, the standard move in philosophy. "The very ideas of *persuading* somebody to become Jewish American like me, much less *showing why and how* everybody ought to pledge my allegiances, are howlers. They are veritable pieces of obscene humor" (Levinson 2004, 39).

On the other hand, this viewpoint is not an emotive commitment that stands apart from criticism. Levinson is willing to be self-critical. He says that his beliefs are subject to modification and change. "When beliefs and desires go *italics* it is time to say kaddish because they have died. That is the occasion either, honorably, to bury them or, more hopefully, to try resurrecting them through some strong misreading or other" (Levinson 2004, 40).

Agreeing with Santayana, Levinson holds that religions are among the institutions that gather light, provide forms of companionship, and give disciplines, "meditative, morally interrogatory, prayerful, humorous," for solitude. Religious naturalists love what good life there is and seek to protect and enlarge it. And their sense of what makes life worth living "is very much derived from our religious traditions in their diversity" (Levinson 2001, 6).

Levinson nourishes his festive naturalism by playing off two traditions or "libraries," the Library of the Varieties of Jewish Experience and the Library of America (Levinson 2001). The latter centers in James and especially Santayana, but also includes Richard Rorty, Cornel West, and Richard Bernstein (see Levinson 2004, 33–39). Among other ideas in the American library Levinson draws on the theme of aesthetic spirituality in Jonathan Edwards, Emerson, and William James noted by William Clebsch (Clebsch 1972). In this theme beauty is to duty as grace is to law. But for our purposes here we will focus on his reading of the Library of Jewish Experience (Levinson 2001, 46–10).

At the core of this tradition are the Biblical Law, Prophets, Wisdom and Talmud which Levinson reads as writings, in order, about creativity, revelating (or revealing), redeeming, and critical reconstruction. The creation stories include not only the cosmological creation, but the entire narrative of social, ethical and cultural creation in the Pentateuch, creation of life-enhancement against life-diminishment. The prophets are about revelation as praxis, the skills to resist idolatry, oppression, to create or embrace the conditions of joy and responsibility, the know-how to live in this particular world in ways that make life worth living. Redemption is not an eschatological transformation as the Christian tradition often sees it, but is wisdom, a process of sagacity, of living wisely in the concrete particularities of this world. It is important for Levinson that the order of the Hebrew scriptures (*Tanakh*), is *Torah, Prophets, Wisdom Literature*, thus not a prequel to the presumptively new as the Christian order of *Torah, Wisdom Literature, Prophets*, would have it. "After Job, *Tanakh* barely mentions God save in—or as—history. It undercuts the out-of-this world kind of flight that informs a lot of *Prophets*. Indeed, it ends with a soft and comic landing, a landing that takes joy as seriously as meanness and disrobes suffering, absurdity and evil of any glory" (Levinson 2004, 41). Finally the Rabbinic tradition, far from settling anything, creates a culture of canonized controversy where majority opinions always come with minority opinions, and where opinions are always open to reconsideration. In this discourse consensus and getting things right are not goals and creeds and dogmas are not aimed at.

Levinson focuses his reading of the Jewish tradition by exploring three early twentieth-century colleagues at the Jewish Theological Seminary: Mordecai Kaplan, Solomon Schechter, and Louis Ginzberg. The first point that Levinson derives from Kaplan is "predicate theology." Where traditional Jewish language spoke of God as just, merciful and forgiving, Kaplan's reconstruction is that justice, mercy and forgiveness are divine. This affirmation that human dispositions and actions are divine forms a bridge to Kaplan's religious naturalism. Levinson also derives from Kaplan the idea of *sancta*, the objects, persons, places, and events that are deemed sacred by Jews. In religious naturalism these sancta are memes or vehicles of cultural memory.

From Schechter's *Aspects of Rabbinic Theology* Levinson first notes a parallel to the American tradition of aesthetic spirituality in Schechter's notion that better than good is good that is beautiful or lovely and lovable. Levinson finds three clusters of ideas in Schechter that are beautiful and lovely and thus divine, creative, revelatory and redemptive traits, practices and institutions. First is "creativity, or life-affirming conduct." Second is moral education, learning to do Mitzvoth, and doing it delightedly, "making compassionate government; becoming considerate citizens; giving work to those who need it, especially the poor, and paying them justly for it; giving voluntary charitable support, at best anonymously, to those whose recompense falls short of sustaining a life of dignity." Third, the redemptive cluster includes "penitence, forgiveness, reconciliation, mercy, graciousness, gratitude," and other acts of loving kindness and mending or salving human faults or wounds (Levinson 2001, 8–9).

Ginzberg's *The Legends of the Jews* is a seven-volume presentation of multilayered and richly textured stories. Concentrating on the stories about Job, Levinson finds Ginzberg giving us accounts of chastened thanksgiving, of loving life in the face of impotence.

Finally Levinson turns, with the help of Richard Bernstein, to a reading of two recent Jewish thinkers. For Sigmund Freud the contribution of Jewish culture is its resistance to idolatry and its devotion to truth and justice. Hannah Arendt sees individuality and thoughtfulness as the characteristics of being human.

Emmanuel Goldsmith has suggested that writings of other Jewish naturalists include Roland Gittelsohn, *Man's Best Hope*; Eugene Kohn, *Religious Humanism*, and Harold Schulweis, *Evil and the Morality of God*.

The Hermeneutics of Culture

A fifth source of religious insight in religious naturalism is the interpretation of culture. We shall explore the work of William Dean and Charles Milligan.

WILLIAM DEAN. According to Dean the creation and appreciation of jazz, football, and the movies manifest America's spiritual culture. A spiritual culture is a vision of the world which orients the impulses of a people. Such a vision may be unconscious, noncognitive and emotional and it need not be explicitly religious (Dean 2002, 20). Jazz, football, and the movies are American creations and they are what many Americans devote much of what little free time they have to. Thus they are reflections of American spiritual culture.

Jazz reflects American appreciation for improvisation. For Dean the immigrant experience in America is that of leaving tradition behind and facing the necessity of improvizing a new culture, of creating new meaning (Dean 2002, 123–126.) For Dean this concern to improvize new meanings was aided by a strand within the Western religious tradition rooted in the Hebrew scriptures. This strand, which Dean terms the Hebraist approach, as distinct from the Hellenist, finds God creatively at work doing new things and attempts to respond appropriately and creatively. This experience was intensified in African American religion, the cradle of jazz. For the Hebraist the past is valued for the inspiration and materials it can provide for the present task. For the Hellenist the past is to be preserved for its normative importance (Dean 2002, 128–134). Dean traces the Hellenist approach from Eusebius and Augustine to Tillich. He finds the Hebraist approach in the Puritans, Hegel, the "sociohistorical" school of the Chicago school of theology, Gordon Kaufman, and others, including himself (Dean 2002, 134–143).

Football, in this view, helps fans relate to their ambivalent negotiation with violence. A football game is about the conquest and defense of territory, summing up the American experience of wresting land from nature and Indians perceived as wild and savage. Dean gives depth to this treatment by an analysis of the reflections of Abraham Lincoln and Richard Nixon on the pervasiveness of violence in the world and on the necessity for violence in struggling with the forces of evil (Dean 2002, 154–161). Dean points out that the implication of God in violence can be seen in several biblical passages in both testaments and that the recent theologians Paul Tillich and Bernard Loomer have reflected further on the moral ambiguity of God (Dean 2002, 162–167).

Movies, according to Dean, represent the desire for self-creation through fantasy. He suggests that people have often turned to the movies to understand who they were as a people or a nation. Dean draws heavily on Neal Gabler's *An Empire of Their Own* and *Life in the Movie* (Gabler 1988; Gabler 1998). He devotes particular attention to two movies, *The Jazz Singer* and *Lone Star* (Dean 2002, 178–181, 183–184). Americans are displaced persons and the lives of the heads of the movie studios are an intense version of this experience. "They were first- or second-generation immigrants, mostly from Eastern Europe, who were born to families in difficult financial straits, often because of the ineptness or absence of the father. . . . Their immigrant and outsider status made these studio heads hyper-American Americans in the sense that they were virtually perfect instances of displaced persons" (Dean 2002, 175).

Drawing on Richard Slotkin, Dean traces how "the changing image of the American is correlative to the changing image of the savage," Indians, gangsers, Nazis, Mexicans, and so forth (Dean 2002, 182; Slotkin, 1998). "Opposition to the savage gave the American the opportunity for 'regeneration through violence,' where protagonists were redeemed by attaining identity through violently overcoming the savage beyond—or, perhaps, within—themselves" (Dean 2002, 183). For a society characterized by a paucity of its own traditions, the movies "created new images of Americans, such as the cowboy, the gangster, the sophisticate, the war hero, the boy and the girl next door, and the urban vigilante, all of whom coped with displacement." These images were not to be emulated literally, but were to symbolize American solutions, even American religious solutions. "Eventually, these images were treated as symbolically true, and then, unexpectedly, they acquired the power to alter American facts. The moviegoers did not become cowboys or gangsters, but took on the simple-mindedness, the idealism, the social protest, and the resentments of cowboys and gangsters" (Dean 2002, 174–175).

For Dean movies, like other forms of art, share in a process that converts fiction into fact. Dean delineates three stages in this process.

> First, when a community confronts a problem that threatens its meaning, a creative artist arises to put forth a new fiction by improvising on or reconstructing the community's traditional identity. Second, if that fiction is widely entertained, curators arise. They set the artist's proposal into the community's tradition, and show how it leads to a minor revision of that tradition. Third, critics arise to defend or attack the creator's fiction and the curator's reinterpretation of tradition by testing how they cope with their community's problem. If their tests

prove negative, they implicitly call for a new creator, one who will offer a fiction better able to confront the community's problems. (Dean 2002, 184)

For Dean all of these aspects of American culture are implicitly, often explicitly, atheistic. They are manifestations of what he calls a "spiritual culture," in that they reflect the overarching vision of the American culture. Nevertheless, this is a secular culture. Religion may be sprinkled in, just as the preacher may be one of the characters in the Western or the priest in the gangster movie. But the major theme, of triumph or despair, is about humans wrestling with their social and natural environments. In that sense American culture is implicitly atheistic, despite our protestations of being religious.

But Dean has a notion of what he calls the "irony of atheism" (Dean 2002 87–110). When secular culture is pursued all the way, there is a religious ground which is found at the end. This is not the old-time theism, but a vision shot through with mystery (Dean 2002, 199–202). There is a strong sense of the *via negativa* here. Whether this takes us beyond the limits of religious naturalism as developed in this essay is hard to say. But it is clear that this is a very powerful and significant theme for Dean and he may be on to something. At least a religious naturalist can respect and agree with his refusal to make definitive statements about this divine mystery. The "irony of atheism" may not be so far different in orientation from the religious naturalist's sense of the sacred in this world.

CHARLES MILLIGAN. Charles Milligan is professor emeritus of philosophy of religion at Iliff School of Theology in Denver. He is has been developing what he terms a naturalistic pantheism, a view which fits into what is here called religious naturalism. "Pantheism is the view that the whole of reality is God. . . . I use the qualifying term *naturalistic* to make clear that this brand of pantheism is significantly different from panentheism, gnosticism, absolute idealism, materialism and spiritualism" (Milligan 1996, 235). This neonaturalism will stress diversity and dynamics, allowing for varying degrees of connectedness from randomly assembled to organically bonded. Unlike some other versions, there is no Oversoul and there is room for individuality.

Milligan stresses "the moral ambiguity of the universe," that it is both supportive of and destructive of life (Milligan 1991, 134). Generally speaking worship has not been of a god with whom one is in moral agreement. "Far more characteristically, the God or gods have been that which evoke the sense of majesty, awesome wonder, the splendor of beauty and mystery. . . . The books of Job and the Psalms tell us more about authentic *spiritual* responses than do Proverbs and Aesop's Fables, but Job and the Psalms are not particularly instructive for morality" (Milligan 1991, 136–137, italics in original). Moral values are not to be found in nature, but are human constructions, ways in which we have found to live together and for which we are responsible (Milligan 1996, 250–251; Milligan 1991, 135, 138).

"God" is not a required term in this philosophy and it is a term open to misunderstanding and misinterpretation, yet Milligan finds it "very difficult to express what I think and how I feel without indulging in God-talk" (Milligan 1991, 146). In addition there is a polytheistic strain here. "Any pantheism needs symbols which are accessible, particular, vivid, and intimate." Indeed, "we need empowering figures and ennobling symbols and places of special meaning. They are not always wisely chosen, but they can represent *particularized* embodiments of courage, values, and commitments. It is not necessary that the symbol be perfect or omniscient . . . but that the symbol be meaningful and cherished" (Milligan 1991, 145). He draws on Samuel Alexander's concept of "deity" here (Milligan 1991, 146; Alexander 1920, 353). He asserts that as long as we are aware that these symbols are "idols or icons (i.e., of our selection and anointment), we do not worship them literally, but we do feel a special affection and affinity for them" (Milligan 1991, 146). Milligan includes Hildegard of Bingen, Luther, Knox, Wesley, Lincoln, Helen Keller, Eleanor Roosevelt, and Martin Luther King Jr. among these particular symbols or embodiments. "My term is 'divinities' by way of admitting that a polytheistic perspective is involved in this, but the label is not important" (Milligan 1991, 146). Pantheism "can have a modest polytheism alongside the wholeness of reality to condition and qualify its temptation toward grandiosity and vagueness. We do not claim our cherished selections to be God, for we remember who selected them. Lesser deities come and go; they inspire and expire" (Milligan, 1996, 244). "The admission of a perspective that is polytheistic need not be disturbing. Trinitarianism has always threatened monotheism." Pantheism must emphasize "the multifariousness of existence, the individuating nature of nature. . . . There is nothing intrinsically good in proclaiming that God is one. If that means you must accept my version of God or be my enemy, as it so often has, it leads to unmitigated evil. But if oneness means integrity, if it means flowing harmony enriched with dissonance . . . it becomes challenging to attempt to conceive God or nature as one" (Milligan 1991, 146–147).

Using his religious term "God," he notes that the earth is "where God is most real and understandable to us. . . . No doubt we can love the earth in ways that are not possible to us to feel toward the whole universe. But, in terms of awesome majesty, we cannot confine nature as God to the earth" (Milligan 1991, 141).

Environmental responsibility is central and obligatory for pantheism. "It requires a lifestyle and social activism on behalf of the environment." In addition to "the motivations which arise from sheer practicality there is the additional religious motivation that this caring about and caring for nature is necessary for our own self-respect and fulfillment as human beings" (Milligan, 1996, 247).

The agenda of Milligan's hermeneutics is to trace the pantheistic motif in some American novelists, essayists, and especially poets. He suggests that these writers have a considerable influence on religious thinking in America. He acknowledges a difficulty in interpretation. "It is a tricky business to discern from poetry what the poet's theological position, if any, is. But in some cases the connection is clear. . . . Sometimes a thinker manages to be both poet and theologian, but in the main the task of vivid particularism and that of coherent systematizing diverge. In view of that, it strikes me that turning to the poets is worthwhile for understanding the religious thought of a people. They may well emphasize views not conspicuously present in the voices of establishment professionals" (Milligan 1987, 585).

Milligan begins his treatment of American pantheism with Walt Whitman who, after a period of a Transcendentalist spiritualizing worldview, has what Milligan calls an "unequivocal pantheism." Milligan quotes from "Gods" in *Leaves of Grass*:

Thought of the Infinite—the All! Be thou my God . . .
Or Time and Space! Or shape of Earth, divine and
  wondrous!
Or shape in I myself—or some fair shape, I, viewing,
  worship
Or lustrous orb of Sun, or star by night: Be ye my Gods.
  (Whitman, 1900, 1, 7)

I hear and behold God in every object, yet understand God
  not in the least,
Nor do I understand who there can be more wonderful
  than myself.
Why should I wish to see God better than this day?
I see something of God each hour of the twenty-four, and
  each moment then. . . .
(Whitman, 1900, "I Celebrate Myself," sec. 48)

What Milligan calls Whitman's dynamic pantheism contains the following themes that separate him from classical pantheism. (1) *Particularization*, "the authentic significance of particular, individual entities . . . not less significant for being temporal." (2) *Interdependence*, "the reality of societal or configurational groupings is recognized and celebrated. Individuality is not isolated but social. He sings his land and people as well as 'Songs of Myself.'" (3) *Urbanization*, "Whitman celebrates the city, with its noise and confusion, and not merely the serene pastoral scene." (4) *Tragedy*, "although extravagantly optimistic at times, he nevertheless dealt poignantly with death, irretrievable loss, oppression and waste, and he did not cover over these stark realities with concluding lines of saccharine piety" (Milligan 1987, 586).

Henry David Thoreau likewise is an unambiguous pantheist. The earth is a living organism. He writes in *Walden:* "There is nothing inorganic . . . not a fossil earth, but a living earth; compared with whose great central life all animal life and vegetable life is merely parasitic" (Thoreau 1992b, 206). Another passage indicative of Thoreau's pantheism is from *A Week on the Concord and Merrimack Rivers*, a book that Milligan finds significant for the subject of pantheism: "I see, smell, taste, hear, feel, that everlasting Something to which we are allied, at once our maker, our abode, our destiny, our very Selves; . . . the actual glory of the universe; the only fact which a human being cannot avoid recognizing" (Thoreau 1893, 226). For Milligan, Thoreau and many later pantheists had rid themselves of sentimentality, that "lingering vestige of anthropoid projection upon nature," although in doing so Thoreau "often disparaged humans and culture." The newer pantheism more often accepts and affirms humanity, but "without maudlin sentimentality or the extravagant praise of Whitman" (Milligan 1987, 592).

Another writer Milligan looks to for his pantheistic affirmations is Sidney Lanier. Milligan does not find him consistent in his pantheistic affirmations, but in some of his poems, such as "Nirvana," he definitely stressed many of the themes of pantheism. Milligan finds this closer to a romantic type of pantheism, but yet recognizing evil as real. "While it is true that he saw evils (and precious values) ultimately absorbed into the All, the comfort of that was not supernal bliss, but relief from the sorrows in life" (Milligan 1987, 587).

Milligan twice quotes "a pantheistic benediction" from Richard Eberhart's autobiographical poem, "The Soul Longs to Return Whence It Came," written after visiting a familiar graveyard. In this poem Eberhart speaks of returning to the "Mother, Great Being" who is the source of life. Milligan comments, "It is not this conclusion which makes this poem religiously significant, but the progression of his thought, travail, and feelings in the graveyard which give meaning to the acceptance of finitude and mortality, and thus rescues the benediction from being merely contrived piety" (Milligan 1996, 239–240). Milligan also suggests. "There is no need of some sacrament intervening as the channel of grace, for the place and the experience are the sacrament" (Milligan 1987, 595).

Milligan finds Robinson Jeffers of interest because he explicitly commented on his own religious views: "I believe that the universe is all one being. . . . This whole is in all its parts so beautiful, and is felt by me to be so intensely in earnest, that I am compelled to love it, and to think of it as divine" (from an interview with Jeffers in Scott, 1986, 29).

In "Shine, Perishing Republic," we find Jeffers's worshipful response:

> I sadly smiling remember that the flower fades to make fruit,
>   the fruit rots to make earth
> Out of the mother; and through the spring exultances, ripeness
>   and decadence; and home to the mother,
> You make haste on decay: not blameworthy; life is good,
>   be it stubbornly long or suddenly
> A mortal splendor: meteors are not needed less than mountains:
>   shine perishing republic. (Jeffers 1937, 168)

Milligan's comment is that: "The older response of wonder, love and praise is there, but exorcised of anthropocentrism and disguised hubris" (Milligan 1987, 596).

Robert Penn Warren joins the list of pantheists for Milligan. Warren has "disavowed a religious perspective." Yet "many of his lines of thought are congruent with modern Pantheism, if not explicitly announcing that view. There is nothing of the perfect beneficence of the eternal ocean of being. Individual characters are treated with recognition of their particular uniqueness, but it is not the older individualism. Above all, these things are not romanticized. He conceives 'the purely private self as incomplete and of the community as analogue or projection of the individual.' 'Time,' Warren has said 'is the dimension in which God strives to define His own being'" (Bloom, Harold 1984, 78). "It is not only an expanding universe, it is an intensifying one in which precious actualities emerge and where the tragic dimension is also real and to be acknowledged" (Milligan 1987, 596). After describing the destruction wrought by a storm in "Summer Storm (circa 1916), and God's Grace," Warren writes of God getting down on his hands and knees and commending the results of his own sadistic idiocies (Warren 1960).

Virginia Woolf expressed a "healing effect" in the contemplation of any part of nature: "if we escape a little from the common sitting-room and see human beings not always in their relation to each other but in relation to reality; and the sky, too, and the trees" (Milligan 1996, 246–247 quoting Woolf 1929, 188).

Without extensive analysis Milligan also mentions among writers who affirmed pantheistic views and whose works were widely loved, including church people among their appreciators: William Cullen Bryant's "Thanatopsis," William H. Carruth's "Each in His Own Tongue" with the line, "Some call it Evolution,/And others call it God" (the whole poem can be read as religious naturalistic); and Elizabeth York Case's "There Is No Unbelief."

Key to understanding Milligan's pantheism is the note of "de-anthropocentrism." He does not mean that "human qualities of value lack significance, rather that humans hold no place of special privilege in the scheme of things. The classic statement," he points out, is in Stephen Crane's lines:

A man said to the universe: "Sir, I exist!"
"However," replied the universe, "The fact has not created in me
A sense of obligation." (Stephen Crane, 1930)

In *A Poet's Life*, Harriet Monroe has also broken from nineteenth-century romanticism in her pantheism: "Call the Force God and worship it at a million shrines, and it is no less sublime; call it Nature, and worship it in scientific gropings and discoveries, and it is no less divine. It goes its own way, asking no homage, answering no questions" (Monroe 1938, 454; see 450). Significant also for Milligan is Shug's speech in Alice Walker's *The Color Purple* (although Milligan suggests that Walker is not herself a pantheist): "God ain't a he or a she, but a It. . . . It ain't something you can look at apart from anything else, including yourself. I believe God is everything, say Shug. Everything that is or ever will be" (Alice Walker 1983, 177–178).

Milligan further uses e. e. cummings, Herman Melville, Gerard Manley Hopkins, and Andrew Hudgins (Milligan 1987, 13; 1996, 239).

For Milligan, "it was a remarkable shift, in less than a century, for the liberal American religious view to move from Deism toward Pantheism. . . . It was due to the transition from the last stages of a mechanistic, Newtonian cosmology, which required an external Designer, to a biologically oriented, evolutionary view of nature, in which God would be more akin to growth and experimentation" (Milligan 1987, 588–589). Pantheism in this view is quite different from those contemporary American religions that conceive the All as Spirit, Mind, the Absolute, Soul or such. The anthropocentrism of the New Thought Movement or "Metaphysical Science" is quite different from the naturalistic and empirical orientation of pantheism.

Both Dean and Milligan turn to American culture as a source of religious insight. Dean is the first major religious naturalist who widens his hermeneutical concern beyond written texts. Their hermeneutical explorations of American culture give a wider scope and richer texture to religious naturalism. For Dean jazz manifests the improvizational character of American experience, football the ambivalent relationship to violence, and movies the remaking of selfhood in a nation of struggling immigrants. For Dean, if one penetrates beneath the surface, one will find that these three characteristics have an implicit and sometimes an explicit religious dimension. For Milligan the American writers selected for examination manifest, with varying degrees of explicitness, a new variety of pantheism that is both dynamic in orientation and allows for the significance of the particular and the human person, although without anthropocentrism and romantic sentimentality.

Chapter Five

Current Issues in Religious Naturalism

The following are a set of questions about which religious naturalists take different approaches.

1. The first question concerns whether all or only part of the world can be considered divine. Some places or events are especially evocative of a sense of the sacred. If we do not experience the sacred sometimes, is that because that time and place is not sacred or because we are not attuned to it or because it has not manifested itself? Is there any aspect of the world that is profane? If one adopts the view of Loomer's *The Size of God* or speaks of the web of life with a tone of sacrality, what becomes of this question?

2. Is the divine best conceived as unitary or plural? Or is a web or matrix that combines unity and plurality a better metaphor? Is the traditional religious analogue to religious naturalism monotheism or polytheism? Or is this a false dichotomy, and an alternation between a monistic and a pluralistic understanding and response the better approach?

3. Which values or experiences can be designated as divine or sacred? Are certain values or experiences the only ones that are sacred or are they paradigmatic, functioning as windows onto a wide range of such values?

4. Do human values and ideals need transformation? What is the basis for a prophetic critique of reigning ideologies?

5. Can religious naturalism exist within more traditional faith communities? Does it create its own communities and traditions as with Reconstructionist Judaism, or the Fellowship of Religious Humanists? Can it find a home within such bodies as the Society of Friends, the Unitarian Universalists, or the North American Buddhist Sangha? Will only its naturalistic theists be at home in more traditional monotheistic faith communities? Or is it primarily a stance for the individual? Or all of the above?

Significant as all of the issues are, we will concentrate on two, the nature of the divine or the object of religious orientation and then on the issue of the term "God."

Power and Goodness of the Object of the Religious Attitude

In his study of recent religious naturalism, Willem Drees points out the tension between those (like Ralph Burhoe) for whom the object of religious orientation is morally ambivalent and those (like Charley Hardwick and myself), for whom it is a term of positive value only (Drees 2000; much of this section is adapted from Stone 2004).

This tension within religious naturalism received classic form in the exchanges between Henry Nelson Wieman and William Bernhardt as the distinction between the power and goodness of God or whether God is a term of selection or a term for a concrete, hence ambiguous, actuality. Bernard Loomer in *The Size of God* opted for the latter (Loomer 1987, 20–51). The issue also surfaces in Bernard Meland's writings. (Tyron Inbody has an excellent treatment of Meland on this issue. See Inbody 1995, 189–192.) In slightly different form the dispute separated George Santayana and John Dewey, and was an echo of the differences, outside the boundaries of naturalism, between Jonathan Edwards or Samuel Hopkins and William Ellery Channing, and earlier between Baruch Spinoza and Gottfried Wilhelm Leibniz and between Thomas Aquinas and William of Occam.

The purpose of this section is to trace, in roughly chronological order, the current form of this dispute in the writings of myself and Charley Hardwick, on the one hand, who conceive of an axiologically determinate object of religious orientation (one that is in some sense creative of the good), and Charles Milligan, William Dean, Brian Swimme and Thomas Berry, and Donald Crosby on the other, who opt for the moral ambiguity of the religious ultimate (as in some sense creative of both and evil, at least from a human pespective). In addition the movement of Sharon

Welch between these views and the subtlety of the stances of Gordon Kaufman and Karl Peters will be discussed. The article will conclude with a possible resolution of this tension.

JEROME A. STONE. The writer holds that many events have what could be called a sacred aspect. I am not referring to a being, a separate mind or spirit. I am saying that some things, like justice and human dignity, and the creativity of the natural world, are sacred. This vision is very pluralistic. What degree of unity there is to this plurality I am reluctant to say.

I have elaborated a technical definition in my book, *The Minimalist Vision of Transcendence*. The transcendent, in my terminology, *refers to norms and creative powers that are relatively or situationally transcendent*, that is, continually compelling norms and resources transcendent to a specific situation yet naturalistically conceived as immanent within the world. A common element in the paradigm cases of religion seems to be what I term an orientation to transcendence. There is also a polarity of norms and of creative power(s). Within the limits of my naturalistic outlook the transcendent dimension of norms and powers is understood as a collection of continually compelling norms and situation transcending creative powers. They are "relatively transcendent" to norms and situations within the world yet are within the world as relevant possibilities and realities beyond a situation as perceived. To illustrate this, the search for the norms of truth or justice means to reach for possibilities relatively transcendent to present attainments and yet relevant to our efforts. Truth and justice remain continually compelling norms no matter how far we come. Likewise openness to the healing or restorative powers of medicine or pedagogy means a readiness to receive creative and re-creative powers relatively transcendent to our present situation and yet located within the world beyond our limited present. This is a philosophy urging openness to norms and resources that are beyond our narrowly perceived present yet are not resident in a different realm (Stone 1992, 9–20).

In this view, when the object of religious orientation is focused on it is axiologically determinate, because the religious orientation is toward relatively transcendent creative resources and compelling norms. The creative and normative aspects are what make them determinate in value.

CHARLEY HARDWICK. Hardwick sees the heart of the Christian life as God's gift of faith as openness to the future and liberation from inauthentic to authentic existence. In traditional terms, this is a Pauline-Lutheran-Bultmannian view, what I call a "twice-born" naturalism.

For Hardwick assertions about God rest on assertions about value which, since the truth about values is physically determined, can be true or false and hence God-language is capable of truth and falsity. "God exists" is a meta-assertion, which means a nonreferential assertion which expresses the theistic valuational stance. This is buttressed by his reading of Wieman for whom God is a valuational term. The Christian valuational stance is openness to the future, the move from bondage to liberation, transformation from inauthentic to authentic existence. "God" means the giftedness of this move, that this transformation is not of ourselves but comes to us.

We now move to the second set of writers who opt for the ambiguity of the object of religion, for axiologically indeterminacy in the object of religion.

CHARLES MILLIGAN. Charles Milligan, professor emeritus of philosophy of religion at Iliff School of Theology in Denver, has advocated a neopantheism emphasizing individuation, distinctiveness, and change. Milligan, drawing especially on his mentor William Bernhardt, clearly advocates the ambiguity of the object of religious orientation. "Naturalistic pantheism does not soften the brutal fact of the moral ambiguity of the universe or the frequent injustices which befall multitudes of human beings" (Milligan 1991, 134; see also Milligan 1987; Milligan 1996).

For Milligan moral values are not to be deduced from a concept of God. We must question the idea that the correct concept of God must provide authority for ethics. To be sure, some significant ethical guidance can be drawn from nature. Cheat on the data and the value of the experiment has been destroyed. On the other hand, "there are moral qualities and principles to which nature is indifferent. Chief among these are justice and compassion. . . . Whatever concept you have of God, it is undeniable that the sun shines and the rain falls (or drought befalls) on the just and the unjust with sublime indifference" (Milligan 1991, 136). What must be realized, according to Milligan, is that worship does not determine one's moral judgment. "Far more characteristically, the God or gods have been that which evoke the sense of majesty, awesome wonder, the splendor of beauty and mystery" (Milligan 1991, 136).

We run into difficulty by speaking of nature in the abstract. Nature is plainly supportive of human life and values in some ways. That we are here speaks to that. In other ways nature is destructive of human life and values, witness disease. Finally there are matters in which nature is morally ambiguous. Poison the earth and there will be suffering and death (Milligan 1991, 137).

Shall we lapse into self-indulgence or destructiveness since we worship the morally ambiguous whole? No. "Worship . . . does not seem uniformly and consistently to culminate in passionate pursuit of peace, daily practice of love, and exercise of impartial justice. . . . The task of sorting out and systematizing ethical claims is a human task." (Milligan 1991, 137–138).

WILLIAM DEAN. William Dean argues in *The Religious Critic in American Culture*, that the sacred is a convention, composed of images carried by the spiritual culture of a people, of what is ultimately important (Dean 1994, 133–139). Although it is constantly subjection to reinterpretaion, it also influences a people's interpretations. As such, it is partially independent of a people's interpretation. It has a life of its own. This independence is seen in that the effects of a sacred convention exceed what is predictable by reference to the images that contribute to that convention. The sacred, like any socially constructed reality, can turn back on the society and act in ways that were not intended. The sacred, then, is a living tradition about what is ultimately significant, is constantly reinterpreted, is completely historical, and is partially independent of its society. (Dean has reminded me that he also talks about the growth of conventions or laws in nature [Dean 1986, 50–55; Dean 1994, 110–115; Dean 2002, 73].)

Such a convention is not a mere projection, first because it has effects on its society, and second, because it works in ways that cannot be strictly predicted. The sacredness of the sacred depends both on its partial independence and on the fact that it involves what is ultimately important, responding to a people's deepest questions and suggesting ultimately important answers. God is such a sacred convention within the life of the American public.

Although it is subject to continual reinterpretation and its effects are unpredictable, a sacred convention is conservative in its own way, since it stands in a line of past conventions. Any convention is tied with a fairly short leash to its previous interpretations.

As a public construction in a chain of interpretations, a sacred convention is neither objective nor subjective, but is formed by an objective public past interacting with current subjective creativity but reducible to neither. To illustrate this Dean refers to the American Constitution which, as a convention, is not reducible either to a written document nor to the interpretations of the Supreme Court. Likewise God, as a sacred convention, is a social construction with a reality of its own, with unpredictable effects on the society within which it operates.

Dean is quite clear that the sacred is morally ambiguous (Dean 1994, 140–148). Our images of ultimacy are morally ambiguous. And since the sacred as a convention is both affected by and affects those images, it follows that the sacred is probably ambiguous. Further, the misery of human histories provides an adequate, if inconclusive, reason for believing that the sacred is implicated in that misery. This affirmation denies that the idea of moral perfection is a deep wisdom. Also language about the divine is an attempt to describe what is, to respond to the whole of reality, rather than a call for what ought to be. To make this affirmation is to follow Martin Luther, John Calvin, Paul Tillich, William Bernhardt, Bernard Loomer, Elie Wiesel, Fred Sontag, and John K. Roth, rather than Whitehead, Wieman, Hartshorne, David Griffin, or Jerome Stone.

Dean gives richness to this affirmation of the morally ambiguous character of the sacred by a discussion of biblical material, drawing on James Crenshaw and Judith Plaskow, by contrasting John Dewey and Bernard Loomer, and by a discussion of American sports. Indeed, "in professional sports lies one of the last public places in America where the brutality of everyday life is ritually dramatized" (Dean 1994, 148). In his latest book, Dean elaborates further on the relationship between sports and American spiritual culture as exemplifying the ambiguity of the sacred (Dean 2002, 148–171; the note of ambiguity is definitely present in this book. See especially chapter 3).

THOMAS BERRY AND BRIAN SWIMME. World religions scholar Thomas Berry and physicist Brian Swimme have been collaborating on articulating a narrative world view informed by the major results of scientific cosmology, evolutionary biology, and human history. This world narrative sees our ecological crisis as necessitating an appreciative yet critical transformation of the modern Western outlook. Combining a careful use of precisely worded empirical generalizations and poetic metaphor, this world narrative seeks to reconnect religious insights and scientific discoveries. Indeed, this universal creative process is sacred and, if the divine be regarded as transcendent, the universe itself should be seen as the primary revelation of the divine.

One guiding thread in this approach is the thrust to restore, in a contemporary fashion, some degree of the lost intimacy between humans and the rest of the world. This thread is part of a wider thread that articulates the interconnectedness, with perhaps varying degrees of relevance and intimacy, of all parts of the universe.

Another thread is that an evolving yet relatively consistent scientific picture, based on disciplines including astrophysics, quantum theory, evolutionary biology, archaeology, and history, shows that the entire universe is a history that can be narrated. The grasp of the significance of this irreversible, temporal dimension is a new element in human understanding, even though it has roots in the Abrahamic outlooks. This is why narrative is crucial for Berry and Swimme. The cosmic scale of this unites us with the mythic stance of primal peoples at the same time as its scientific underpinnings provide a new element in the history of worldviews and helps prevent naive romanticism. This narrative, cosmic yet inclusive of each person, helps bridge scientific inquiry and religious wisdoms. The universality of this cosmic epic also opens the way to intercultural conversation.

When the threads of historicity and of interconnectedness are woven together, what is perhaps the nodal point of this tapestry is discovered, namely that humans are an integral part of the ongoing universe-process, indeed, humans are the universe-process become self-conscious. Hence they can say that "the mathematical formulations of the scientists are the way in which the multiform universe deepens its self-understanding" (Swimme and Berry 1992, 40).

Berry and Swimme are self-consciously willing to use emotionally charged language, such as "instant by instant the universe creates itself as a bonded community." From the perspective of the dominate worldview that we now need to outgrow, they claim, such language was derided as an anthropomorphic stain. "Anthropomorphic language was abandoned in favor of mechanomorphic language," in order to abandon wishful thinking and establish contact with the essence of things. Besides, given the processive-relational nature of things, to know carbon we need to know what it can do in the right contexts. We can refer to carbon as the "thinking element" or "the element of life," abandoning univocal for analogical language (Swimme and Berry 1992, 35–36; Swimme 1984, 64–66, 77–79). This epic narrative is close to a Whiteheadean approach, differing in emphasis partly by its self-conscious melding of current science and the world's wisdom traditions, by its construction of a single grand narrative with room for local traditions, and by its reference to the sacredness of the creative process and its evolving products.

Berry's background as a scholar of Teilhard de Chardin shows in the controversial concept of the "interiority" or "subjectivity" of things.

> Things emerge with an inner capacity for self-manifestation. Even an atom posses a quantum of radical spontaneity. In later developments in the universe this minimal dimension of spontaneity grows until it becomes a dominant fact of behavior, as in the life of the gray whale. (Swimme and Berry 1992, 75–76; see also 71–72)

The integrity of the universe must be respected, so we must not think of consciousness as a radical departure. Its possibility is latent from the beginning and its actuality is dimly present in many life forms. This emphasis on the interiority of things provides the basis for a feeling of intimacy or communion with both the universe at large and with all the many things within it. Indeed, this intimacy is not only for humans, but for all beings. Rather than a collection of objects, the universe is a communion of subjects.

Although Berry and Swimme do not use our term "axiological ambiguity," their treatment of the role of destruction in the universe clearly sets them in the camp of those who see the object of religious orientation to be inclusive of good and evil. Violence and destruction are part of the universe. They are present at all levels of existence: the elemental, the geological, the organic, the human. It is even difficult to decide when violence is simply destructive or when it is linked to creativity. "Yet it is out of such violence—even in some mating cycles and in some processes of nurturance—that the stupendous variety displays its beauty throughout the planetary system" (Swimme and Berry 1992, 51; see also Swimme 1984, 70–82).

Indeed, three pervasive features of existence are the roots of violence and destruction: the resistance of matter, the need for energy, and the tendency of things to fulfill their nature. Many inventions in nature come from beings meeting constraints with creative responses. "The violence associated with the hawk starving to death or the vole being consumed are intrinsically tied to the creativity of each. The beauty of their response arises from an inherently difficult situation" (Swimme and Berry 1992, 56). With the rise of self-reflective consciousness, "life understands that it is precious and liable to destruction." Out of this fear humans devote themselves to eliminating violence and destruction. "The determination to dominate the universe so that all insecurity, limitation, destruction, and threat of destruction could be eliminated eventuated in racism, militarism, sexism, and anthropocentrism, dysfunctional maneuvers of the human species in its quest to deal with what it regarded as the unacceptable aspects of the universe" (Swimme and Berry 1992, 56).

Swimme and Berry conclude this treatment with a nuanced reflection on the necessity of legitimate sacrifice which justifies neither cruelty nor masochism. Indeed our esteem for heroes and those who sacrifice comfort, wealth or prestigious work for the betterment of the Earth community, reveals our "recognition that the individuals who act this way make clear a sacred dimension of existence" (Swimme and Berry 1992, 59). I recognize the importance of this notion of legitimate sacrifice. However, after reading Rita Nakashima Brock and Rebecca Ann Parker's powerful *Proverbs of Ashes*, I wish to surround this notion with extreme cautionary warnings, since it is often the powerless who are called on to be the sacrifice (Brock and Parker 2001).

DONALD CROSBY. In *A Religion of Nature* Donald Crosby has developed a viewpoint in which nature is both metaphysically and religiously ultimate. He starts by asserting three theses: (1) nature is religiously ultimate, (2) nature is metaphysically ultimate in that it is self-sustaining and requires no explanation for its existence beyond itself, and (3) humans are "at home" in the universe and our moral and religious responsibilities extend to one another, to the human community, and to the whole of nature (Crosby 2002, xi; see also Crosby 2003a, 117–120; Crosby 2003b, 245–259; Crosby, 2007a; Crosby 2007b; Crosby 2007c; Crosby 2008).

In part one of *A Religion of Nature* Crosby develops a sophisticated process-relational conception of nature, drawing heavily on William James and Whitehead. By means of this he is able to address many of the standard objections to naturalism that are based on a nineteenth-century mechanistic conception of nature.

After developing his conception of nature, Crosby proceeds to clarify and justify his assertion that nature is religiously ultimate. He does this by articulating a complex theory of the functions of a "religious object," that is, "the fundamental focus of thought and practice in a particular religious system or outlook" (Crosby 2002, 180, n. 2). The six functions of a religious object are uniqueness, primacy, pervasiveness in relation to everything else, rightness in the sense of defining the goal as well as a standard for human existence, permanence in the face of declining health and impending death, and hiddenness, in the sense of being a source of mystery and awe and something that can only be spoken of elliptically. Crosby then goes on to show how nature fulfills each of these six functions and thus is the appropriate religious object.

Flesh can be put on Crosby's conception by noting how he responds to six standard objections to a view like his. The first three objections, that nature is wasteful, cruel, and indifferent to humans, he classifies as moral objections. His approach can be seen by examining his answer to the second objection, that nature is cruel.

Crosby first notes that to speak of the cruelty of nature is a category mistake, to treat nature anthropomorphically. But we must face the fact that pain, suffering, and death are serious disvalues. Good and evil are mixed in nature and constitute its axiological ambiguity. "The system of nature that makes these wide-scale intrinsic evils necessary is *to that extent* an evil system. . . . It is partly good but also partly evil. It contains rampant disvalues as well as rampant values" (Crosby 2002, 138, italics in original). This means that we cannot base our moral outlook on nature.

Crosby's response to the third objection, the alleged indifference of nature, is similar. He points out first, that the objection is a category mistake, since nature itself is not personal and thus could not be indifferent. Then we realize that, along with apparent indifference, nature can have redemptive significance for humans, that it can "rejuvenate, inspire and redeem" us (Crosby 2002, 142).

The next two objections to the view of nature as religiously ultimate, that nature is not personal and that it is contingent, Crosby calls metaphysical objections. His response to the first, that nature is not intentional, has no conscious awareness, is multiple: (1) Just because we would like for something to be true, does not make it so. (2) The advantage of realizing that the religious ultimate is not personal is that there is no need for theodicy. (3) While there is no purpose of nature as a whole, there is purpose in nature in humans and some animals. (4) Many religious outlooks do not include personality in their religious ultimate. (5) The objection seems presumptuous and hubristic. (6) In religions with a personal deity prayers of petition have the theoretical difficulty of God's partiality and of violating the principle of parsimony. On the other hand, it is "possible to express gratitude, trust, and personal resolve in meditations upon nature" (Crosby 2002, 153).

Crosby's response to the objection that nature is contingent is also complex. (1) All questions about nature as self-existent apply also to God. Where did God come from? If God is self-caused, why cannot nature? (2) While it is legitimate to seek for explanations of things within nature, we need not think that we need an explanation for nature as a whole. (3) It is possible to think of nature as existing necessarily, provided we think of it as *natura naturans* rather than as *nature naturata*. (4) Nature as a metaphysical and religious ultimate has the advantage of being open to scientific investigation. Thus it is a more plausible candidate for the given to which all explanations appeal than a vague and elusive spirit.

The final objection to nature as a religious ultimate is practical. The religion of nature has no organization, tradition, ritual, symbols or practice. Crosby's response is that there is already potential material in existing religious traditions from which a religion of nature can draw in developing beliefs, evocations and practices appropriate to itself.

What Crosby calls his "final set" of reasons for according religious ultimacy to nature is that nature, while not itself good, is the principal source of good for all its creatures. Specifically, nature has produced the beauty and sublimity of the physical universe, through biological evolution it is the source, sustainer, and restorer of life, it is the ultimate source of human life and the specific goods of human history, and nature has evolved humans so as to implant in them a yearning for the attainment and preservation of good. Thus, "we have no need of God, gods, animating spirits . . . nor do we need to pine for another life. . . . Nature itself, when we rightly conceive of it and comprehend our role within it, can provide ample context and support for finding purpose, value, and meaning in our lives" (Crosby 2002, 169).

We conclude our survey of the issue of the axiological determinacy or ambiguity in the object of religious orientation by reference to two thinkers who seems to span the gap and one who has moved across the gap between these two views.

GORDON KAUFMAN. Gordon Kaufman has been moving into a religious naturalist position in recent writings, particularly *In Face of Mystery*, chapters 19–22, and *In the Beginning . . . Creativity*, although he does not use that term (Kaufman 1993; Kaufman 2003; Kaufman 2007 is a good introduction). Recently Kaufman has been willing to use the term "naturalism" to describe his approach, although he would prefer the qualifier "biohistorical" to "religious" (Kaufman 2003, 97, 99).

In an article on "Power and Goodness of the Object of the Religious Attitude," I misinterpreted Kaufman as belonging with those naturalists for whom the object of religious orientation was axiologically determinate, that is, "good." However, conversation with him and a rereading of *In the Beginning . . . Creativity* have convinced me that I was wrong (Kaufman 1904, 59–66). Instead I would now see Kaufman as one for whom the cosmic and abstract scope of God is valuationally neutral to the human perspective, but that the specific trajectory productive of us is indeed good from our perspective. Thus he stands with one foot on both sides of this issue.

Kaufman's analysis of the term "God" is that it refers to that which produces and leads us to a fuller human existence and at the same time that which relativizes all our projects, accomplishments, and values. In short, God is that which humanizes and relativizes (Kaufman 1993, 316). Although this symbol is a construction of disciplined imagination for which we are responsible, it refers to a reality that is "neither a simple fantasy of ours nor something that we can manipulate or control, make or remake as we choose; God is a reality genuinely distinct from us and all our imaginings, that which—quite apart from our own doing—has given us our being as humans and continues to nurture and sustain us" (Kaufman 1993, 317).

In place of the personal-agential model for divine creativity, Kaufman develops a model based on the serendipity of the long cosmic and historical process, referring to the surprising, unforeseen and unexpected results of a process, results which are not always happy or fortunate. Although he seems to find history to be the area most suggestive of serendipity, by analogous extension he finds it a fruitful concept to apply to both biological and cosmological processes (Kaufman 1993, 268, 274, 279). This cosmic serendipity has "trajectories," series of events which, building on each other, seem in retrospect to take a certain direction. These trajectories move in many "directions," humanity being one of them. "Thus the appearance of human modes of being in the world would be properly regarded not as a metaphysical surd but rather as grounded in the ultimate nature of things, in the ultimate mystery" (Kaufman 1993, 284).

This complex notion of trajectories of serendipitous creativity provides an overall vision which gives significant, but not dominant place, to human life within the cosmic and biological processes. This can provide an orientation encouraging people to take responsible roles, a ground of hope (though not certainty), which can help motivate people to devote their lives to bringing about a more humane world (Kaufman 1993, 294). "On this view the symbol 'God' refers us not to a particular existent being within or beyond the world, but rather to that trajectory of cosmic and historical forces which, having emerged out of the ultimate mystery of things, is moving us toward a more truly humane and ecologically responsible mode of existence: it is *that* to which I commit myself; it is that which I will serve with my life" (Kaufman 1993, 347–348, italics in original). Thus the term "God" is used, not simply to designate the collection of disparate cosmic powers that have produced us, but to focus our attention and commitment to this process. At this point there are parallels to Henry Nelson Wieman and to Shailer Mathews.

Why continue to use the ancient term? "Why not just speak of 'cosmic and historical forces' working toward humanization and ecological order?" The answer is part lies in the need to connect ourselves with the historical past in order to see our place in the trajectory moving into the future. By using this symbol to focus our attention and devotion, we make clear, to ourselves and others, that we do not think of ourselves as a generation disconnected from our forbears, but rather as participants in an ongoing history and community. "The idea of 'cosmic and historical forces' working toward humanization and ecological responsibility . . . is much too abstract and intellectual to be able to generate universal interest and support. To commit ourselves to *God*, however, is to express just such a stance and loyalty by means of a symbol which is capable of drawing together and unifying persons of differing degrees of sophistication in all walks of life" (Kaufman 1993, 348). In addition the term focuses our attention on the gradually increasing unity and directness of the specific cosmic trajectory toward humaneness. " 'God,' as a proper name . . . focuses our minds so they will grasp as significantly unified and of existential import to us what we might otherwise take to be simply diverse processes and powers" (Kaufman 1993, 348). And further, "The God-symbol is well worth keeping. Not only can it help keep us humble; thought of in the way I am proposing, it can continue to orient us to what is of greatest importance for us" (Kaufman 2003, 99).

In a passage reminiscent of George Burman Foster, Kaufman writes that to speak of "God" does not commit us to the existence of some additional "being," in or beyond the world, from which these evolutionary forces proceed, any more than selfhood commits us to an individual "something" alongside the body. What we are doing by using the name "God," rather, is attending to the significance for us humans of the unity and direction which gradually developed in this particular evolutionary-historical trajectory. " 'God' " (with its accent on that which grounds our humanness) is the principle word available in our language for focusing our minds on this growing unity of *directedness toward the human*" (Kaufman 1993, 349, italics in original).

Implicated in this notion of serendipitous creativity is a transcendent point of criticism that challenges our standards and dreams. It is important for religious naturalism that he has this principle of criticism and prophetic protest. "What is needed is a nonreified version of the normative, a version according to which it is never expected that life 'on earth' will perfectly conform to the ideal—there will always be room for criticism and further transformation . . . but at the same time it is not held that the perfect or ideal 'exists' somehow or somewhere 'outside' or 'beyond' the world" (Kaufman 1993, 327).

It is significant that Kaufman's use of the term "creativity" is different from that of Wieman, although he recognizes the inspiration of Wieman in his use of the term (Kaufman 2004, 60). For Kaufman creativity is the coming into being of the new, new evils as well as new goods from the human perspective, whereas for Wieman the "creative event" is always "the source of human good." If we think of serendipitous creativity in the abstract on a cosmic scale we will see that it gave rise to many trajectories, some of them in conflict with others. This creativity in the abstract is not appropriate to take as normative for us humans. The creativity that is normative is the productive creativity on planet Earth and its environment, the trajectory that produced us. In this trajectory the attitude and behavior we call "loving" becomes significant, although it is not proper to say without qualification that "God is love" without seeing this term in a configuration of other terms, including "power" and "eternity." Any human acts, practices or institutions that are destructive of the biohistorical constraints within which we must live are "evil," while whatever facilitates the forward movement of the evolutionary/historical trajectory of which we are a part and is in harmony with Earth's wider ecological order is "good" (Kaufman 2004, 59–66). One also admires the courage of skirting so close to a demiurge in deifying the trajectory toward humanity.

KARL PETERS. What Karl Peters, co-editor of *Zygon*, calls serendipitous creativity is a two-part process: the recurrence of variations in cosmic, biological, and human history and the selection of some of these variations to continue (Peters 2002). In short, God is the creative process that is made up of a set of interactions that create variations plus a set of interactions that preserve some of them. Following Ralph Wendell Burhoe, God is the twofold process of innovation and selection in cosmic, cultural, and personal evolution. This means that cosmic and biological evolution and individual life can be thought of in Daoist fashion as a dance or conversation where no one leads and there is no goal but where each mutually influences the others. The pay-off is participation in the dance itself.

What this means is that for Peters, if I read him correctly, the creative process in Darwinian fashion selects for creative innovation and survival, and is in this sense axiologically determinate, but in the process is destructive of what does not survive and in this sense is axiologically ambiguous. On this reading, for Peters it is a matter of perspective. From the viewpoint of the total process selection is for the good. From the viewpoint of anything left behind in the process, selection will appear evil. (Ursula Goodenough probably comes out close to Peters at this point.)

SHARON WELCH. Sharon Welch has made a fundamental shift on our issue. In the first edition of *A Feminist Ethic of Risk* in the 1980s she clearly took the view of the axiologically determinate character of the object of religious orientation. "Grace is not the manifestation of the divine in our lives, the gift of a separate or foundational being . . . grace is all there is or need be of the divine" (Welch 2000, 175). Here she is clear on the connection between the divine and worthiness of worship. Divinity "connotes a quality of relationships, lives, events, and natural processes that are worthy of worship, that provide orientation, focus, and guidance to our lives" (Welch 2000, 176). Further, "divinity, or grace, is the resilient, fragile, healing power of finitude itself. . . . The divinity of these forces does not lie in their absolute power but in the quality of life they enable." There is much that is divine: "work for justice, love, creativity itself, the web of life, joy, and beauty, innumerable states and qualities of acting are divine. By naming joy as divine, we affirm that these aspects of human existence are worthy of worship" (Welch 2000,

178–179). However, by the time she wrote *Sweet Dreams in America* Welch had moved toward a sense of the ambiguity of the divine.

> The solace and challenge of belonging to a community, the joy and challenge of finding a purpose in life, may seem unambiguously good. . . . Nothing could be further from the truth. Religious experience, while most certainly real and compelling, is fundamentally amoral. Belonging to a religious group, feeling connected to other people and to the sacred, can as easily fuel campaigns of genocide and coercion as movements of compassion and social transformation. Slave owners and abolitionists, participants in the Civil Rights movement and members of the Ku Klux Klan, alike drew comfort and challenge from their religious beliefs and their participation in religious communities. (Welch 1999, 127)

For Welch this calls, not for a denial of ethics and spirituality, but for irony. "Is it possible to hold together a recognition of the power and value of spirituality without denying its intrinsic dangers? To do so requires developing an ironic spirituality, one fueled by audacity and an appreciation of the perverse contradictions of life" (Welch 1999, 128). It also calls for a critical humanism, for an analysis of the actual effects of concrete actions. Religious experience is amoral. The experience of transcendence is not foundational. "It is an experience of creativity, connection, and energy that is as likely to be evoked by the Religious Right and by the Klan, as by politically progressive religious groups. The sense of religious ecstasy in each is the same: the sense of being energized, of being connected with forces outside oneself." Welch argues that "we need a critical humanism to check our claims about deity, about the good, and that the check to fanaticism is not religious but political, a critical examination of the actual impact on people of a community's constructions of good, order, truth, and power" (Welch 1999, xxii).

So now what? What about the power and goodness of the referent of our religious attitude? Shall we say that we have here two different approaches to the religious object, shall we finally prefer one as more adequate, or shall we be left with a yin-yang alternation?

The answer, I believe, is to recognize the complex nature of the religious orientation. There is, simply put, a difference between the moral and what we could call "the transmoral" attitudes and corresponding to these a difference between the moral and the transmoral aspects of the object of religious devotion. There is a time for moral inspiration and dedication and a time for the recognition of the transmoral aspects of the universe that call for such attitudes as consent and resignation. We need at times to hear the call of righteousness and at other times to yield and surrender, to relate in awe and wonder. It may take more wisdom than we have to know the difference, which is why this is a matter of risk and courage, sailing between the Scylla of fanaticism and the Charybdis of aimlessness.

Put another way, a healthy religious life should strive for complementarity, to balance moral earnestness with adoration, humility, and a covenant with mystery, to use Goodenough's term. In that case, my emphasis in *The Minimalist Vision of Transcendence* on relative transcendence as referring to constructive forces and ideals needs to be enriched by the balanced view of Kaufman and Peters (Stone 1992, 10–17). We need to be inspired by the elements of constructive goodness we select for devotion and also to humble ourselves in awe before the power of the entire creative process.

The Use of God-language

In the contemporary scene the question of the viability of a naturalistic conception of God is a live issue. Some religious naturalists employ theistic language. God is either the totality of the entire universe, usually considered from a religious perspective, or else God is one strand within the universe, such as the creative process. Occasionally the distinction is not clear.

Among religious naturalists at least five positions can be discerned concerning this question. I am urging us to see this issue as more complicated than a mere yes or no to the use of the term "God." That is, unless one wishes to adopt a strictly nontheistic position, as some humanists and naturalists advocate. But this would exclude Wieman, Burhoe, and Karl Peters, for example, from the ranks of religious naturalists.

In the first place there are those, like Loomer who think the concept of God is vitally important, at least in the Western tradition, provided that it is drastically rethought. Gordon Kaufman, for example, takes the relativizing and humanizing function of the concept of God to be of paramount significance.

There are those who would use the concept of God for devotional use, but who understand that an analysis of the concept would reveal something so far removed from the traditional concept that the concept has no theoretical use. The early Meland is probably the clearest example of this type. For Meland, as for Wieman, there must be an alternation between the language of devotion and the language of theoretical reflection (Meland 1933b; Wieman 1968, 30, 32; Wieman 1987, 99–100, 190; Stone 1992, 157–167). The term "God" unifies the multiplex conditions on which we are dependent and gives them a cosmic import, but the language of critical reasoning recognizes the plurality of these conditions and uses instead carefully crafted rational and instrumental concepts designed for understanding and practical adjustment.

Further there are those who think the concept of God is generally to be avoided, but for purposes of communication or joint celebration or repentance are willing to employ a hermeneutical translation device. I am willing to invoke the name of deity when I take an oath in order to convey the seriousness with which I take my obligation. When I attended the bedside of a patient wracked with pain and was asked to pray, I did so with fervor. It was not about me. When I attended my mother's memorial service I knew there would be prayers, so rather than grumble, I used my translation device: "God is the traditional term for the sum of the constructive and challenging aspects of the universe." Yet when I see the demonic and destructive possibilities of religion in today's world, especially when mixed with political fervor, I wish to urge extreme caution in the use of religious language. And I definitely wish to defend the right of atheists and agnostics. If they are silenced, religious naturalists will be next.

Fourth there are those who think the concept of God is not helpful, but accept, indeed often appreciate, its use by other people. Ursula Goodenough is a representative of this view.

Finally there are those who think the concept of God is so dangerous as to be beyond rehabilitation. William Jones and David Bumbaugh are examples of this view.

Chapter Six

Other Current Religious Naturalists

Robert Corrington

Professor of Philosophical Theology at Drew University, Robert Corrington is the author of a number of significant works developing what he calls an "ecstatic naturalism." He draws on a rich metaphysical tradition including Schopenhauer, Schelling, C. S. Peirce, and Justus Buchler and also on current hermeneutical theory, including Kristeva. Corrington departs from much postmodern hermeneutics by following Peirce in anchoring the semiotic relation within the natural world. For example, bacteria interpret their environment for food and toxins. Sign interpretation does not require consciousness. Like that of Robert Neville, this is a theory that embeds humans as language users firmly within that natural, physical world.

Corrington is a metaphysician in that he develops a set of categories by which to see the fullness of the world as we can experience and know it, to see life and to see it whole. His religious outlook, especially as developed in *Nature's Religion*, is one part of his total outlook, definitely not an afterthought, but more of a capstone. His religious outlook, which is explicitly post-Christian, is a metaphysics without God, resting on a rhythm alternating between ecstatic encounters with the sacred and intervals of what could be called recuperation, culminating in "the eros of spirit." Of special note is that he wishes to cleanse the religious life from anthropocentrisms as far as possible, to eschew false consolation and to avoid fanaticism. (In his first major statement of his position, *Ecstatic Naturalism*, he had a concept of God, which he later rejected [Corrington 1994]. See *Nature's Religion*, xvii. The Introduction and first chapter of his earlier book are recommended as background for his philosophical theology. See also Corrington, 2007.)

His vocabulary is carefully thought through, deeply informed by both the history of Western metaphysics and psychoanalytic theory, and requires careful reading. It is rich, evocative, and rewarding.

Basic to Corrington's thought is his notion of "the ontological difference" between *nature naturing (natura naturans)* and *nature natured (natura naturata)*. Nature is the most general idea of all. "Nature per se cannot be conceived in any but the *most* elliptical way. . . . In the barest sense, nature is the availability of orders, as well as the 'sum' of the orders themselves. Nature has no location, that is, it is not *in* anything. It is the nonlocated location within which all container relations obtain, as well as the innumerable relations that are *not* container relations, such as laws" (Corrington 1997, 3, italics in original). *Natura naturans* might be thought of as the world as productive of everything and *natura naturata* as the attained and emerging orders of the world. This distinction is basic to Spinoza and was developed in a distinctive way by Heidegger. However, before Spinoza "this distinction emerges in the twelfth century Latin tradition," although "it is as old as thought itself" (Corrington 1997, 4).

While it might be argued that the idea of *natura naturans* is ontologically distinct and superior, and thus falling outside our working definition of naturalism, I prefer to take Corrington's explicit statements as well as the general tenor of his thought to include him within this history of religious naturalism. According to him, naturalists must reject the notions of providence and theodicy, and "there can be no principle of sufficient reason to explain the existence of the world" (Corrington 1997, 30).

Corrington's naturalism is similar to that of Spinoza, Bernhardt, and Crosby in that there is an austerity to his outlook. The recognition that humans occupy a minor and vulnerable place in the grand scheme of things is central to his outlook.

In many senses, ecstatic naturalism insists on a rich universe of signs and objects. . . . But when it comes to the final object of religious semiosis, a kind of holy minimalism enters into that framework, a minimalism that struggles to protect the human process from importing personal predicates where, for good or ill, they simply do not obtain. Once one has made the primary move of rejecting the concepts of providence and theodicy, as all naturalists must, it follows that no honest naturalism can then somehow discover that the universe was created to be congenial to human desire. (Corrington 1997, 58)

In explicating Corrington in detail we can follow the major divisions of *Nature's Religion*. First there is the concept of "sacred folds." This is a metaphor for especially meaningful events, ones that are "thick" or "folded back," what in religious studies we have come to call "hierophanies," although they need not be manifestations of personal deities (Corrington 1997, 23). The "form-shattering momentum" of nature's sacred folds enters into "the region of ultimacy" (Corrington 1997, 56). In an interesting semantic move, Corrington explicitly rejects the term "atheism," equating this with the "absurd claim that there can be no power that we might call divine (or, sacred in an extrahuman sense) within nature" (Corrington 1997, 38).

> Nature's sacred folds . . . have no collective integrity, nor do they embody a common teleological pattern. They obtain prior to the divide between good and evil precisely because they unfold their power without any regard whatsoever for the desires and needs of the human process. As epiphanies of power they represent those uncanny moments in which nature, for whatever reason, folds back upon itself to achieve a dimension of enhanced semiotic scope and density. The increase in semiotic scope is manifest in the ability of the fold to enter into many intersecting transference fields simultaneously, while the increase in semiotic density is manifest in the dramatic enhancement of projective and counterprojective meaning that hovers around the fold. The human process cannot help but be caught up in these manic swirls of energy and meaning. . . . The image of manic power . . . signal(s) that any encounter with nature's folds would accelerate and heat up the human process with material that might be too strong to integrate." (Corrington 1997, 61–62)

This image of the manic power of these hierophanies overheating the human process will lead us to the recuperative value of "intervals," which we treat below.

These sacred folds are inexplicable and have no governing logic. "We cannot say why nature has epiphanies of power. By the same token we cannot isolate some alleged principle of unity that would bring all of nature's folds under some governing logic or schema. There is a sense in which we encounter an ultimate form of irrationality when we become exposed to nature's folds" (Corrington 1997, 29).

Now the image shifts. The fold becomes "an overwhelming wave that comes crashing into finite structures." The wave itself has no self-awareness. "No one would say that the wave is conscious of its power or that it is a person who looks toward specific agents or structures as it expends its energy" (Corrington 1997, 29). To use colloquial language, the wave does not have it in for me. The intrusion of nature's sacred folds into our lives follows no rhyme or reason. "They are simply there like grand presences that come and go as our species makes its fitful way toward probable extinction" (Corrington, 1997, 58).

However, humans project human-like qualities on the waves. When humans encounter the wave, "strong unconscious complexes are activated that are compelled to see the wave *as* something other than what it is." We are inclined to see the wave "as a unique locus of power and meaning for our tribe, or as a message-laden epiphany that holds a specific revelation" (Corrington 1997, 29, italics in original). The sacred folds are magnets for human projections.

The destructive possibilities of these projections are extremely dangerous in Corrington's eyes. Rushing too quickly to divinize the folds of nature "has had disastrous social and political consequences . . . turning the adherents of one fold, or fold-cluster, against another." The folds have a power to "pull forth projections, thereby magnifying them, thus giving them their own divine status. It is as if you were to take something dangerous and dramatically amplify its power." Corrington is quite strong in his language. "For example, the failure to deal with one's contrasexual dimension could turn into a massive patriarchal projection, supported by a fold that is divinized, that in turn could generate violence" (Corrington 1997, 32). One of Corrington's illustrations is the Battle of Blood River in 1838 when the Afrikaners defeated the Zulus, "thus showing their election from god to control the southern part of Africa." There can develop a system of competing epiphanies, with sign systems jealous of each other. "Thus the three gods of Western monotheisms remain at war with each other" (Corrington 1997, 44).

Note that Corrington does not say that the sacred folds are projections, but that they attract projections. The type of austere philosophical theology that Corrington advocates does not take a totalizing Feuerbach-like approach. If an approach based on psychoanalysis deconstructs the totality of the gods and goddesses that have emerged in human history, a better approach would be open to the possibility that "it is possible to become permeable to something that is not a human projection, even if it extremely difficult to find out what that something is. What psychoanalysis provides, and it is absolutely indispensable, is a constant reminder that in almost all cases we will create a god or goddess of our own making, and that this transference object will come to dominate the psyche even though it is partially a product of that very psyche (in consort with the relevant fold(s) of nature)" (Corrington 1997, 36). The numinous powers fill finite selves with content that it both dangerous and transforming. "For some, self-divinization is the result, which has often produce horrendous social and political consequences. For others the shattering of form may produce a crippling affective or thought disorder" (Corrington 1997, 42).

Thus Corrington does not *reduce* nature's folds to human projection. "Folds have power in themselves, regardless of how they are colored by the human process" (Corringon 1997, 35). Put in a pithy statement, "Folds exist and projections exist and they find each other" (Corrington 1997, 55).

We have seen that Corrington uses the terms "divine" and "sacred" in describing these folds. But he holds that it is important to strip away these projections. "There is something like a divine power within the orders of nature." However, this power is not supernatural. "It is a momentum within nature that has a compelling presence. However, in the process of working past and through projections and transference relations, one traditional trait after another drops away." The "witch" burnings of the sixteenth and seventeenth centuries attest to "the blind ferocity of projections to assault the personal and social orders." Unconsciousness is a sin. To put it strongly, "unconsciousness can lead to a violent overturning of form, measure, and justice" (Corrington 1997, 38–39).

The second major concept Corrington employs is that of "intervals" between the sacred folds. The term comes from an older medical vocabulary that indicated the calmer periods between the paroxysms of a fever. The manic power of sacred folds could heat up the human process so that it cannot achieve integration. In these intervals of decompression the human organism can recover its equilibrium and become open to life-transforming goals. These periods of recovery provide space for the probing and assimilation of the material absorbed from the sacred folds. One thing that can happen is a humbling process, when the self realizes that the "all-powerful sacred fold is in fact a circumscribed and finite event that stands over and against other events that do not honor its claims to ultimacy." In these rare moments "religious self-consciousness can become free from a demonic temptation toward divinized origins, while giving content to the goals that seem to come so effortlessly out of the decompression in the world" (Corrington 1997, 69–70). These are religious goals, that is, goals "which live in and out of the infinite"

(Corrington 1997, 75). "The transformation of finite instrumental goals into the infinite goals of religion takes place through the opening power of the interval as it frees the self from the intense semiotic noise that comes to it from those sacred folds that threaten to envelop it" (Corrington 1997, 84). This period of decompression allows the self to make judicious choices, but they are not merely instrumental choices, for they are done in the light of the self's glimpse of the infinite. The loss of the manic psychic inflation can turn to mourning, irony, betrayal, rage, or a sense of liberation. However, if the self can hold itself open in courage and insight, it can return in a transformed way to the lost object. Otherwise, the epiphany may return with greater power and shatter the boundaries of the ego. We cannot domesticate the religious powers of nature. But with "insight, luck, natural convergence, and natural grace, we can enter into a religious sphere that does not destroy the very creatures who intensify it with their abjected desires" (Corrington 1997, 96).

The third concept is that of "the unruly ground." Corrington challenges the romantic notion of nature as a great nurturing mother, "forgetting that the image of the web is derived from a creature who uses it primary [sic] as a finally-tuned killing machine" (Corrington 1997, 97). The unruly ground both enables and destroys without intentionality or consciousness awareness. The unruly ground can be understood through analogy with a churning sea that is indifferent to whatever may occurs below its surface, yet which also furnishes nourishment to its creatures. "What does this unruly ground provide? Everything whatsoever . . . both actualities and possibilities, goods and absences, life and death, space/time and things in space/time" (Corrington 1997, 102). Given this fecundity, finite sign users will select-out regnant features for emphasis. Another image which Corrington uses is that of the continual spawning of the constituents of *nature natured*. This image suggests an ejection and we, and everything else, are orphans or foundlings. "On the deepest level, the world itself is a foundling, an eject that has no direct link to the inaugurating and unruly ground" (Corrington 1997, 119).

This is a nontheistic conception of grace. "So we have providingness but no provider, natural grace but no bestower of grace, sheer availability but no intentionality, and a seed bed for consciousness with no consciousness in the seed bed." From particular instances of consciousness, a universal conscious intentional agent is projected. "From finite instances of purpose, evident in only a few of the orders of the world, a kind of grand purpose is read into the unruly ground" (Corrington 1997, 103). In another of his striking images he writes, "The sheer providingness of nature . . . could no more bestow love than could the water coursing through the gills of a fish" (Corrington 1997, 136). This notion of grace without a bestower results in a mixed attitude. "For the ecstatic naturalist, stoicism, which makes the most sense when applied to a material substrate of some kind, must be augmented by a kind of fitful *jouissance* that appears whenever the unruly ground somehow breaks into the world in specific ways." These "primary experiences" include both "various forms of shipwreck or boundary situations," but also "moments of high creativity, sexual connection and release, a sudden illumination and expansion of a meaning horizon, and a rapturous sense of the sublime" (Corrington 1997, 104–105). It does not require superior strength to be open to the intermittent grace. "The correlation between providingness and natural grace provides the self with the courage to enter into what puts its deepest self-portrayal at risk" Providingness, despite its roots in the unruly ground, has a quiet presence. There are "no apocalyptic dramas . . . only the endless quiet availability of orders. Providingness is not a sustaining and conscious agent to whom the self can turn" (Corrington 1997, 131). Nevertheless, providingness provides an ontological courage. The self cannot expect from the unruly ground some ally in negotiating through life. "It cannot answer a petition or be quickened by prayer. . . . Strictly speaking, there is no it that could be addressed." Instead, "providingness can only make available a type of healing and transformation that is far more subtle than most that we desire" (Corrington 1997, 132). This is a very minimalist theory of grace indeed, but I am in agreement with Corrington that this minimal, purged of illusion, can be very real.

The last concept is that of "spirit's eros." There is a sadness in the face of recognition of our status as foundlings, but this sadness can give way to an ecstatic transformation, an eros toward the sacred. "If the utter indifference of nature to human need makes us melancholy, the transformative prospects emergent from the spirit bring us into the erotic embrace of something that transcends all other orders" (Corrington 1997, 3).

We must strip anthropomorphic categories from this concept as much as possible. "It is impossible to *fully* remove anthropocentric and anthropomorphic categories from philosophical theology. We are always left with some measure of the human in a fundamental perspective." Nevertheless, "whenever it seems compelling to use a human trait at a key juncture in the framework, every effort must be spent to assure that it is rendered as generically as possible. We will see that this final qualification applies to the ways in which the concept of eros will be reconstructed" (Corrington 1997, 136–137). Indeed, parallel to the way Corrington embeds signs in nature, the spirit, and its eros, are embedded in the how or way of nature.

Although when we reduce the anthropomorphic language to a minimum, we can say that eros is not a conscious agent, its central characteristic is movement and transformation. It is a longing, desire, drive, without intentionality. (Corrington 1997, 136–137). Summarizing several pages, he writes that "Spirit's eros is thus the posttemporal, trans-ordinal, lack generated, infinity evoking, connecting, and differentiating momentum that lies deeply within the transference field (of the human order)." The Greek experience witnesses to the often "ferocious power of this field of relation manifest in both pathology and creativity." The final step probes into "that from which and through which eros comes. Eros is the outer circumference of the even more elusive spirit; it is its how under the conditions of finitude" (Corrington 1997, 159). This last, put differently, states that spirit is the heart of eros.

Following in the long tradition from St. Paul to Josiah Royce, spirit is the great interpreter. "This spirit-interpreter intersects with the human community whenever that community is called upon to interpret and ramify signs of great complexity and depth." Signs, especially religious ones, have "traces and potentialities that conscious agents will always fail to exhaust. The spirit does not add new signs to this mixture, nor does it have an antecendent interpretive code that could somehow be accessed." The spirit does not furnish "a semiotic blueprint for life" and does not "provide an absolute barrier against nonbeing. It is not a body of signs waiting to be decoded, perhaps in some liminal state of consciousness. It cannot give the individual or community a road map of the future." What the spirit can do is to open up "interpretive prospects without providing an actual interpretation. As an open or opening infinite, the spirit pro-vides the connective tissue between and among signs, and opens up each relevant sign so that the sign's own inner momentum can become less hindered." This means that the spirit "has no internal semiotic content. It does not hold at its heart great life secrets. It is much more akin to the opening power of water as it washes away barriers to understanding" (Corrington 1997, 160–161).

As a final word, part of the significance of Corrington's work in relation to the story of religious naturalism can be seen in his appraisal of John Dewey's *A Common Faith*. The brunt of this appraisal, somewhat echoing Santayana, is that Dewey "utterly fails to probe into the depth dimension of nature's epiphanies and decompressions, while providing a kind of ersatz comfort to those humanisms that refuse to look into the ways in which the ontological difference enters into the human pro-cess." Dewey's "stress is always on how the human process can unify its instrumental and aesthetic nature." For Dewey religious ideals function as Kantian regulative principles which unify human life. However, they do not "connect the self to the depth-dimension of nature nor do they acknowledge the extrahuman (but not extranatural) powers that enter into the human process." Dewey's descriptive naturalism seems to ride "on the surfaces of *nature natured* while being simultaneously oblivious to the transference field and the pulsations of *nature naturing*. His humanistic religion is no religion at all." Corrington grants that for Dewey the world is a mixture of the precarious and the stable, but this doesn't get to the heart of the matter: the world is "a realm in which many overwhelming powers can enter into and transform (or even destroy) human life" (Corrington 1997, 76–77, italics in original).

I would suggest that this is a deficient religion, rather than no religion at all. My appraisal of Dewey is similar to that of Corrington but, as might be expected, not as harsh (Stone 1992, 202–207). Even within a naturalistic framework we can speak of occasional transformation by powers not of our own making. At this point Wieman is a better guide than Dewey.

Additional Writers

LARRY AXEL. An able historian of Chicago naturalism and a major figure in the American Journal of Theology and Philosophy and Highlands Institute for American Religious and Philosophical Thought, Larry Axel was developing Bernard Meland's elementalism at his untimely death. Readers will want to explore his "Reshaping the Task of Theology" and "Religious Creaturalism and a New Agenda for Theology" (Axel 1987 and Axel 1989).

DAVID BUMBAUGH. Unitarian Universalist minister, now Professor of Ministry at Meadville/Lombard Theologial School, has been arguing for a *humanist* theology of reverence. He says we are called to reverence before "this miraculous world of our everyday experience, . . . a world in which neither god nor humanity is at the center; in which the center is the void, the ever fecund matrix out of which being emerges." He writes also of "a deep reverent, mystical sense of being an integral part of a sacred and holy reality which is the interdependent web of being." Further, "we are called to define the *religious* and *spiritual* dimensions of the ecological crisis confronting the world and to preach the gospel of a world in which each is part of all, in which every place and every one is sacred, and every place is holy ground" (Bumbaugh 1994, 37, italics in original).

Drawing on the scientific picture of evolution and ecology, he affirms that "It is a religious story in that it calls us out of our little local universes." Our struggles with meaning and purpose, our search for insight and understanding are not limited to the human enterprise alone, but are part of the emergence of the universe itself. "It is a religious story in that it implies a broader ethic for our lives" enlarging "our sense of responsibility" to include all living things and their habitats. He goes on. "Our existence, our struggles and our failures are lent moral significance by the fact that they occur within a larger context—within the largest context our imaginations can conceive. . . . This is a religious story; it invites us to awe; it demands a vocabulary of reverence" (Bumbaugh 2001, 57–59).

TOM CLARK. In his Web site *naturalism.org* Tom Clark offers suggestive explorations of the meaning of spirituality in a naturalist sense. There is sense of adventure in these probings and Clark clearly invites cooperative inquiry in these matters. He has published *Encountering Naturalism* (Clark 2007).

ROGER GILLETTE. Trained as a scientist, Roger Gillette's "Theology Of, By, and For Religious Naturalism" is a concise statement of religious naturalism as a belief system, an ethics, and a path of spiritual transformation. His article affirms that we can treat the whole process and product of evolutionary emergence in the universe as holy and sacred. For him religious naturalism is a religion "in that it is a system of belief and practice that demands and facilitates one's intellectual and emotional reconnection with one's self, one's family, one's local and global community and ecosystem, (and) the universe" (Gillette 2006). Through this reconnection we can find meaning and purpose and joy and an ethical imperative of love and concern toward self, family, local community and ecosystem, and global community.

WILLIAM HAMMOND. Unitarian, later Unitarian Universalist minister, William D. Hammond published *Ecology of the Human Spirit: Fourteen Discourses in Reverential Naturalism* (Hammond 1996). The twelfth sermon, "Return to Earth Reverence," is an excellent example of religious naturalism. As a child he "was supposed to honor the invisible high-order abstraction *G-o-d* rather than the first-order fact of the self-existing, *creating universe*" (Hammond 1996, 97, italics in original). As he matured he felt the inadequacies of "thinned-out Theism" and "hubristic Humanism," and developed what he called "nature mysticism" or "earth reverence" or *"A Reverential Naturalism."* The central affirmation was that "the universe is a vast, wondrous, *creating* system. *The universe itself is "The Creator!"* (Hammond 1996, 98; italics in original).

STUART KAUFFMAN. Director of the Institute for Biocomplexity and Informatics at the University of Calgary has been working on the concept of emergence. He gives a tentative yes to the use of the God word for the creativity of the universe. This invites spirituality, awe, reverence, and responsibility for the earth (Kauffman 2007, 913–914). See also his *Reinventing the Sacred* (Kauffman, 2008).

ROBERT MESLE. Chapter 17 of Robert Mesle's *Process Theology: A Basic Introduction* introduces his "process naturalism," process thought without God (Mesle 1993). Process naturalism, shares many of the ideas of process theism, except replacing the term "God" with "sacredness," "a powerful sense of what really matters to us" (Mesle 1993, 128). Sacredness is not derived from a divine source. It is a way of experiencing the world.

> I would say that I experience my wife and children as sacred. This means to me, first, that they themselves are of ultimate importance to me. But at the same time, they also act as powerful symbols for, or windows through which I see, the importance of all children, all people, and to some degree, all life. . . . Secondarily, I might speak of other things as sacred, too: an act of self-sacrifice, the beauty of a symphony, or the quest for truth. (Mesle 1993, 128–129).

WILLIAM R. MURRY. Some recent humanist writers have developed what William Murry, past-president of Meadville Lombard Theological School, calls the new humanism, embedding humanity within the natural world (Murry 2000). The best statement of this is his own *Reason and Reverence* (Murry 2006). This is one of the best systematic affirmations of humanism as a way of life since Corliss Lamont's *The Philosophy of Humanism*, anchoring humanism in a scientifically based religious naturalism.

DAVID OLER. Rabbi of Congregation Beth Or in Deerfield, Illinois, David Oler has been leading his congregation from a secular toward a more religious humanism. Picking up the theme so common among our writers, in his Shabbat Service, he writes about "an awesome sense of wonder when we contemplate the tremendous mystery of existence. The grandeur of our world amazes us, and we are also radically amazed by our own capacity for such awe in response to our surroundings. Jacob awoke from his dream of a ladder and said 'how awesome is this place!' " To this mystery we should respond "with humility and awe. . . . Let us continue, in the spirit of Israel, to wrestle with ourselves to find the courage to face that which frightens us so that we can live most fully in the presence of the tremendous mystery of existence" (Oler 2005, 4). Melded with this is the strong humanist emphasis on human values: "To seek to be holy as human beings means to strive for truth and justice to pursue righteousness, and to bring love and compassion into all that we do" (Oler 2005, 8. We do not have time to explore his contributions to the psychology of religion. See Dayringer and Oler 2004, xiii–xiv).

CREIGHTON PEDEN. Author of *The Chicago School* and co-editor of *The Chicago School of Theology—Pioneers in Religious Inquiry* and other historical studies in American radical religion, including F. E. Abbot, Eustace Haydon, and William James Potter, Creighton Peden's inestimable contribution to the cause of religious naturalism has been as founding co-editor of the *American Journal of Theology and Philosophy*, and as the organizing and administrative enabler of the Highlands Institute for American Philosophical and Religious Thought. Basically a humanist in his orientation, he makes the following statement in his autobiographical reflections: "If one's philosophy requires, as one Nobel laureate dubbed, a 'God Particle' . . . I would suggest a god-idea which represents our highest evolving ideals and is conceived as part of evolving nature without a personal relationship with humans. . . . Having come to understand humans as social animals who have evolved as a part of nature, I no longer find satisfactory the pre-scientific mythologies concerning human beings. . . . The way to solve problems is, as President Roosevelt proclaimed, through experimentation" (Peden 2006, 113–114).

CHET RAYMO. In his delightful *Skepticism and True Believers*, Chet Raymo has given us a very readable accout of the attitudes of these two groups. A teacher of physics and astronomy, Raymo has a weekly column in the *Boston Globe*. "Science cannot nor should be a religion, but it can be the basis for the religious experience: astonishment, experiential union, adoration, praise" (Raymo 1998, 255). After debunking pseudoscience, he goes on to write: "The pieces are in place for a renaissance of religion: cosmic knowledge, the power for good, awareness of mystery, a sense of responsibility for all creation, and a longing for union with the Absolute. What is required is imagination, self-confidence, courage. The world is charged with the grandeur of God" (Raymo 1998, 267). Although I am a little hesitant about "Absolute" and "God," having read his book I am not put off. Basic to Raymo is his sense that "[A]ll scientific knowledge that we have of this world, or will ever have, is as an island in the sea [of mystery]. . . . We live in our partial knowledge as the Dutch live on polders claimed from the sea" (Raymo 1998, 47, quoted from his previous *Honey from Stone*). As a corollary, "the growth of the island increases the length of the shore along which we encounter mystery" (1998, 48). The term "mystery" does not seem to be used in Gabriel Marcel's sense of the distinction between a problem and a mystery, but in the sense that we cannot claim to have a scientific explanation for everything. Also key to Raymo is that he opposes Wordsworth's "meddling intellect" who "murders to dissect" with Richard Feynman's reply that scientific knowledge adds to the excitement of a flower. It adds. It does not subtract (Raymo 1998, 52–53). Also important is his *When God is Gone Everything is Holy* (Raymo 2008).

MARVIN SHAW. Two major contributions to religious naturalism have been made by Marvin Shaw. The first is *The Paradox of Intention: Reaching the Goal by Giving Up the Attempt to Reach It* (Shaw 1988). Here he reflects on the paradox that we often reach a goal only after we stop striving for it. To do this he explores five writers, Epictetus, Paul of Tarsus, Lao Tzu, the Tantric Buddhist Saraha, and Viktor Frankl. Any reflection on a naturalistic (or theistic) theory of grace would benefit from these explorations.

The other contribution is his study of Wieman, *Nature's Grace: Essays on H. N. Wieman's Finite Theism* (Shaw 1995). Here he sets Wieman in the context of Santayana, Dewey, the Chicago naturalists Ames and Mathews, and Bernhardt. He uses the term "naturalistic theism" and finds that Wieman's "openness to gifts" allows for the "theistic stance without the supernatural God." He finds great value in Wieman's middle period, specifically *Methods of Private Religious Living* and Wieman's contributions to *Normative Psychology of Religion* and *The Growth of Religion* (Wieman 1929; Wieman and Westcott-Wieman 1935; and Wieman and Horton 1938).

CHARLENE SPRETNAK. In *States of Grace* Charlene Spretnak pulls together much of the thinking behind her environmental political activism, eco-feminism, and women's spirituality. She develops an "ecological postmodernism" as distinct from both the fragmentation and mechanization of the modernist worldview and from what she sees as the nihilism and alienation from nature of deconstructive postmodernism. This view is based on a perception of the interconnectedness of everything, resulting in a sense of "the grand unity, the ground of the sacred" (Spretnak, 1991, 20). In this worldview the awareness of the larger reality (which includes the perceiving being) can be called revelation. While this revelation may be *extra*ordinary, it is not *super*natural. Indeed, she calls this *ultra*natural (Spretnak 1991, 208). She holds that we need to feel ourselves to be part of something important and that nothing is more important than our place in the story of the earth and our responsibility and contribution to its unfolding (Spretnak 1991, 228–229). Here she strikes a note echoed by many of today's religious naturalists.

Spretnak explores four wisdom traditions as resources for developing and practicing this ecological postmodernism: Buddhist, indigenous, Goddess, and the Abrahamic traditions. She buttresses her argument with detailed and suggestive historical analyses of the development of modern and postmodern ideas.

Spretnak's *The Spiritual Dimension of Green Politics* should also be consulted (Spretnak, 1986; see also Bodian and Windfall, 1988). Here she valorizes attention to bodily feelings and awareness of interconnectedness as aspects of the resacralization of the natural world. I resonate with her notion of "a state of grace" where she says that "Awe at the intricate wonders of creation and celebration of the cosmic unfolding are the roots of worship" (Spretnak 1986, 42). My only demurral is that there are other roots, such as the moral consciousness.

Conclusion

Living Religiously as a Naturalist

What Is Religious About Religious Naturalism?

Speaking as a pragmatist, the worth of any theology or "atheology" is not only its apparent theoretical adequacy in terms of internal consistency and compatibility with all of the rest of human experience in our various insights and disciplines, but also what it "feels like" to live by this viewpoint and what kind of attitudes, character, and ethics it encourages. Robert McAfee Brown maintains that the test of any theology is whether it is good for children (Brown 1980, 546). Religious naturalism is good for children!

This conclusion will be very personal. I have been trying to expound and analyze the views of other religious naturalists. However, for this conclusion I shall revert to a personal voice, reflecting what I have learned in the process of writing this volume and in the hope that some of my naturalist companions will agree. John Haught, in his thoughtful reply to religious naturalism, *Is Nature Enough?*, has said that there are sunny and sober religious naturalists (Haught 2006, 10). I hope that I am presenting a view for all weather.

I understand why many people wish to have a belief in God. We seek an explanation as to why there is anything, not nothing. But I have come to think that God does not suffice as an explanation. Why is there a God? Naturalism respects limit-questions, but it retains an agnostic attitude toward them.

There is an upside and a downside to living as a religious naturalist. The upside, the good news, is that you can lead a religiously fulfilling life without many of the disadvantages of traditional religion. You do not have to wonder "if God has it out for me," or why bad things happen to the relatively innocent. And you do not have to feel guilty for breaking some of the irrational taboos of a childhood religion. Also much of what we ordinarily mean by religious resources for living can be found within a naturalistic framework.

But what are these religious values? Put differently, what is religious about religious naturalism? "Religion," like "nature" (indeed, like most valuable words), has a great deal of ambiguity. Reflection on the term "religion" suggests that we should avoid a too simple approach in defining the essence of religion. *One way of getting at what we mean by religion is that it is our attempt to make sense of our lives and behave appropriately within the total scheme of things.* This may not be a complete definition, but it points to a couple of crucial issues. First, when we try to "make sense" of something, what we are doing is not "empirical" in the strict sense, but it need not, it should not, side-step empirical inquiry. In other words, insight should be informed by the best sciences available. Second, when we try to make sense of our lives there is a dimension of this that asks about "everything." How does my joy, my pain, my dilemma, fit into the grand scheme of things? This striving to make sense "of it all" can be thought of as what makes us religious. It is what unites naturalistic and other religious orientations. As a naturalist I try to be open to the graces and challenges this life affords me. Occasionally I picture myself as a minor partner in one of the growing edges of the cosmos.

Religion can be a quest or an answer. Likewise religious naturalism can have the adventure or loneliness or angst of a search or it can have the assurance of a settled conviction. It can lead to transformation or to stability.

To lead a religious life does not mean that one accepts or identifies with any particular religion. I am agreeing with Dewey here. Thus a religious naturalist need not be a member of any normally recognized religious group. Santayana and Dewey, for example, were not members of any religious group in their mature years. Whether they needed a religious upbringing is another question. I suggest that there is enough religiousness in popular culture to provide grist for a naturalistic mill for some people, although popular religiousness generally provides a poor diet and a lack of critical distance. Some people are joiners, others are not. Some people find a compatible group to join, others do not. Some naturalists are alienated from their childhood religion, others have learned a critical acceptance of it. Some religious naturalists find resources and discipline in a particular faith community and its tradition. Some of us have even learned how to live lives of integrity with multiple religious identities, as Robert Neville suggests in *Boston Confucianism* (Neville 2000). Such a concept might seem strange to a monotheist.

Religious values are multiplex. Most religions will include beliefs, affects, practices, and ethics. These, of course, are part of human life in general. However, religion is not to be equated with any of these components. How they orient oneself to the big picture is what makes them religious. This conception of religion translates Joachim Wach's "orientation to the dimension of the ultimate" naturalistically into "an orientation to the cosmos" (Wach 1958; see Rue 2005). Let us look briefly at the conceptual, affective, and ethical components of a naturalistically oriented religion.

Clearly a naturalistic religion does not require a belief in God, although it may include belief in God naturalistically conceived. For many religious naturalists the intellectual component of our religious life takes the form of insight rather than specific beliefs. For many religious naturalists the epic of evolution is a main part of the ideational content of their religion.

Religions can involve many possible affects and no one feeling or mood should be taken to be defining. Celebration, courage, guilt, repentance, a sense of alienation or of being at home, a feeling of dependence or of independence are among many affects that have been involved in religion and which naturalists may also share.

Religion normally involves an ethical imperative, but many nonreligious people also lead ethical lives. What religion often adds to the ethical imperative is a motivation to act morally and sometimes a way to deal with moral failure. Religion often adds a dimension of continuing challenge or perpetual unrest to the moral life. Finally religion often gives some specificity to the moral imperative. In particular, many religious naturalists have a strong sense of urgency in protecting, nurturing, and renewing the natural systems and ecosystems that nurture life on this planet.

My claim is that the upside, the good news of religious naturalism, is that we can have the values of religion within a naturalistic framework. We can celebrate the wonders of life. We can aspire to nobler living (Drees 2006, 120). One does not need a god who is a conscious agent, supermind, or intelligent designer to enjoy ecstasy or sustaining moods or to lead a moral life.

The downside of religious naturalism is that one does not have the solace and comfort of a super mind, of divine intervention, of an ultimate explanation, nor of immortality. There is no cosmic companion to assuage moments of loneliness, although some of us have found many neighbors and distant kin among the nonhuman peoples of this world. When an earthquake devastates Lisbon, when tsunamis or hurricanes strike, or when the depth of human evil is revealed in holocaust, child abuse, torture, or the holds of slave ships, there is no God to cling to. We cannot take refuge in God's will to make sense of it all or rely on God to save us. It is our responsibility to strengthen the levees and prepare for emergencies. It is our job to comfort the bereaved. It is our job to resist genocide and to remember those who perished. Furthermore, God does not bear responsibility for those who are not spared as if their guilt is stronger or their prayers not as effective as those who do not perish.

To live without appeal to God may take some mourning. However, mourning is part of maturity. This does not mean that nonnaturalists are immature, but that moving into a naturalistic framework may require maturity to do some grief work.

Some religious naturalists use the term "God" in a revised sense. Either way, they share in the upside and the downside, the good news and the needed maturity of religious naturalism.

To live without hope of immortality may also take some mourning. To be sure, since patterns of information can outlast their original physical substratum, just as music can outlive its composer, immortality is not definitively foreclosed in a naturalistic framework. However, most religious naturalists live richly and fully without hope of immortality. Karl Peters, with his notion that our larger selves include streams of cultural, biological, and physical information, extending long before and after our conscious physical selves, is helpful here.

The good news is that naturalists need not debate with science, do not fan the flames of religious hostility and wars, are not burdened with unnecessary guilt or outdated moral codes, and are not raised to be dogmatic. Many other religious people share these freedoms, but naturalists do not have to fight rearguard action against the sorrier aspects of religion as many religious liberals have to fight.

The good news is that religious naturalists can nurture in themselves an openness to the world, human, nonhuman, and domesticated. They can train themselves in mindfulness. They can often find joy in useful work and the consolation of love. Religious naturalists appreciate the draba flower, the *Calypso borealis*, the fierceness of Mt. Ktaadin, the beauties of the Shasta nation bioregion, the life-and-death struggles at Tinker Creek, and the power of the evening star on a clear northern New Mexico night. (These allusions are to Aldo Leopold, John Muir, Henry David Thoreau, Gary Snyder, Annie Dillard, and an evening with my wife under the canopy of stars north of Hernandez, New Mexico.) Religious naturalists are not the only ones to appreciate these concrete particulars, but we claim them as our sacraments and burning bushes.

There is the issue of idolatry, of absolutizing the finite. Modern theologians, especially Wieman, Kaplan, Reinhold Niebuhr, Tillich, Langdon Gilkey, and James Luther Adams, have pointed out the human propensity to deify finite values and causes. Tillich was aware of what he saw as the easy move from an empty autonomy to a dangerous heteronomy. A naturalistic outlook will be accused of having no defense against the human tendency to fashion absolutes. But the traditional religions are just as prone to absolutism. The defense against idolatry lies not in monotheism, but in the constant nurturing of the institutions and spirit of criticism.

How humans can fashion a sustainable and just life for all creatures on our fragile Earth is our most pressing issue. The religious resources of naturalism provide orientation, healing, and motivation for some of us. We also need to figure out how to talk about responsible choice.

The final question concerns our attitude, our orientation, our aspirations, and response to the values and worth that we discern in our experience.

Is nature enough? No. Nature is not self-explanatory. Nature is not completely meaningful. Nature does not offer complete and final fulfillment of our deepest longings. Nature does not give us the answer to our moral dilemmas. Nature does not give us a foundation for our epistemological, metaphysical, or valuational searches. Nature is not enough for all our wishes. But nature, including human culture, is all we have and often it suffices magnificently (adapted from Stone 2003b, 783). In short, there are pockets of meaning that sometimes we can enlarge. With Thoreau I say, "I have great faith in a seed" (Thoreau 1993, vii).

Bibliography

Adams, James Luther. 1965. *Paul Tillich's Philosophy of Culture, Science, and Religion.* New York: Harper & Row Publishers.

Albanese, Catherine L. 1990. *Nature Religion in America: From the Algonkian Indians to the New Age.* Chicago: The University of Chicago Press.

Alexander, Samuel. 1920, 1966. *Space, Time and Deity: The Gifford Lectures at Glasgow, 1916–1918.* Two volumes. London: Macmillan & Co. (Repr. New York: Dover Publications)

———. 1927. "Lessons from Spinoza," *Chronicon Spinozanum,* vol. V (1927), 14–29.

———. 1939. *Philosophical and Literary Pieces.* Edited by John Laird. London: Macmillan & Co., Ltd. (Repr. Westport, CT: Greenwood Press Publishers, 1970).

Ames, Edward Scribner. 1929. *Religion.* New York: Henry Holt and Company.

Arnold, Charles Harvey. 1966. *Near the Edge of Battle: A Short History of the Divinity School and the 'Chicago School of Theology' 1866–1966.* Chicago: The Divinity School Association.

Avery, Jon Henry. 1989. *An Analysis and Critique of Roy Wood Sellars' Descriptive and Normative Theories of Religious Humanism.* Unpublished Ph.D. dissertation. The Iliff School of Theology and University of Denver.

Axel, Larry. 1980. "Bernard Meland and Religious Humanism," *Religious Humanism* 14: 21–29.

———. 1987. "Reshaping the Task of Theology," *American Journal of Theology and Philosophy* 859–862.

———. 1989. "Religious Creaturalism and a New Agenda for Theology," in *God, Values, and Empiricism: Issues in Philosophical Theology,* edited by W. Creighton Peden and Larry E. Axel. Macon: GA: Mercer University Press.

Barlow, Connie. 1997. *Green Space, Green Time: The Way of Science.* New York: Springer-Verlag.

Bateson, Gregory. 1991. *A Sacred Unity: Further Steps to an Ecology of the Mind.* Edited by Rodney E. Donaldson. New York: HarperCollins Publishers.

Bateson, Gregory and Mary Catherine Bateson. 1987. *Angels Fear: Towards an Epistemology of the Sacred.* New York: Macmillan Publishing Company.

Beck, Peggy V., Walters, Anna Lee, Francisco, Nia. 1992. *The Sacred: Ways of Knowledge, Sources of Life.* Tsaile, AZ: Navajo Community College Press.

Bernhardt, William H. 1932. "The Significance of the Changing Function of Religion," *The Journal of Religion* 12 (October), 556–570.

———. 1942. "An Analytic Approach to the God-Concept," *Religion in the Making* 2 (March), 252–263.

———. 1943a. "The Cognitive Quest for God," *The Journal of Religion* 23, (April), 91–102; published also in Bernhardt 1971.

———. 1943b. "God as Dynamic Determinant," *The Journal of Religion* 23, (October), 276–285.

———. 1958a. *A Functional Philosophy of Religion.* Denver: The Criterion Press.

———. 1958b. "A Metaphysical Basis for Value Theory and Religion," *The Iliff Review* 15 (Spring), 11–36.

———. 1959a. "Operational Theism," *The Iliff Review* 16 (Winter), 21–33. Published also in Bernhardt 1971.

———. 1959b. "The Reality Principle in Religion," *The Iliff Review* 16 (Spring), 25–42.

———. 1971. *The Cognitive Quest for God and Operational Theism.* Denver: Iliff School of Theology.

Berry, Thomas. 1988. *The Dream of the Earth.* San Francisco: Sierra Club Books.

———. 2006. *Evening Thoughts: Reflections on Earth as Sacred Community.* Edited by Mary Evelyn Tucker. San Francisco: Sierra Club Books and University of California Press.

Bloom, Harold. 1984. "Sunset Hawk: Warren's Poetry and Tradition," in *A Southern Renascence Man: Views of Robert Penn Warren.* Edited by Thomas L. Connelly and Walter B. Edgar. Baton Rouge, LA: Lousiana State University Press, 1984.

Bodian, Stephan and Florence Windfall. 1988. "Seeing Green," *Yoga Journal* 79 (March/April), 57.

Boisvert, Raymond D. 1988. *Dewey's Metaphysics.* New York: Fordham University Press.

Breed, David R. 1992. *Yoking Science and Religion: The Life and Thought of Ralph Wendell Burhoe.* Chicago: Zygon Books.

Bretall, Robert W., ed. 1963. *The Empirical Theology of Henry Nelson Wieman.* New York: The Macmillan Company.

Brightman, Edgar Sheffield. 1940. *A Philosophy of Religion.* New York: Prentice-Hall.

Brock, Rita Nakashima and Rebecca Ann Parker. 2001. *Proverbs of Ashes: Violence, Redemptive Suffering, and the Search for What Saves Us.* Boston: Beacon Press.

Brown, Delwin. 1994. *Boundaries of Our Habitations: Tradition and Theological Construction.* Albany: State Univesity of New York Press.

Brown, Robert McAfee. 1980. "Starting Over: New Beginning Points for Theology," *Christian Theology* XCVII (May 14), 546.

Broyer, A. John and William S. Minor, eds. 1982. *Creative Interchange.* Carbondale, IL: Southern Illinois University Press.

Bumbaugh, David. 1994. "The Heart of a Faith for the Twenty-First Century," *Unitarian Universalism Selected Essays 1994.* Boston: Unitarian Universalist Ministers Association, 28–38.

———. 2001. "Toward a Humanist Vocabulary of Reverence," *Religious Humanism* XXXV (Winter/Spring), 49–59.

Burhoe, Ralph Wendell. 1981. *Toward a Scientific Theology.* Belfast: Christian Journals Limited.

Cajete, Gregory. 2000. *Native Science: Natural Laws of Interdependence.* Santa Fe: Clear Light Publishers.

Callicott, J. Baird. 1989. *In Defense of the Land Ethic: Essays in Environmental Ethics.* Albany: State University of New York Press.

Cassara, Ernest, ed. 1997. *Universalism in America: A Documentary History of a Liberal Faith,* rev. ed. Boston: Skinner House Books.

Cavanaugh, Michael. 1996. *Biotheology: A New Synthesis of Science and Religion.* Lanham, MD: University Press of America.

———. 2000. "What Is Religious Naturalism? A Preliminary Report of an Ongoing Conversation," *Zygon: Journal of Religion and Science* 35 (June), 241–252.

Chan, Wing-tsit. 1963. *A Source Book in Chinese Philosophy.* Princeton: Princeton University Press.

Charlton, Noel G. 2006. *Mind, Beauty and the Sacred: An Introduction to the Thought of Gregory Bateson.* Albany: State University of New York Press.

Clark, Thomas W. 2007. *Encountering Naturalism: A Worldview and Its Uses.* Somerville, MA: Center for Naturalism.

Cleary, Maryell. 2006. "Kenneth Leo Patton." *Dictionary of Unitarian Universalist Biography.* http://www.uuhs.org/htmlduub (accessed August 27, 2006).

Clebsch, William. 1972. *American Religious Thought.* Chicago: University of Chicago Press.

Cohen, Jack. 1958. *The Case for Religious Naturalism: A Philosophy for the Modern Jew.* New York: The Reconstructionist Press.

———. 1999. *Guides for an Age of Confusion: Studies in the Thought of Avraham Y. Kook and Mordecai M. Kaplan.* New York: Fordham University Press.

Cohen, Michael P. 1984. *The Pathless Way: John Muir and American Wilderness.* Madison: The University of Wisconsin Press.

Corrington, Robert S. 1994. *Ecstatic Naturalism: Signs of the World.* Bloomington, IN: Indiana University Press.

———. 1997. *Nature's Religion.* Lanham, MD: Rowman & Littlefield Publishers.

———. Forthcoming. "Deep Pantheism," *International Journal for the Study of Religion, Nature and Culture.*

Crane, Stephen. 1930. *The Collected Poems of Stephen Crane.* Edited by Wilson Follett. New York: Alfred A. Knopf.

Crosby, Donald A. 2002. *A Religion of Nature.* Albany: State University of New York Press.

———. 2003a. "Naturism as a Form of Religious Naturalism," *Zygon: Journal of Religion and Science* 38, (March), 117–120.

———. 2003b. "Transcendence and Immanence in a Religion of Nature," *American Journal of Theology and Philosophy* 24 (September 2003), 245–259.

———. 2007a. "Religious Naturalism." *The Routledge Companion to Philosophy of Religion.* Edited by Paul Copan and Chad V. Meister. New York: Routledge, 1145–1162.

———. 2007b. "A Case for Religion of Nature," *International Journal for the Study of Religion, Nature and Culture* 1, 489–502.

———. 2007c. "Further Contributions to the Dialogue," *International Journal for the Study of Religion, Nature and Culture* 1, 508–509.

———. 2008. *Living with Ambiguity: Religious Naturalism and the Menace of Evil.* Albany: State University of New York Press.

Danto, Arthur C. 1967. "Naturalism," in *The Encyclopedia of Philosophy*, Paul Edwards, Editor-in-Chief. New York: The Macmillan Company.

Dayringer, Richard and Oler, David. 2004. *The Image of God and the Psychology of Religion.* Binghamton, NY: The Haworth Pastoral Press, published simultaneously as *American Journal of Pastoral Counseling* 7, 2004.

Deacon, Terrence W. 1998. *The Symbolic Species.* New York: W. W. Norton.

———. 2001. "How I Gave Up the Ghost and Learned to Love Evolution," in Clifford N. Mathews, Mary Evelyn Tucker and Philip Hefner, eds. *When Worlds Converge: What Science and Religion Tell Us About the Story of the Universe and Our Place Within It.* Peru, IL: Open Court Publishing. 136–154.

———. 2003. "The Hierarchical Logic of Emergence: Untangling the Interdependence of Evolution and Self-organization," in B. Weber and D. Depew, eds. *Evolution and Learning: The Baldwin Effect Reconsidered.* Cambridge: MIT Press.

———. 2005. "Interview with Terry Deacon" *Science and Theology News.* (Fall)

Dean, William. 1986. *American Religious Empiricism.* Albany: State University of New York Press.

———. 1988. *History Making History: The New Historicism in American Religious Thought.* Albany: State University of New York Press.

———. 1991. "Naturalistic Historicism and Humanistic Historicism," in Sheila Davaney, ed., *Theology at the End of Modernity.* Philadelphia: Trinity Press International.

———. 1992. "Empiricism and God," in Randolph Crump Miller, ed., *Empirical Theology: A Handbook.* Birmingham, AL: Religious Education Press.

———. 1994. *The Religious Critic in American Culture.* Albany: State University of New York Press.

———. 2002. *The American Spiritual Culture: And the Invention of Jazz, Football, and the Movies.* New York: The Continuum International Group.

Deloria, Vine, Jr. 1973. *God Is Red.* New York: Dell Publishing Co.

———. 1999. *For This Land: Writings on Religion in America.* New York: Routledge.

Dewey, John. 1927. *The Public and Its Problems.* Chicago: The Swallow Press.

———. 1933a. "A God or the God," review of "Is There a God?—A Conversation by Henry Nelson Wieman, Douglas Clyde Macintosh and Max Carl Otto," *The Christian Century* February 8, 193–196.

———. 1933b. "Dr. Dewey Replies," *The Christian Century*, March 22, 394–395.

———. 1934a. *A Common Faith*. New Haven: Yale University Press.

———. 1934b. "Letter to the Editor," *The Christian Century*, December 5, 1551–1552.

———. 1944. *Human Nature and Conduct*. Madison, WI: US Armed Forces Institute.

———. 1958. *Art as Experience*. New York: Capricorn Books.

———. 1980. *Essays in Experimental Logic, Middle Works*, vol. X, ed. Jo Ann Boydston. Carbondale: Southern Illinois University Press.

———. 1984. *Essays, Reviews, Miscellany, and "Impressions of Soviet Russia, The Later Works, 1925–1953*, vol. 3, ed. by Jo Ann Boydston. Carbondale: Southern Illinois University Press.

———. 1988. *Experience and Nature*, 2nd ed. *Later Works, Vol. I*. Carbondale: Southern Illinois University Press.

Dietrich, John H. 1989. *What if the World Went Humanist?: Ten Sermons*. Edited by Mason Olds. Yellow Springs, OH: Fellowship of Religious Humanists.

Dorrien, Gary. 2003. *The Making of American Liberal Theology: Idealism, Realism, & Modernity, 1900–1950*, Louisville: Westminster John Knox Press.

Drees, Willem. B. 1996. *Religion, Science and Naturalism*. New York: Cambridge University Press.

———. 1997. "Postmodernism and the Dialogue Between Religion and Science: Naturalisms and Religion." *Zygon: Journal of Religion and Science*. 32 (December), 525–541.

———. 1998. "Should Religious Naturalists Promote a Naturalistic Religion?" *Zygon: Journal of Religion and Science* 33 (December), 617–633.

———. 2000. "Thick Naturalism: Comments in *Zygon 2000*," *Zygon: Journal of Religion and Science* 35 (December), 849–860.

———. 2002. *Creation: From Nothing Until Now*. New York: Routledge.

———. 2006. "Religious Naturalism and Science," *The Oxford Handbook of Religion and Science*, ed. Philip Clayton. Oxford: Oxford University Press, 108–123.

Edwards, Rem. 1972. *Reason in Religion: An Introduction to the Philosophy of Religion*. New York: Harcourt, Brace, Jovanovich.

Einstein, Albert. 1936. "Einstein to P. Wright, 24 January 1936." Einstein Archive, reel 52–337, quoted in Max Jammer, *Einstein and Religion: Physics and Theology*. Princteon: Princeton University Press, 1999, 93.

———. 1947. "Einstein to M. W. Gross. 26 April 1947." Einstein Archive, reel 58–243, quoted in Max Jammer, *Einstein and Religion: Physics and Theology*. Princteon: Princeton University Press, 1999, 138–139.

Eliot, Frederick May. 1926. *Fundamentals of Unitarian Faith*. St. Paul, MN: Unity Church.

———. 1928. *Toward Belief in God*. St. Paul, MN: Unity Church.

Emerson, Ralph Waldo. 1982. *Selected Essays*. Edited by Larzer Ziff. New York: Penguin Books.

Emmet, Dorothy. 1966. "Foreword to the 1966 Reprint Edition," in Samuel Alexander, *Space, Time, and Deity*, vol. I. New York: Dover Publications.

Engel, J. Ronald. 1983. *Sacred Sands: The Struggle for Community in the Indiana Dunes*. Middletown, CT: Wesleyan University Press.

Ferm, Vergilius. 1950. "Varieties of Naturalism," in *A History of Philosophical Systems*. Edited by Vergilius Ferm. New York: The Philosophical Library.

Flanagan, Owen. 2006. "Varieties of Naturalism," in *The Oxford Handbook of Religion and Science*, ed. Philip Clayton and Zachary Simpson. New York: Oxford University Press.

Foster, George Burman. 1909. *The Function of Religion in Man's Struggle for Existence*. Chicago: The University of Chicago Press.

———. 1913. "The Status and Vocation of Our Colored People," *The Survey* (Feb. 1), 567–569.

———. 1914. "The Philosophy of Feminism," *The Forum* 52 (July), 10–22.

———. 1921. "The Ethics of the Wage," *The Sewanee Review* 29 (January), 39–43.

Frankenberry, Nancy. 1987. *Religion and Radical Empiricism*. Albany: State University of New York Press.

Gabler, Neal. 1988. *Empire of Their Own: How the Jews Invented Hollywood*. New York: Doubleday.

———. 1998. *Life the Movie: How Entertainment Conquered Reality*. New York: Alfred A. Knopf.

Gaylor, Annie Laurie. 1997. *Women Without Superstition*. Madison, WI: Freedom From Religion Foundation.

Gillette, P. Roger. 2006. "Theology Of, By, and For Religious Naturalism," *Journal of Liberal Religion*, 6 (Spring) www.Meadville.edu.

Goldman, Eric. F. 1977. *Rendezvous with Destiny: A History of Modern American Reform*. New York: Random House, Vintage Books.

Goldsmith, Emanuel S. 1990. "Mordecai M. Kaplan's Synthesis of Judaism and American Religious Naturalism," *American Journal of Theology and Philosophy* 11 (January), 5–24.

———. 1993. "Salvational Zionism and Religious Naturalism in the Thought of Mordecai M. Kaplan," *Process Studies* 22 (Winter), 204–210.

Goldsmith, Emanuel S., Mel Scult and Robert M. Seltzer, eds. 1990. *The American Judaism of Mordecai M. Kaplan*. New York: New York University Press.

Goodenough, Ursula. 1994. "The Religious Dimensions of the Biological Narrative," *Zygon: Journal of Religion and Science* 29 (December), 603–618.

———. 1998. *The Sacred Depths of Nature*. New York: Oxford University Press.

———. 2000a. "Reflections on Scientific and Religious Metaphor," *Zygon: Journal of Religion and Science* 35 (June), 233–240.

———. 2000b. "Religiopoiesis," *Zygon: Journal of Religion and Science* 35 (Sept.), 561–566.

———. 2001. "Vertical and Horizontal Transcendence," *Zygon: Journal of Religion and Science* 36 (March 2001), 21–31.

———. 2003. "Religious Naturalism and Naturalizing Morality," *Zygon: Journal of Religion and Science* 38 (March), 101–109.

Goodenough, Ursula and Terrence W. Deacon. 2003. "From Biology to Consciousness to Morality." *Zygon: Journal of Religion and Science* 38 (December 2003), 801–819.

———. 2004. "Religious Naturalism Defined," *Encyclopedia on Religion and Nature.* http://www.religionandnature.com/ern.

———. 2006. "The Sacred Emergence of Nature," in *The Oxford Handbook of Science and Religion.* ed. Philip Clayton. New York: Oxford University Press, 853–871.

Goodenough, Ursula and Paul Woodruff. 2001. "Mindful Virtue, Mindful Reverence," *Zygon: Journal of Religion and Science* 36 (December 2001), 585–595.

Griffin, David Ray. 2000. *Religion and Scientific Naturalism: Overcoming the Conflicts.* Albany: State University of New York Press.

Hall, David L. and Ames, Roger T. 1987. *Thinking Through Confucius.* Albany: State University of New York Press.

Hammond, William D. 1996. *Ecology of the Human Spirit: Fourteen Discourses in Reverential Naturalism.* Minneapolis: Rising Press.

Hardwick, Charley D. 1996. *Events of Grace: Naturalism, Existentialism and Theology.* Cambridge: Cambridge University Press.

———. 2003. "Religious Naturalism Today," *Zygon: Journal of Religion and Science* 38 (March), 111–116.

Hargrove, Eugene C. 1989. *Foundations of Environmental Ethics.* Englewood Cliffs, NJ: Prentice-Hall.

Harnack, Adolf. 1902. *What Is Christianity?* Translated by Thomas Bailey Saunders. New York: G. P. Putnam's Sons.

Harrison, Paul. 1999. *The Elements of Pantheism: Understanding the Divinity in Nature and the Universe.* Shaftesbury, Dorset: Element Books Limited.

Haught, John F. 2006. *Is Nature Enough? Meaning and Truth in the Age of Science.* Cambridge: Cambridge University Press.

Hefner, Philip. 1993. *The Human Factor: Evolution, Culture and Religion.* Minneapolis: Fortress Press.

Hershock, Peter D. 2005. *Chan Buddhism.* Honolulu: University of Hawai'i Press.

Huang, Siu-chi. 1999. *Essentials of Neo-Confucianism: Eight Major Philosophers of the Song and Ming Periods.* Westport, CT: Greenwood Press.

Humanist Manifestos I and II. 1973. Buffalo: Prometheus Books.

Huxley, Julian. 1941. *Religion without Revelation.* London: Watts & Co.

Inbody, Tyron. 1995. *The Constructive Theology of Bernard Meland: Postliberal Empirical Realism.* Atlanta: Scholars Press.

Ingersoll, Robert G. 1983. *The Best of Robert Ingersoll.* Ed. Roger E. Greeley. Buffalo: Prometheus Books.

James, William. 1942. *A Pluralistic Universe and Other Essays.* London: Longmans, Green and Co.

———. 1947. *Essays in Radical Empiricism* and *A Pluralistic Universe.* London: Longmans, Green and Co.

——. 1961. *The Varieties of Religious Experience.* New York: Collier Books.

——. 1983. *Talks to Teachers on Psychology, The Works of William James*, ed. Frederick H. Burkhardt, Fredson Bowers, and Ignas K. Skrupskelis. Cambridge: Harvard University Press.

Jammer, Max. 1999. *Einstein and Religion: Physics and Theology.* Princeton: Princeton University Press.

Jeffers, Robinson. 1937. *The Selected Poetry of Robinson Jeffers.* New York: Random House.

——. 1977. *The Double Axe and Other Poems.* New York: Liveright Publishing Corporation.

Jenkins, Philip. 2004. *Dream Catchers: How Mainstream America Discovered Native Spirituality.* New York: Oxford University Press.

Johnson, Cassandra and J. M. Bowker. 2004. "African-American Wildland Memories," *Environmental Ethics* 26, 57–75.

Jones, William R. 1978. "The Case for Black Humanism," in *Black Theology II*, ed. Calvin E. Bruce and William R. Jones. Lewisburg, PA: Bucknell University Press.

——. 1998. *Is God a White Racist?: A Preamble to Black Theology.* Boston: Beacon Press.

Kalton, M. 2000. "Green Spirituality: Horizontal Transcendence," in *Paths of Integrity, Wisdom and Transcendence: Spiritual Development in the Mature Self*, ed. M. E. Miller and P. Young-Eisendrath. London: Routledge, 187–200.

Kaplan, Mordecai M. 1934. *Judaism as a Civilization: Toward a Reconstruction of American Jewish Life.* New York: The Macmillan Company, republished by the Jewish Publication Society of America and Reconstructionist Press, 1981.

——. 1948. *The Future of the American Jew.* New York: Macmillan Company; reprinted by Reconstructionist Press, 1981.

——. 1956. *Questions Jews Ask: Reconstructionist Answers.* New York: Reconstructionist Press.

——. 1958. *Judaism Without Supernaturalism: The Only Alternative to Orthodoxy and Secularism.* New York: Reconstructionist Press.

——. 1962. *The Meaning of God in Modern Jewish Religion.* New York: Reconstructionist Press (first published in 1937).

——. 1970. *The Religion of Ethical Nationhood.* New York: The Macmillan Company.

——. 1985. *Dynamic Judaism: The Essential Writings of Mordecai M. Kaplan.* Edited by Emanuel S. Goldsmith and Mel Scult. New York: Fordham University Press.

Karman, James. 1987. *Robinson Jeffers: Poet of California.* San Francisco: Chronicle Books.

Kaufman, Gordon D. 1993. *In Face of Mystery: A Constructive Theology.* Cambridge: Harvard University Press

——. 2003. "Biohistorical Naturalism and the Symbol 'God,' " *Zygon: Journal of Religion and Science* 38 (March), 95–100.

———. 2004. *In the Beginning . . . Creativity*. Minneapolis: Fortress Press.

———. 2006. *Jesus and Creativity*. Minneapolis: Fortress Press.

———. 2007. "A Religious Interpretation of Emergence: Creativity as God," *Zygon: Journal of Religion and Science* 42 (December 2007), 915–928.

Kaufman, William E. 1990. "Mordecai M. Kaplan's Transnaturalism and American Naturalism," in *American Journal of Theology and Philosophy* 11 (Jan. 1990), 25–34.

Kauffman, Stuart. 2007. "Beyond Reductionism: Reinventing the Sacred," *Zygon: Journal of Religion and Science* 42 (December 2007), 903–914.

———. 2008. *Reinventing the Sacred: A New Science, Reason, and Religion*. New York: Basic Books.

King, Winston L. 1954. *Introduction to Religion*. New York: Harper.

Krikorian, Yervant H. 1944. *Naturalism and the Human Spirit*. New York: Columbia University Press.

LaChapelle, Delores. 1988. *Sacred Land, Sacred Sex, Rapture of the Deep: Concerning Deep Ecology and Celebrating Life*. Durango, CO: Kivaki Press.

———. 1996. *D. H. Lawrence: Future Primitive*. Denton, TX: University of North Texas Press.

LaChapelle, Delores and Janet Bourque. 1985. *Earth Festivals*. Silverton, CO: Finn Hill Arts.

Lao Tzu 1963. *Tao Te Ching*. Translated by D. C. Lau. Baltimore: Penguin Books.

Lazaroff, Allan. 1990. "Kaplan and John Dewey," in Emanuel S. Goldsmith, Mel Scult and Robert M. Seltzer, eds, *The American Judaism of Mordecai Kaplan*. New York: New York University Press.

Leopold, Aldo. 1966. A *Sand County Almanac: With Essays on Conservation from Round River*, eds. Carolyn Clugston Leopold and Luna Leopold. New York: The Oxford University Press.

Levinson, Henry S. 1992. *Santayana, Pragmatism, and the Spiritual Life*, Chapel Hill: Univ. of N. Carolina.

———. 2001. "Festive Naturalism and *The Legends of the Jews*," *Harvard Divinity School Bulletin* 30 (Summer/Fall 2001).

———. 2004. "Festive Jewish Naturalism and Richard Bernstein's Work on Freud and Arendt." The Malcolm L. Diamond Memorial Lecture. Princeton University. March 30 (unpublished).

Lewis, David Levering. 2000. *W. E. B. DuBois: The Fight for Equality and the American Century, 1919–1996*. New York: Henry Holt and Company.

Locke, Alain. 1924. "Apropos of Africa," *Opportunity* (February): 37–40.

Loomer, Bernard. 1974. "S-I-Z-E Is the Measure," *Criterion* 13, The Divinity School, The University of Chicago, 5–8; reprinted in *Religious Experience and Process Theology*, ed. Harry James Cargan and Bernard Lee. New York: Paulist Press, 1976.

———. 1976. "Two Conceptions of Power." *Process Studies* 6: 5–32.

———. 1987. *The Size of God: The Theology of Bernard Loomer in Context*, ed. William Dean and Larry Axel. Macon, GA: Mercer University Press; also available in *American Journal of Theology and Philosophy* vol. 8, no's. 1&2 (January & May).

Main, C. F. ed., 1970. *A College Book of Verse*. Belmont: CA: Wadsworth, 1970.

Mathews, Shailer, ed. 1924. *Contributions of Science to Religion*. D. Appleton and Company.

———. 1929. Untitled article in *Religious Life*, ed. E. Sapir. New York: D. Van Nostrand Company.

———. 1931. *The Growth of the Idea of God*. New York: The Macmillan Company.

———. 1940. *Is God Emeritus?* New York: The Macmillan Company.

Mead, George Herbert. 1934. *Mind, Self, and Society from the Standpoint of a Social Behaviorist*. Edited by Charles W. Morris. Chicago: The University of Chicago Press.

Meland, Bernard E. 1931. "Toward a Valid View of God," *Harvard Theological Review* 24, 197–208.

———. 1933a. "Kinsman of the Wild: Religious Moods in Modern American Poetry," *Sewanee Review* 41, 443–453.

———. 1933b "Is God Many or One?" *The Christian Century* 50: 725–726.

———. 1934. *Modern Man's Worship: A Search for Reality in Religion*. New York: Harper & Brothers.

———. 1935. "Mystical Naturalism and Religious Humanism," *The New Humanist*. 8:72–74.

———. 1937. "The Mystic Returns," *The Journal of Religion* 17: 146–160.

———. 1947. *Seeds of Redemption*. New York: The Macmillan Company.

———. 1948. *America's Spiritual Culture*. New York: Harper & Brothers.

———. 1949 *The Reawakening of the Christian Faith*. New York: The Macmillan Company.

———. 1953. *Higher Education and the Human Spirit*. Chicago: The University of Chicago Press; reprinted Chicago: Seminary Cooperative Bookstore, 1965.

———. 1955. "The Roots of Religious Naturalism," unpublished. [This manuscript is undated, but internal evidence in the form of footnotes suggests this date.]

———. 1955 *Faith and Culture*. London: George Allen and Unwin Ltd.

———. 1962. *Realities of Faith: The Revolution in Cultural Forms*. New York: Oxford University Press.

———. 1966. *The Secularization of Modern Cultures*. New York: Oxford University Press.

———. 1969a. "The Empirical Tradition in Theology at Chicago," in *The Future of Empirical Theology*, ed. Bernard Meland. Chicago: The University of Chicago Press.

———. 1969b. "Can Empirical Theology Learn Something from Phenomenology?," in *The Future of Empirical Theology*, ed. Bernard E. Meland. Chicago: The University of Chicago Press.

———. 1970. "The New Realism in Religious Inquiry," *Encounter*, XXXI, No. 4 (Autumn) 311–324.

———. 1976. *Fallible Forms and Symbols: Discourses on Method in a Theology of Culture*. Philadelphia: Fortress Press.

———. 1984. "Reflections on the Early Chicago School of Modernism," *American Journal of Theology and Philosophy* 5 (January), 3–12.

———. 1988. *Essays in Constructive Theology: A Process Perspective*, edited by Perry LeFevre. Chicago: Exploration Press.

Mesle, C. Robert. 1993. *Process Theology: A Basic Introduction*. C. Robert Mesle with final chapter by John B. Cobb, Jr. St. Louis: Chalice Press.

———. 1999. "Seeking the Welfare of Children within the Limits of Nature Alone: Pragmatism, Naturalism and the Inner Life," *Religious Humanism* xxxiii, 1 & 2.

———. 2000. "Creativity, Freedom, Ambiguity, and God," *American Journal of Theology and Philosophy* 21:2 (May), 99–117.

Miller, Randolph Crump. 1974. *The American Spirit in Theology*. Philadelphia: United Church Press.

———, ed. 1992. *Empirical Theology: A Handbook*. Birmingham, AL: Religious Education Press.

Milligan, S. Charles. 1987. "The Pantheistic Motif in American Religious Thought," in Peter Freese, ed., *Religion and Philosophy in the United States of America*, vol. 2. Essen: Die Blaue Eule.

———. 1991. "The Philosophical Venture: A Personal Account," *American Journal of Theology and Philosophy* 12: 2 & 3. (May, September), 121–148.

———. 1996. "The Eco-Religious Case for Naturalistic Pantheism," in Donald A. Crosby and Charley D. Hardwick, editors, *Religious Experience and Ecological Responsibility*. New York: Peter Lang, 235–255.

———. 1999. Letter from Charles Milligan to author. July 16, 1999.

Minor, William Sherman. 1977. *Creativity in Henry Nelson Wieman*. Metuchen, NJ: The Scarecrow Press, and The American Theological Library Association.

Monroe, Harriet. 1938. *A Poet's Life*. NY: The Macmillan Company.

Morgan, C. Lloyd. 1923. *Emergent Evolution*. New York: Henry Holt and Company.

———. 1925. *Life, Mind, and Spirit*. New York: Henry Holt and Company.

Murry, William. 2000. "Religious Humanism Yesterday, Today, and Tomorrow." *Religious Humanism* XXXIV (Summer/Fall), 55–90.

———. 2006. *Reason and Reverence: Religious Humanism for the 21st Century*. Boston: Skinner House Books.

Neville, Robert Cummings. 2000. *Boston Confucianism: Portable Tradition in the Late-Modern World*. Albany: State University of New York Press.

Oelschlaeger, Max. 1991. *The Idea of Wilderness: From Prehistory to the Age of Ecology*. New Haven: Yale University Press.

Olds, Mason. 1996. *American Religious Humanism*, rev. ed. Minneapolis, MN: Fellowship of Religious Humanists.

Oler, David. 2005. *Shabbat Service, Congregation Beth Or*. Deerfield, IL: Congregation Beth Or.

Oliver, Mary. 1992. *New and Selected Poems*. Boston: Beacon Press.

Patton, Kenneth L. 1954. *Man's Hidden Search: An Inquiry in Naturalistic Mysticism* Boston: Meeting House Press.

———. 1964. *A Religion For One World: Art and Symbols for a Universal Religion.* Boston: Beacon Press.

Peden, Creighton. 1987. *The Chicago School: Voices in Liberal Religious Thought.* Bristol, IN: Wyndham Hall Press.

———. 2006. "Recollections," *American Journal of Theology and Philosophy.* 27 (January), 104–114.

Peden, W. Creighton and Larry E. Axel. 1989. *God, Values, and Empiricism: Issues in Philosophical Theology.* Macon, GA: Mercer University Press.

Peden, W. Creighton and Jerome A. Stone. 1996. *The Chicago School of Theology—Pioneers in Religious Inquiry.* 2 vols. Lewiston, NY: The Edwin Mellen Press.

Pepper, Stephen C. 1942. *World Hypotheses: A Study in Evidence.* Berkeley: University of California Press.

Peters, Karl E. 2002. *Dancing with the Sacred: Evolution, Ecology, and God.* Harrisburg: Trinity Press International.

———. 2008. *Spiritual Transformations: Science, Religion, and Human Becoming.* Minneapolis: Fortress Press.

Phenix, Philip Henry. 1954. *Intelligible Religion.* New York: Harper & Brothers.

Pinn, Anthony. 2001. *By These Hands: A Documentary History of African American Humanism.* New York: New York University Press.

Post, John. 1987. *The Faces of Existence: An Essay in Nonreductive Metaphysics.* Ithaca: Cornell University Press.

Radhakrishnan, Sarvepalli and Moore, Charles A. 1957. *A Sourcebook in Indian Philosophy.* Princeton: Princeton University Press.

Randall, John Herman, Jr. 1958. *The Role of Knowledge in Western Religion.* Boston: Starr King Press.

———. 1968. *The Meaning of Religion for Man.* New York: Harper & Row, Publishers.

Raymo, Chet. 1998. *Skeptics and True Believers: The Exhilarating Connection Between Science and Religion.* New York: Walker and Company.

———. 2008. *When God is Gone Everything is Holy: The Making of a Religious Naturalist.* Notre Dame, IN: Sorin Books.

Riggan, George Arkell. 1973. "Epilogue to the Symposium on Science and Human Purpose," *Zygon: Journal of Religion and Science* 8: 1973, 443–481

Rockefeller, Steven C. 1991. *John Dewey: Religious Faith and Democratic Humanism.* New York: Columbia University Press.

Rodman, John. 1986. "Ecological Sensibility." *People, Penguins, and Plastic Trees: Basic Issues in Environmental Ethics*, eds. Donald Van De Veer and Christine Pierce. Belmont, CA: Wadsworth Publishing Company. Reprinted from Donald Scherer and Thomas Attig, *Ethics and the Environment.* Englewood, NJ: Prentice-Hall, 1983.

Rogers, Delores Joan. 1990. *The American Empirical Movement in Theology.* New York: Peter Lang Publishing.

Rosenkranz, Z. 1998. *Albert through the Looking-Glass.* Jerusalem: Jewish National and University Library.

Rue, Loyal. 1989. *Amythia: Crisis in the Natural History of Western Culture.* Tuscaloosa: The University of Alabama Press.

———. 1994. "Redefining *Myth* and *Religion*: Introduction to a Conversation," *Zygon: Journal of Religion and Science* 29 (September), 315–319.

———. 2000. *Everybody's Story: Wising Up to the Epic of Evolution,* Albany: State University of New York Pres.

———. 2005. *Religion Is Not About God: How Spiritual Traditions Nurture Our Biological Nature and What to Expect When They Fail.* New Brunswick, NJ: Rutgers University Press.

Ryder, John, ed. 1994. *American Philosophic Naturalism in the Twentieth Century.* Amherst, NY: Prometheus Books.

Santayana, George. 1899. *Lucifer: A Theological Tragedy.* Chicago: Herbert S. Stone.

———. 1905. *Reason in Religion,* vol. III of *The Life of Reason, or the Phases of Human Progress.* New York: Charles Scribner's Sons.

———. 1913. *Winds of Doctrine: Studies in Contemporary Opinion.* New York: Charles Scribner's Sons.

———. 1923. *Scepticism and Animal Faith: Introduction to a System of Philosophy.* New York: Charles Scribner's Sons.

———. 1925. "Dewey's Naturalistic Metaphysics," in John Dewey, *Essays, Reviews, Miscellany, and Impressions of Soviet Russia, The Later Works,* vol. 3, 1927–1928. Edited by Jo Ann Boydston. Carbondale: Southern Illinois University Press, 1984, 367–384.

———. 1926. *Dialogues in Limbo.* New York: Charles Scribner's Sons.

———. 1936. "Ultimate Religion," in *Obiter Scripta: Lectures, Essays and Reviews,* ed. Justus Buchler and Benjamin Schwartz. NY: Charles Scribner's Sons, 280–298.

———. 1942. *Spirit, The Fourth Realm of Being.* New York: Charles Scribner's Sons.

———. 1946. *The Idea of Christ in the Gospels; or, God in Man: A Critical Essay.* New York: Charles Scribner's Sons.

———. 1953. *The Life of Reason,* one-volume edition. New York: Charles Scribner's Sons.

———. 1989. *Interpretations of Poetry and Religion,* ed. William G. Holzberger & Herman J. Saatkamp Jr. Cambridge, MA: The MIT Press.

Sarett, Lew. 1925. *Slow Smoke.* New York: Henry Holt and Company.

Scott, Robert Ian. 1986. "The Great Net—The World as God in Robinson Jeffers' Poetry," *The Humanist* vol. 46, no. 1 (Jan.–Feb.).

Scult, Mel. 1985. "Mordecai M. Kaplan: His Life," in *Dynamic Judaism: The Essential Writings of Mordecai M. Kaplan,* Emanuel S. Goldsmith and Mel Scult, eds. New York: Fordham University Press.

Schulz, William F. 2002. *Making the Manifesto: The Birth of Religious Humanism.* Boston: Skinner House Books.

Seigfried, Charlene Haddock. 1996. *Pragmatism and Feminism: Reweaving the Social Fabric.* Chicago: The University of Chicago Press.

Sellars, Roy Wood. 1916. *The Next Step in Democracy*. New York: The Macmillan Company.

———. 1918. *The Next Step in Religion: An Essay Towards the Coming Renaissance*. New York: The Macmillan Company.

———. 1922. *Evolutionary Naturalism*. New York: Russell and Russell.

———. 1926. *The Principles and Problems of Philosophy*. New York: The Macmillan Company.

———. 1928. *Religion Coming of Age*. New York: The Macmillan Company.

———. 1931. "Humanism Viewed and Reviewed," *New Humanist* 4 (July–August), 15–16.

———. 1932. *The Philosophy of Physical Realism*. New York: The Macmillan Company.

———. 1933a. "Religious Humanism," *The New Humanist* 6 (May–June), 7–12.

———. 1933b. "In Defense of the Manifesto," *New Humanist* 6 (November–December), 11.

———. 1934. "Nature and Naturalism," *The New Humanist* 7, 1–8.

———. 1941. "Notes and Communications in Response to Henry Nelson Wieman's 'On Using Christian Words,' " *Journal of Religion* XXI, 50–52.

———. 1947. "Accept the Universe as a Going Concern!," in *Religious Liberals Reply*. Edited by Henry Nelson Wieman. Boston: The Beacon Press.

———. 1950. "The New Materialism," in Vergilius Ferm, ed. *A History of Philosophical Systems*. New York: The Philosophical Library.

———. 1961. "American Realism: Perspective and Framework," in *Self, Religion and Metaphysics: Essays in Memory of James Bissett Pratt*, ed. Gerald E. Myers. New York: The Macmillan Company.

Shaw, Marvin Cabrera. 1968. "Naturalism and the Divine: The Possibility of a Naturalistic Theism Based on the Philosophies of Santayana and Dewey." Unpublished dissertation. Columbia University, New York.

Shaw, Marvin C. 1988. *The Paradox of Intention: Reaching the Goal by Giving Up the Attempt to Reach It*. Atlanta: Scholar's Press.

———. 1995 *Nature's Grace: Essays on H. N. Wieman's Finite Theism*. New York: Peter Lang.

———. 1999. "Assessing Wieman's Contribution: The Theistic Stance Without the Supernatural God," *American Journal of Theology and Philosophy*, vol. 20 (Sept.), 241–257.

Shea, William M. 1984. *The Naturalists and the Supernatural: Studies in Horizon and an American Philosophy of Religion*. Macon: Mercer University Press.

Skinner, Clarence R. 1945. *A Religion for Greatness*. Boston: Murray Press.

Sleeper, Ralph W. 1986. *The Necessity of Pragmatism: John Dewey's Conception of Philosophy*. New Haven: Yale University Press.

Slotkin, Richard. 1992. *Gunfighter Nation: The Myth of the Frontier in Twentieth-Century America*. Norman, OK: University of Oklahoma Press.

Smith, Gerald Birney. 1925. "Is Theism Essential to Religion?" *The Journal of Religion* V, 356–377.

———. 1928. *Current Christian Thinking*. Chicago: University of Chicago Press.

Smith, Kimberly K. 2004. "Black Agarianism and the Foundations of Black Environmental Thought," *Environmental Ethics* 26, 267–286.

——. 2005. "What Is Africa to Me? Wildness in Black Thought from 1860 to 1930," *Environmental Ethics* 27, 279–298.

Smuts, Jan. 1961. *Holism and Evolution*. New York: Viking Press. [Originally published by Macmillan and Co., 1926.]

Snyder, Gary. 1990. *The Practice of the Wild*. San Francisco: North Point Press.

——. 1992. *No Nature: New and Selected Poems*. New York: Pantheon Books.

——. 1995. *A Place in Space: Ethics, Aesthetics, and Watersheds*. Washington, DC: Counterpoint.

Spretnak, Charlene. 1986. *The Spiritual Dimension of Green Politics*. Santa Fe: Bear.

——. 1991. *States of Grace: The Recovery of Meaning in the Postmodern Age*. San Francisco: HarperCollins Publishers.

Stone, Jerome A. 1983. "Samuel Alexander," *Thinkers of the Twentieth Century: A Biographical, Bibliographical and Critical Dictionary*, ed. Elizabeth Devine, et al. Detroit: Gale Research Company, 12–13.

——. 1992. *The Minimalist Vision of Transcendence: A Naturalist Philosophy of Religion*. Albany: State University of New York Press.

——. 1993a. "The Viability of Religious Naturalism," *American Journal of Theology and Philosophy* 14 (January), 35–42.

——. 1993b. "Broadening Care, Discerning Worth: The Environmental Contributions of Minimalist Religious Naturalism," *Process Studies* XXII (Winter), 194–203.

——. 1995. "Bernard Meland on the New Formative Imagery of Our Time," *Zygon: Journal of Religion and Science* 30 (September), 435–449.

——. 1996a. "Caring for the Web of Life: Towards a Public Ecotheology," in Donald A. Crosby and Charley D. Hardwick, eds, *Religious Experience and Ecological Responsibility*. New York: Peter Lang.

——. 1996b. "Charley Hardwick's Dichotomies: God-language, Determination, and the Subject-Object Dichotomy," *American Journal of Theology and Philosophy* 17 (Sept.), 279–293.

——. 1997. "On Listening to Indigenous Peoples and Neo-pagans: Obstacles to Appropriating the Older Ways," in *Pragmatism, Neo-Pragmatism, and Religion: Conversations with Richard Rorty*. Edited by Charley D. Hardwick and Donald A. Crosby. New York: Peter Lang.

——. 1998. "The Resacralazation of Nature: A Religious Naturalist's Contribution." Paper delivered at the Highlands Institute for American Religious Thought, Bad Boll, Germany, August 1998 (unpublished).

——. 1999. "The Line Between Religious Naturalism and Humanism: G. B. Foster and A. E. Haydon," *American Journal of Theology and Philosophy* 20 (September), 217–240.

——. 2000. "What Is Religious Naturalism?" *Journal of Liberal Religion* (Fall) http://www.meadville.edu. [Reprinted with addendum, *Religious Humanism*, Winter/Spring 2001, 60–74.]

———. 2002a. "Religious Naturalism and the Religion-Science Dialogue: A Minimalist View," *Zygon: Journal of Religion and Science* 37 June 381–394.

———. 2002b. "Itinerarium Mentis ad Naturam" [Intellectual autobiography], *American Journal of Theology and Philosophy* 23, 252–267.

———. 2003a. "Introduction" and "Varieties of Religious Naturalism" *Zygon: Journal of Religion and Science* 38 March, 85–93.

———. 2003b. "Is Nature Enough? Yes," *Zygon: Journal of Religion and Science* 38 December, 783–800.

———. 2004. "Power and Goodness of the Object of the Religious Attitude," *American Journal of Theology and Philosophy* 25 September, 225–246.

———. 2005. "Is God Emeritus?" *Journal of Liberal Religion*, www.Meadville. edu., 5, no. 2 (Spring 2005).

Stout, Jeffrey. 2004. *Democracy and Tradition*. Princeton: Princeton University Press.

Stroh, Guy W. 1968. *American Philosophy from Edwards to Dewey: An Introduction*. Princeton: D. Van Nostrand Company.

Swimme, Brian. 1984. *The Universe Is a Green Dragon: A Cosmic Creation Story*. Santa Fe: Bear & Company.

Swimme, Brian and Thomas Berry. 1992. *The Universe Story: From the Primordial Flaring Forth to the Ecozoic Era—A Celebration of the Unfolding of the Cosmos*. San Francisco: HarperCollins Publishers.

Thoreau, Henry David. 1893. *A Week on the Concord and Merrimack Rivers*. Boston: Houghton Mifflin & Co.

———. 1988. *The Maine Woods*. New York: Penguin Books.

———. 1992a. *Journal, Volume 4: 1851–1852*, ed. Leonard N. Neufeldt and Nancy Craig Simmons. Princeton: Princeton University Press.

———. 1992b. *Walden and Resistance to Civil Government*, 2nd ed., ed. William Rossi. New York: W. W. Norton & Company.

———. 1993. *Faith in a Seed: The Dispersion of Seeds and Other Late Natural History Writings*. Edited by Bradley P. Dean. Washington, DC: Island Press.

Tillich, Paul. 1952. *The Courage To Be*. New Haven: Yale University Press.

———. 1957. *Systematic Theology*, Volume Two. Chicago: The University of Chicago Press.

———. 1963. *Systematic Theology*, volume three. Chicago: The University of Chicago Press.

———. 1969. *What Is Religion?* Translated by James Luther Adams et al. New York: Harper & Row, Publishers.

Toland, John. 1721. *Pantheistikon*. Sam Paterson, London; reprinted by Garland Publishing, New York.

Towne, Edgar. 1977. "A 'Singleminded' Theologian: George Burman Foster," *Foundations* 20 (Jan.–Mar.), 36–59; (April–June), 163–180.

Tucker, Mary Evelyn and Berthrong, John. 1998. *Confucianism and Ecology: The Interrelations of Heaven, Earth, and Humans*. Cambridge: Harvard University Press.

Untermeyer, Louis. 1923. *American Poetry Since 1900*. New York: Henry Holt and Company.

Van Huyssteen, J. Wentzel.1997. *Essays in Postfoundationalist Theology.* Grand Rapids, MI: William B. Eerdmans Publishing Company.

———. 1999. *The Shaping of Rationality: Toward Interdisciplinarity in Theology and Science.* Grand Rapids, MI: William B. Eerdmans Publishing Company.

———. 2006. *Alone in the World?: Human Uniqueness in Science and Theology.* Grand Rapids, MI: William B. Eerdmans Publishing Company.

Wach, Joachim. 1958. *The Comparative Study of Religions,* ed. Joseph M. Kitagawa. New York: Columbia University Press.

Walker, Alice. 1982. *The Color Purple.* New York: Harcourt Brace Jovanovich.

———. 1983a. *The Color Purple.* New York: Washington Square.

———. 1983b. "From an Interview," "Only Justice Can Stop a Curse," from *In Search of Our Mother's Gardens* (New York: Harcourt, Brace, Jovanovich, 1983), 244–272, 338–342.

Walls, Laura Dassow. 1995. *Seeing New Worlds: Henry David Thoreau and Nineteenth-Century Natural Science.* Madison: University of Wisconsin Press.

Warren, Karen. 1990. "The Power and the Promise of Ecological Feminism," *Environmental Ethics* XII/2 (Summer), 125–146.

Warren, Robert Penn. 1960. *Selected Poems: New and Old, 1923–1966.* New York: Random House.

Waters, Anne, ed. 2004. *American Indian Thought.* Malden, MA: Blackwell Publishing.

Welch, Sharon D. 1999. *Sweet Dreams in America: Making Ethics and Spirituality Work.* New York: Routledge.

———. 2000. *A Feminist Ethic of Risk,* rev. ed. Minneapolis: Fortress Press.

———. 2004. *After Empire: The Art and Ethos of Enduring Peace.* Minneapolis: Fortress Press.

Whitehead, Alfred North. 1938. *Modes of Thought.* New York: The Macmillan Company.

Whitman, Walt. 1900 *Leaves of Grass,* Philadelphia: David McKay.

Wieman, Henry Nelson. 1929. *Methods of Private Religious Living.* New York: The Macmillan Company.

———. 1930. *The Issues of Life.* New York: The Abingdon Press.

———. 1933. "Is God Many or One?" *The Christian Century,* vol. L, April 31, 726–727.

———. 1943a. "Can God Be Perceived?" *Journal of Religion* 23 (January).

———. 1943b. "Power and Goodness of God," *Journal of Religion* 23 (October).

———. 1944. "Reply to Dubs and Bernhardt," *Journal of Religion* 24 (January).

———. 1946. *The Source of Human Good.* Carbondale, IL: Southern Illinois University Press.

———. 1952. "Contribution of Mordecai Kaplan to the Concept of God," in *Mordecai Kaplan: An Evaluation,* ed. by Eisenstein and Kohn. New York: Jewish Reconstructionist Foundation.

———. 1958. "Naturalism," in *A Handbook of Christian Theology,* ed. Marvin Halverson and Arthur A. Cohen. New York: Meridian Books.

———. 1968. *Religious Inquiry: Some Explorations.* Boston: Beacon Press.

———. 1975. *Seeking a Faith for a New Age: Essays on the Interdependence of Religion, Science and Philosophy*, ed. Cedric L. Hepler. Metuchen, NJ: Scarecrow Press.

———. 1982. *Creative Freedom: Vocation of Liberal Religion*, ed. Creighton Peden and Larry E Axel. New York: Pilgrim Press.

———. 1985. *The Organization of Interests*, ed. Cedric Lambeth Hepler. Lanham, NY: University Press of America.

———. 1987. *Science Serving Faith*, ed. Creighton Peden and Charles Willig. Atlanta: Scholars Press.

Wieman, Henry Nelson and Walter Marshall Horton. 1938. *The Growth of Religion*. Chicago: Willett, Clark.

Wieman, Henry Nelson and Bernard Eugene Meland. 1936. *American Philosophies of Religion*. Chicago: Willett, Clark & Company.

Wieman, Henry Nelson and Regina Westcott-Wieman. 1935. *The Normative Psychology of Religion*. New York: Thomas Y. Crowell Company.

Wilson, Edwin H. 1995. *The Genesis of a Humanist Manifesto*, ed. Teresa Maciocha. Amherst, NY: Humanist Press.

Woodruff, Paul. 2001. *Reverence: Renewing a Forgotten Virtue*. New York: Oxford University Press.

Woolf, Virginia. 1929. *A Room of One's Own*. New York: Harcourt Brace.

Wordsworth, William. 1947. "Lines Composed a Few Miles Above Tintern Abbey," in *Seven Centuries of Verse*. Edited by A. J. M. Smith. New York: Charles Scribner's Sons.

Yu-lan, Fung. 1953. *A History of Chinese Philosophy*, vol. II. Translated by Derk Bodde. Princeton: Princeton University Press.

Index

29488783R00155

Made in the USA
Middletown, DE
21 December 2018